T0247655

The Perfectionist's Dilemma

Also by Tara Cousineau

The Kindness Cure: How the Science of Compassion
Can Heal Your Heart and Your World

The Perfectionist's Dilemma

Learn the Art of Self-Compassion and Become a Happy Achiever

TARA COUSINEAU, PhD

alcove
press

Published in the United States by Alcove Press, an imprint of
The Quick Brown Fox & Company LLC.

Alcove Press and its logo are trademarks of
The Quick Brown Fox & Company LLC.

Library of Congress Catalog-in-Publication data available upon request.

ISBN (hardcover): 978-1-63910-946-3
ISBN (ebook): 978-1-63910-947-0

Cover design by Ashley Santoro

Printed in the United States.

www.alcovepress.com

Alcove Press
34 West 27th St., 10th Floor
New York, NY 10001
First Edition: January 2025
10 9 8 7 6 5 4 3 2 1

AUTHOR'S NOTE

Perfectionism is a very human dilemma. As a so-called "recovering perfectionist," this book represents a personal quest for understanding and also draws on my background as a clinical psychologist working with many people who also identify as perfectionists. While individual circumstances, narratives, and recollections differ, I have found that the inner critic's sway is remarkably similar among many of my clients and students. As such, the profiles of perfectionists presented in this book are composites, reflecting common experiences; any names and personality traits are fictitious. The dialogues and situations depicted are drawn from my perfectionism workshops and clinical practice and stem from authentic discussions, notes, and feedback shared by past participants. This book imparts psychoeducational insights about perfectionism, weaving insights from diverse fields, including clinical psychology, complementary and alternative medicine, social sciences and neuroscience, to underpin my particular—and unconventional—approach in helping people overcome the negative effects of perfectionism.

The content provided in this book is intended solely for informational purposes and is not a substitute for professional medical advice, diagnosis, or treatment. Always seek the advice of your physician, psychologist, or other qualified health provider with any questions you may have regarding a medical or mental health condition.

*This book is dedicated to all of those
who learn to love their inner critics and
to my family for putting up with and healing mine.*

CONTENTS

INTRODUCTION

Being a straight A student in high school came easy to Mariah. In fact, she could literally leave her studying to the last minute, whip off a paper, often using her cell phone, and still ace the class. While Mariah's friends suffered with the enormity of the work in Advanced Placement US History, Mariah could easily pack in the info and regurgitate it—it was just how her brain worked. This natural ability allowed Mariah to easily fill her days with choral practice, student council, and be a Best Buddy to students with disabilities. It was no surprise that Mariah got accepted to every college she applied to. But when she got to college, it was totally different. She could no longer put things off until the last moment. After failing a physics quiz, Mariah freaked out. She doubled down, pulled all-nighters, and would not accept failure. Once carefree and giddy, Mariah became tightly wound. She could not relax or sleep. Mariah became controlling, and her new friends stopped hanging out with her.

Justin was recruited to college for football—his great love in life. Justin was a hefty linebacker who loved being part of the team. His three roommates were also football players. From the get-go Justin knew he had friends for life. But the team practice schedule was relentless. He couldn't figure out how to get everything done—putting off his papers and problem sets—and wondered why none of his teammates seemed to be struggling too. Justin's anxiety became crippling. He lost his appetite and, ultimately, lost weight needed for his position. He started to oversleep. Worst of all, Justin's heart was no longer in football. He found himself crying several times a day and felt ashamed. The tough guy became homesick.

Luis had worked hard to earn his doctorate in computational neuroscience. Now thirty-five, he was part of a prestigious think tank. Luis had global collaborators and grant funding. As a first-generation college student, Luis worked hard to overcome many barriers and expected the same of others. But there were growing complaints to senior faculty about his condescending attitude toward his research associates, who saw him as a bully. Luis was confused by this feedback. The more he thought about the complaints, which he viewed as unjustified, the more enraged he became. After all, he was contributing to institutional excellence. They should feel lucky to have him.

As an avid climate change activist, Kayla decided to pursue environmental design and architecture in grad school. What she didn't expect was the evaluation process where professors judged students' work in open forums. It was crushing to get feedback in front of peers and visiting scholars. Kayla's comparing mind tortured her. She dreaded every assignment. In an effort to gain peace of mind and ease of productivity, Kayla insisted on having a tidy, minimalist space with her ideal design table set up. She wanted to begin each day with a "clean slate." Yet, Kayla found herself spending more time perfecting her workspace rather than making progress on her portfolio. Procrastination took hold.

Reed, an early career financial analyst with a major investment firm, had entered business school with a singular focus on cultivating a deep and wide network of connections. After all, you never knew which conversation might lead to a coveted internship or job offer on Wall Street. It paid off. He kept a detailed "who's who" spreadsheet of every person he met—a coffee meetup, handshake, or B-school trip to exotic places. His résumé glittered with accomplishments. In business school, he was co-president of two organizations, a conference organizer, and a member of multiple student clubs: fintech, consulting living the good life. These powerful social narratives shape how you live and learn, and importantly, what you believe about yourself and your world.

The second driver of perfectionism is an *individual* one. This includes your own inner stories about your worthiness, or what I call *inner algorithms*, that influence how you feel about yourself, about others, and about your place in your community. In addition, you have an essential human need for love and belonging. Because humans evolved to survive in groups, we long to matter, to be useful to and accepted by our family, friends, and community. Finding a role, having purpose, and feeling kinship sustains us. Naturally, the threat of failure or rejection is a deep human fear.

It's understandable, then, that we seek perfection as a solution to the human need for belonging. Unfortunately, it is a solution that tends to only make things worse. This is the perfectionist's dilemma: the very thing you strive for—acceptance, love, security, validation— becomes ever elusive.

It's noble to strive for excellence and meaning. Of course! But you likely picked up this book because the way you've been trying to achieve your dreams isn't working all that well. You may feel anxious, stuck, or exhausted. You may feel like an imposter or isolated. You may be wondering about how you can do things differently without giving up your drive for excellence or need for acceptance.

I can't promise a fix to the societal causes of perfectionism, but I can help show you how to rewrite your unique inner algorithms and find more balance and ease. Once you do, those societal causes don't have the same sway.

The key to overcoming perfectionism isn't to work harder or to banish those anxious thoughts. It's to make friends with the source of those inner algorithms through the practices of self-compassion, mindfulness, and acceptance. This includes cultivating *kindfulness*— learning to be present to your life with compassion—and having an attitude of *kindsight*, an ability to view your life experiences with curiosity, patience, and understanding instead of beating yourself up. These practices will help ease the fear of failure or the shame of rejection, and will help you bravely forge a new path.

Why do I care about overcoming perfectionism? Because I have been where you are and came through to the other side. My moment of recognition happened not long after earning my PhD in clinical psychology. We were having a summer barbecue, and my toddlers were playing on the swing set. With a food tray in one hand and grilling utensils in the other, I suddenly felt a seizing pulsation from the right side of my face to the end of my fingers. I thought I was having a stroke. I couldn't articulate a sound other than muttering "911" to my husband. The fear was: "I'm going to die in front of my children." As I heard my girls giggling in the distance, I passed out.

It took being carried out on a stretcher in front of my confused little family for me to eventually recognize I just had a panic attack. After years of striving and achieving to make something of myself, being a workaholic, and feeling like my efforts were never enough, my body had had enough. Although I had such a clear wake-up call, it took me a long time to find the remedies to rewrite my inner algorithms. I want to share what I've learned so that it won't take you as long as it did for me to find your way to happy achieving. After countless conversations with people of all ages, and especially young adults, I have developed a method that can help you understand perfectionism in a new way, honor the upside of striving for excellence in all its aspirational glory, and tend to the dark side of perfectionism—the patterns that are entangled in criticism and self-doubt that ironically can hold you back from living your best life.

In working with many people who struggle with the negative effects of perfectionism, I have found a constellation of practices that help ease its grip. I can help you change the inner algorithms for perfectionism, procrastination, or workaholism into a new code for self-acceptance and agency with a method to help you EVOLVE in living your life with joy, pride, and generosity.

EVOLVE is a six-step process that my clients have used again and again to free themselves from the negative effects of perfectionism, and it's something I've taught in a series of workshops called "Overcome Perfectionism Through Self-Compassion" and "Befriending the Inner Critic," conducted through Harvard University's Counseling and Mental Health Service for undergraduate and graduate students, online via the Insight Timer app for the general public, and through executive coaching for business professionals. The EVOLVE process combines mindfulness, compassion-based therapy methods, and nuggets from neuroscience, with basic energy medicine skills, such as gentle touch, tapping, and movement, that you can practice on your own whenever you need help finding a new way to relate to yourself and the people around you. Whether you are just starting out as a young adult or fully engaged in professional pursuits, evolving perfectionism into happy achieving is a game changer at any age.

The EVOLVE approach helps you cultivate three powerful resources that are in you, just waiting to burst forth: *Inner worth*, a basic sense of being OK that helps you treat yourself with respect, care, and safety. *Inner leadership*, a resilient and courageous orientation to life that empowers you to advocate for yourself, find strength in failure, connect with a sense of purpose, and experience joyful effort in your work. *Inner humanity*, a wellspring of self-compassion that is a powerful antidote to shame and compassion for others, which helps you forge meaningful relationships. These resources require your nurture and patience. The following pages offer the tools to tend to your unfolding, allowing you to clear the emotional and mental blocks of perfectionism that serve to constrain you—and thereby free you to happily achieving your full potential.

Part 1, **Perfectionism: When the Solution Is the Problem**, begins by helping deepen your understanding of the triggers and different manifestations of perfectionism. Chapter 1, **Perfectionism: It's Not Your Fault**, offers a wide lens on the variability of perfectionism—how it is an honorable intention that creates unintended consequences. You'll get to know perfectionism from the point of view of your nervous system, personality traits, as well as the outside influences. Chapter 2, **What's Energy Got to Do With It? A New Lens for Understanding**

Perfectionism, invites you to consider a nontraditional and refreshing new way to see yourself—one that helps you become aware of your "subtle energy" and tune into your vibes. Chapter 3, **Discover Your Inner Critic**, walks you through getting to know the inner narratives that drive your thoughts, emotions, and behaviors. Importantly, you'll learn why self-compassion and having kindsight are crucial and how to cultivate them.

Starting in part 2, **The New Solution (That Actually Helps)**, we'll embark on a journey together. Each chapter that follows describes the six steps in the EVOLVE process:

1. E: Embody the Present Moment
2. V: Validate Your Experience
3. O: Open Your Heart
4. L: Love Your Inner Critic
5. V: Make a Vow
6. E: Spark the Energy of Excellence

These steps are grounded in mindfulness, self-compassion, and self-acceptance, and they offer exercises to connect your head and your heart. As such, each of the chapters in part 2 offers step-by-step instructions on befriending your inner critic, bringing you into balance, and experimenting with new, lighter ways of being. Importantly, each step concludes with practical Happy Achiever Tools to help you get grounded, get energized, and get connected.

As you practice these tools, you will naturally spark the *energy of excellence*, the last E in EVOLVE. When your unique energy patterns are in balance, your mind, body, heart, and spirit are aligned—and primed—for success. As you choose to live consciously, new algorithms emerge, allowing you to create soul habits for life.

Throughout the book, you'll meet people who have traveled a unique path to evolve into happy achievers. By working your way through this book, you'll be able to do what Mariah, Justin, Luis, Kayla, and Reed (and the many other perfectionists, myself included, you'll meet in this book) did. You will become less reactive, transform the inner algorithms for unhealthy perfectionism, raise your self-awareness and self-compassion, and release your inner critics so that you can create, play, and live with ease and joy. Through their experiences—and through taking your own steps along your unique path—you'll see that you're not alone, and there is a way forward.

EVOLVE-ing doesn't need to be a solo affair. In fact, when you learn that others are struggling with similar fears of failure and rejection, or feel like an imposter among exceptional peers, a new kinship arises. So I encourage you to read this book with a friend or two. Not only will you befriend yourself, but you can befriend others along the way.

PART I

Perfectionism

When the Solution Is the Problem

Don't be afraid of perfection. You will never attain it!

— *Salvador Dali*

Perfection is a paradox.

It's compelling, yet ultimately disheartening. An ideal that is as likely to wear you down as it is to inspire you to greater heights. A dearly held value that can exact a personal cost.

It's a very understandable solution—to feelings of unworthiness, unbelonging, or fear—that creates its own problems: burnout, stress, overwhelm, procrastination, difficult relationships, social isolation, and/or a dependency on self-medicating strategies.

If perfection is a quality of flawlessness, a state of being complete and correct in every way, an absence of defect, or an unsurpassable degree of excellence (no pressure there, right?), then perfection*ism* is a human desire—no, *need*—to be perfect, flawless, or exceptional in order to achieve recognition, security, belonging, and happiness.

An *ism* is a socially constructed doctrine or theory that, when taken to an extreme, can become an oppressive attitude or belief. The *ism* in perfectionism is associated with an understandable but misguided personal belief shaped by society that if you are perfect, you are protected. And therefore, you must be perfect in order to be safe, valued, and worthy. Perfectionism often becomes an entrenched personal doctrine that is accompanied by an overly critical evaluation of yourself and others. You can sum up this *ism* by the acronyms:

I see mistakes.
I sabotage myself.
I strive for more.

Not very helpful, right?

No one is perfect, *obviously*. Yet, we can't help believing that there is a perfect job, partner, or body type, not to mention the material stuff like a perfect car, home, or vacation. (I still want a red Mini Cooper with white racing stripes someday.) But perfectionism is much more complicated than a wish list of achievements, attributes, and possessions that we think will make us happy or complete. Perfectionism is, at its essence, a very human dilemma. We want to be perfect so we will never be rejected, yet our quest creates negative effects that keep us from getting the very fulfillment we crave. Now, no one says *I have to be perfect or else no one will love me* out loud, because it sounds absurd. Yet we crave acceptance. We want to be seen and recognized. We want to be loved. But no one really wants to admit that.

You probably already have a sense that harboring unrealistic ideals results in more stress than happiness. But there are just so many examples of perfection being churned out by the media, the entertainment industry, online influencers, and even our "friends" on social media that it can feel impossible to give up that longing to be perfect—even though it keeps you trapped in a loop of comparing and dissatisfaction.

At its root, perfectionism is a protective shield. It's a body-mind solution to the problem of anxiety and risk of failure and rejection—an understandable but misguided solution that, sadly, breeds problems of its own. As neuroscientist Lisa Feldman Barrett writes, "Ironically, each of us has a brain that creates a mind that misunderstands itself."[3]

The inner algorithm of perfectionism says: *If I work harder, stay up late, do all the right things without mistakes, then I won't expose myself to that risk.* Unfortunately, that inner algorithm is flawed. Luckily, it can also be rewritten.

But before you can change a subconscious thought pattern, you need to be able to recognize that it's there. Be curious. And the more you can understand *how* you developed it in the first place, the more compassion, care, and effectiveness you can bring to the task. So let's take a look at where those perfectionistic tendencies are coming from so that we can start to rewrite them to something more useful—and more loving.

Perfectionism

It's Not Your Fault

The biggest dreams aren't fueled by belief.
They're fueled by doubt.

— Kobe Bryant

Chloe was a lovely twenty-three-year-old woman who came to see me shortly after a stint on an early season of *The Bachelor*. Instead of receiving a red rose and finding her one true love, Chloe didn't make the first cut and left the show after just one episode. She was totally devastated. Because the season hadn't yet aired, Chloe was bracing for a tidal wave of embarrassment and shame. The experience had left her obsessing over her possible faults, in search of an answer to the question, *Why didn't I measure up?* That the leading young man randomly picked half of the women to continue to the next episode did not make her feel better.

It wasn't even that Chloe had hoped she might last to the final cut. She just wanted to be part of the opportunity. To belong. To feel desirable. Being dismissed at the starting gate—and on a global stage—confirmed her deepest fear: she was not good enough.

You don't have to be on a nationally broadcast reality TV show to experience that feeling of being rated and falling short. Middle school boys have been known to hold up numbers from 1 to 10 as unknowing girls walk into the school cafeteria. Facebook was originally designed as a means to rate others' appearance, and many social media apps that have since followed are not much different—swipe right on Tinder if someone's hot, swipe left if they're not. Frustratingly, classifying people based on looks is a familiar human habit. You love to hate it, yet—even if it's subconscious—the tendency is to rely on superficial visual criteria to quickly judge who and what is a sure bet. It's such an ingrained habit influenced by your social reality. No wonder it's so easy to turn that judgment toward yourself.

Chloe had entered the competition believing that if she looked perfect—stood at the right angle, wore the sexiest dress, and smiled just so—she would be *safe*. Her thought process was a classic example of how perfectionism is a misguided belief that being exceptional or flawless will ensure your safety and your acceptance. It's a seductive disguise for fear of rejection or failure that comes packaged with overly critical self-evaluations and self-doubt. And the negative effects of perfectionism influence how you behave and conduct yourself.

Social scientists have measured and documented a rise in perfectionism among young people for the past several decades, starting in the late 1980s and steadily rising from there.[1] Perfectionist traits (and the corresponding emotions of shame and fear of rejection) are also associated with other afflictions that have been steadily increasing in prevalence, including eating disorders, anxiety, and depression.

Here is the hard truth: The last three decades of college students surveyed find their world more demanding of them and are more critical of themselves. This trend holds no matter your gender or part of the westernized world you live in.[2] Unless you live under a rock, no one is immune from perfectionism.

Why do so many of us suffer from this pervasive dilemma?

It's just so sticky. Like crazy glue, once we get fixated on wanting things to be a certain way, or needing to feel exceptional, it's hard to get unstuck. The brain is also tricky. Its predictive nature repeats the familiar algorithms or narratives of unworthiness learned over time, and when unchecked, leads to chronic self-doubt. If there is any measure of comfort, just know that you are not alone. Even if perfectionism is in part heritable—about 30 to 40 percent, according to a hallmark study in Spain with 600 pairs of twins—there are many other factors in play and plenty of room to thrive.[3] It is possible to grow and evolve away from the negative effects of perfectionism and find a way to balance both success and achievement with happiness and fulfillment. I believe this from my own personal challenge with perfectionism and from witnessing my clients evolve. As such, I've come to my own framework in understanding perfectionism.

A Definition of Perfectionism

Many excellent definitions of perfectionism exist in the psychology literature. Various assessments tease out a milieu of characteristics and factors, which is so helpful when looking at perfectionism trends, identifying correlates and predictors of distress and well-being, and creating evidence-based interventions. Yet, sitting face to face with students in a harried counseling center or in the quiet of private practice, the toll that perfectionism takes is hardly abstract. It is heartbreaking to witness. Pressure lingers in the air, and the energy feels dense and contracted. And so I've come around to my own description:

> *Perfectionism is the paradox created by the need for belonging—and fear of rejection—paired with unrealistic expectations for achievement and approval that sap your energy or life force.*

This paradox can manifest throughout your being in different ways:

- At the **body** level, perfectionism is an energetic survival pattern intimately tied into sensory experiences to avoid pain and seek pleasure—especially to evade exclusion from the circle of humanity and a quest to optimize acceptance, belonging, and love.
- At the **heart** level, perfectionism ignites momentary disruptions in your heart alchemy—considered sacred and powerful in many spiritual and healing traditions—and invites you to cultivate the heart qualities of courage and self-compassion.

- At the **mind** level, perfectionism is a conditioned algorithm and an exaggerated fear of rejection and disconnection that gives rise to self-protective inner critical parts, which yearn for kindness and healing.
- At the **spirit** level, perfectionism is a veil obscuring your true essence and soul purpose. Yet your unique spiritual vibration continually seeks to illuminate your natural wellspring of inner strengths and guides and is just waiting for you to recognize this powerful source of subtle energy.

The Costs of Perfectionism

Even if a more holistic mind-body understanding of perfectionism may feel like a stretch, it's hard to deny the prevalence of perfectionism, worn like a badge of honor by many. One reason perfectionism is so pervasive and on the rise is that we often idolize people whose perfectionistic ways are in full view. Take, for example, Kobe Bryant, the professional basketball player who dominated the sport—and our public imagination—for decades. In many ways, Kobe was a perfectionism influencer, making a total devotion to being the best a coveted lifestyle. And you didn't need to be a basketball fan to be influenced by Kobe's example. My daughter Sophie, a cocaptain of her college soccer team, was heavily influenced by him.

In her second year, a new coach came on board. Set on turning her scrappy team into champions, he gave them a new tagline: "Just Us." The coach's aim was to turn the team into a unified force with a singular focus on skills and success. At first, it was miserable. The players were up at 5:30 AM, no matter rain, snow, or shine, but it was always cold and dark in New England at that hour. The girls persisted—they had no choice if they wanted to play. The training seemed militant from a parent's point of view. But the new coach was aiming for excellence. He was guided by reverence for his hero, Kobe. He had the players read or watch every Kobe Bryant documentary, interview, book, and meme. They wore workout T-shirts with slogans like *Passion and Perseverance*, and *Drive and*

Discipline. The girls bravely stuck it out. It's hard to tell if the pressure made an impact. They secured one regional championship—and a lifetime of friendship, which happened despite any one coach's philosophy.

Shooting guard Kobe Bryant professed allegiance to five pillars: resilience, fearlessness, obsessiveness, relentlessness, and passion. Perfectionism oozed out of his pores. Nicknamed "Black Mamba," Kobe brought his #mambamentality to the basketball court, as a way to singularly focus on elevating the game.⁴ He motivated and awed his teammates and fans with his determination.

Kobe wanted nothing more than to be the best at basketball. A compulsive student of the sport, he endlessly watched films of every basketball game, and not just of the Los Angeles Lakers but of all teams across the history of the game. Where did his relentless drive come from? In his documentary *Kobe Bryant's Muse*, Kobe admitted to being an insecure and sensitive child. His father, Joe Bryant, was an international basketball player. Little Kobe fell in love with the game his dad was so good at. The players, the court, and the practices—it was an exclusive club, and he wanted in. Like all perfectionists, he wanted to *belong.*

Beyond the allure, basketball was also Kobe's refuge as his family moved for his dad's professional basketball career. He became obsessed with the game as a way of avoiding the possible rejection involved in making new friends in a new town. It was a coping mechanism. (Perfectionism, as an understandable protective factor and personality feature, is not an obsessive compulsive disorder or OCD, which is a diagnoseable mental health condition that can significantly interfere with a person's daily functioning.⁵) Even later as Kobe reached the pinnacle of his career, he reflected, "I always wanted to be better, wanted more . . . This fueled me until the day I hung up my sneakers."⁶ Yet at some point all coping mechanisms lose their efficacy, generally because they exact too high a toll.

There is a personal cost when striving for excellence that goes beyond high standards and becomes a necessary means to an end: to secure your place in the world and have a coherent sense of self. There were times when Kobe's perfectionism, or his "obsession" with basketball as he often referred to his unparalleled drive, had costs to himself and others. During his twenty years as a Laker, Kobe was known to be brutal in his feedback to his teammates, said to alienate players with his own narrative of being destined for greatness, and known for his unflinching ruthlessness—not exactly a recipe for the human connection that so often drives perfectionism. A *Sports Illustrated* article summed it up well: "Kobe Bryant may never be happy, and perhaps that's what makes him great."[7]

Perfectionism reliably swings from one extreme to another. Perhaps you lean into workaholism or retreat into procrastination. Or maybe you, like many perfectionists, have a pattern of being in overdrive, then sputtering to a halt. You may be hyperfocused for a period of time and overthink things by constantly improving upon your efforts, yet find yourself spinning in place. Then you scamper to meet deadlines. Or you may start out by pushing things off to the last minute, pulling an all-nighter and ending up doing less than quality work, reinforcing a negative core belief that you're "not good enough" or that you're "an imposter."

Remember, perfectionism is an understandable solution to a deep need to belong. Therefore, two common thinking patterns—or what I call inner algorithms—that accompany it are: *If I don't do this, then that bad thing will happen—and it will be my fault*, and, *If I just work hard enough and do things perfectly, I will be accepted.* Chloe came to refer to this as "bad mental math." A natural consequence of the algorithm is that you might work really, really hard to be the best, to be flawless, to ensure your status. And guess what that's a recipe for? Overwork. Disconnection. Stress. Burnout.

Perfectionism can also lead to avoidance behavior. Meaning, it can cause you to procrastinate in an attempt to delay or outright avoid the anxiety and shame that the possibility of failure, social humiliation, and rejection brings. And who wouldn't want to avoid such a primal fear? So you might stop short of putting in your best effort. The inner algorithm in this instance is: *Why bother to even try? I'll never be as good as them. It's not worth the risk.* And this, of course, leads to a self-fulfilling prophecy of never feeling good enough.

Some perfectionists also have a fixation on *appearing* flawless to others, or conversely, a need to *hide* any shortcomings or mistakes—it's called a perfectionistic self-presentation style.[8] This constant attention to reputation management and living up to unrealistic ideals can involve putting enormous energy into promoting one's image as perfect, concealing any felt imperfection, or avoiding any verbal acknowledgement of weakness or faults. This constant attempt to keep up appearances and be vigilant about public perceptions can cause psychological distress. Chloe, the rejected bachelorette, not only worried about her outward appearance, but she also internalized a sense of herself as inherently flawed. While rejection stings for even nonperfectionists, Chloe's mortal fear of public scrutiny once the televised season aired took her down a wormhole of anxiety that dragged her plummeting self-esteem along with it.

Perhaps the most pervasive toll of perfectionism is that it's hard to be happy when you believe there is always room for improvement. It's exhausting, and taxes your mental well-being. Perfectionists are more vulnerable to chronic stress, burnout, and workaholism.[9] In the business world, researchers analyzed ninety-five studies over several decades, amounting to about 25,000 working age adults. They found that perfectionism is *not* associated with performance on the job. Sure, employees with an amplified drive to do their best might put in more hours, be totally engrossed in their work, and display a high level of commitment to doing a good job. Yet, in the final analysis, perfectionists' job performance wasn't better or worse than other employees'. Meaning, all that extra effort and care didn't pay off.

I have found this to be true in my clinical work with high achievers. They are so identified with their research, projects, portfolios, or career track that they virtually exclude any other part of their self-concept. They wear their workaholism as a badge of honor, their body habituates to high stress levels, and they are typically anxious and depressed. Perfectionists can become isolated and lonely because they are always looking for something better around the corner. They can demand that others meet their high standards and miss opportunities for authentic connection. Perhaps worst of all, they tend to overlook all the other beautiful aspects of life—relationships, appreciation of nature, fun, and meaning. You have to wonder, what's the point?

The Pursuit of Excellence vs. the Pursuit of Perfection

Here's the hitch. So many people I work with believe their perfectionism gives them an edge. After all, that's how they got into a top university or graduate school or landed a sweet deal in their career. They ask me, "How do you know when your perfectionism is helping or hurting you?"

Great question.

I invariably answer them with another question as a kind of personal litmus test: "What do you notice about your energy and emotions when you are being so-called perfectionistic?" Some students will say, "I'm stressed, tense, sit at my computer all day, I have to get everything right, there is no room for failure because everyone else is so accomplished, I worry and I can't sleep" and on and on. They clearly neglect self-care and see it as an inconvenience.

Other students describe how they can get hyperfocused, are excited about what they are doing, feel a sense of purpose, and manage to take care of themselves. They take brain breaks, exercise, and have dinner with friends. This litmus test inevitably leads to a rich conversation about the differences between perfectionism and striving for excellence. The latter is associated with ease, flexibility, and inspiration, while the former is fraught with tension, rigidity, and disenchantment. Another difference, as explained by thought leader and researcher Brené Brown, is that "Healthy striving is self-focused—How can I improve? Perfectionism is other-focused—What will they think?"[10]

But it's very complicated. Pursuing excellence is something to appreciate and encourage in people for whom it matters. The "good enough" mantra that runs counter to our perfectionism culture, while useful and well-intentioned, minimizes the healthy and aspirational pursuit of striving for legitimate goals and dreams. Perfectionists also seek excellence, yet they set themselves up for constant struggle. For them, goal attainment is fraught with unhealthy striving, and as mounting research shows, perfectionism offers little to no advantage in getting ahead.[11] So where is the line?

Canadian researcher Patrick Gaudreau offers a distinction between the pursuit of excellence and the pursuit of perfection in his novel work. Across several studies with over 2,000 university students, he tackles the question of whether perfectionism is helpful, harmful, or offers any advantage at all in the academic setting.[12] Spoiler alert: perfectionism holds you back in more ways than one. In his theoretical "Model of Excellencism and Perfectionism," he defines the pursuit of excellence, or *excellencism*, as "a tendency to aim and strive toward very high yet attainable standards in an effortful, engaged, and determined yet flexible manner."[13] In contrast, he defines *perfectionism* as "the tendency to aim and strive toward idealized, flawless, and excessively high standards in a relentless manner."[14] While these distinctions are related, you can begin to see the slippery slope of perfectionism. Gaudreau's twenty-two-item research measure, called the *Scales of Perfectionism and Excellencism* (SCOPE), illuminates the striving *excellencism-perfectionism* spectrum related to life goals.[15] For example, how might you respond to the following prompt on the extent to which the sample items reflect your life goals, using a scale of 0 (not at all) to 7 (totally)?

As a person, my general goal in life is to:	
. . . have very good performances.	. . . have perfect performances.
. . . be very productive.	. . . be exceptionally productive all the time.
. . . reach excellence.	. . . reach perfection.
. . . perform very well.	. . . perform perfectly.
Excellencism <———> *Perfectionism*	

Gaudreau writes, "An excellence striver will still want to be a competent person and have very good performances, whereas a perfection striver will want to be a perfect person and have perfect performances."[16] He puts it another way: "Perfection is not excellence, because excellence can be attained without perfection, although perfection cannot be attained without excellence."[17] Naturally, your ratings aren't black and white or either/or—it's a continuum—but you likely get the point.

This distinction in the pursuit of excellence or perfectionism resonates with what I see all the time with students and clients as the negative costs of perfectionism accrue. At some point the constant tinkering with papers and dissertations, the late nights at the office, or overconditioning for that 5K race simply backfire. There is a burden on your inner resources. Gaudreau offers a useful economic analogy called the theory of diminishing returns.[18] For the perfectionist, the amount of effort made in the pursuit of goals may initially be beneficial and efficient, but at a certain point any additional effort will yield marginal improvement. Even worse, the cost of the effort can lead to negligible personal gains or worse outcomes and affect mental health and wellbeing. This flies in the face of the popular phrase, "What doesn't kill you makes you stronger." It's simply not true.

The Psychology of Perfectionism

While the social forces that spin high standards and unrealistic ideals may seem obvious, what happens in the mind and body are not. So much occurs below our level of awareness. And so much is in service to survival.

At its root, perfectionism is your nervous system's attempt to predict and avoid the potential threat of exclusion. Once the nervous system signals an interpretation that rejection is possible, it cues responses that cascade throughout your being. Let's take a look at these factors one by one. You will notice reflection questions to ponder for yourself at the end of each.

Mental Factors

Our quirky brains are optimized for adapting to an ever-changing world. The brain is a network of 128 billion neurons bathed in neurochemicals that constantly communicate throughout the brain and the body.[19] It's a complex system geared toward efficiency. We are wired to predict potential dangers in the world and remember each moment that caused distress or harm, so we don't find ourselves in that vulnerable position again. The attention networks in the brain are shaped by what psychologists refer to as a "negativity bias," an inner surveillance system that attunes our attention to possible trouble.[20] The dangers we fear are not just about physical survival, like jumping out of harm's way as an oncoming car runs a stop light. There are also perceived dangers, like a fear of rejection, disappointing someone, or the feeling of being an imposter, that can feel every bit as real and as threatening as a near collision. Yet, because the brain is wired for learning and flexibility—what's known as plasticity—you can intentionally counter those negative biases by honing your attention toward intentional experiences of hope, optimism, and joy (as you will learn in later chapters).

Whether you realize it or not, you create inner algorithms about your standing in the world and feeling good enough. Maybe you start negatively comparing yourself to other people, see yourself as a fraud, and entertain a host of inner critical voices. Chloe was riddled with what ifs and should haves. *What if I were prettier? Should I have put my hair in a French twist and worn the red dress?*

To start to raise your awareness of your own mental factors, ask yourself, *What mental images and scripts do I have about my self-worth?*

Physiological Factors

While your brain may operate like command central, calling on executive functions, intellect, and imagination, the body's nervous system is constantly monitoring functions to optimize self-preservation and safety. Our nervous system, with the familiar fight/flight/freeze response to life's challenges, is highly attuned to stress before the mental gears in the brain even begin to interpret it. Maybe you experience a real or imagined threat as muscle tension or tightness, a racing heart, sweaty palms, or panic. Maybe there are times when you feel paralyzed or numb, or suffer from insomnia. Perhaps you experience illness, chronic pain, or symptoms like headaches, digestive pain, or fatigue. These can all happen as your nervous system continually adapts to bodily fluctuations, daily hassles, or any threat to your sense of well-being—meaning, physical signals can influence your beliefs of not being good enough and trigger perfectionist tendencies in search for acceptance, relief, or certainty (and vice versa).

What sensations do I notice when I'm stressed about being good enough?

Emotional Factors

Our human biological blueprint evolved to help us flexibly adapt to the world, including giving rise to varied emotional responses to the environments and social conditions we are born into. On a basic level, we are wired to making meaning of sensory input from inside and outside of the body, largely in relation to people around us—our friends, family, neighbors, teachers, colleagues, and so on. From our earliest experiences of temper tantrums, bellyaches, and skinned knees to the delights and pleasures of ice cream, puppies, and sunsets, we learn various expressions for feelings and emotions. Simple feelings, referred to as *affect*, include *arousal* states (low to high intensity) such as calm or agitated/excited, and *valance*, such as pleasant (positive) or unpleasant (negative) states.[21] Contrary to what most of us believe, emotions are not feelings. Rather, emotions are the mental labels we give to such states and are learned by socialization. Our caregivers and culture reinforce emotion labels like happy, sad, flummoxed, irritated, hygge, schadenfreude, and so on that serve to shape our perceptions and social reality.[22] Advances in the neuroscience of emotions suggest that we are not so much "triggered" into having emotional experiences located in various brain regions, but we construct "instances of emotions" as the brain produces simulations based on several factors, such as past experiences, interoception (noticing what's happening in the body currently), and our social reality.[23]

Moreover, having a broad vocabulary for emotion words or experiences, sometimes referred to as emotional intelligence, granularity, or agility, is helpful when it comes to making meaning about life events.[24] Feeling bad or good, giving thumbs up or down, texting a smiley or sad emoji is a fairly narrow way of expressing an affect or emotion. Cultivating a wide range of human emotion words and expressions—an expansive affective niche—helps the brain make more accurate predictions. Naturally, if you feel threatened, you would run or hide using all your metabolic resources to attain safety, which informs how you label a corresponding emotion using expressions familiar to you. A broad emotion category label might be *overwhelm*, and getting more granular might be labeled *scared sh!tless, angry as hell, shell-shocked, down in the dumps*, with each phrase insinuating a different kind of experience. Similarly, on the upside, let's say if you want to make friends, date, or seek a skill or career, you may feel *inspired, excited, stoked, focused*, and *determined* and put your efforts toward such goals. There are also times when you need to recover from both the stresses and strivings in life, moments when *relaxation, rest*, and *peace* are needed. Having a robust vocabulary to express feeling states and emotions is good for overall well-being. In a way, life is about finding a rhythm or emotional balance in spite of the fluctuations and variety of human experiences.

> *What am I feeling in my body? How would I describe my emotions? Can I make space for a wide range of positive and negative emotions?*

Relational Factors

I've already mentioned that perfectionism is largely about a sense of belonging (or not), but it's worth unpacking this further. Naturally, nurturing relationships foster the capacity for healthy emotion regulation and a stable sense of self. But we hardly ever have perfect upbringings. Good enough, hopefully. But perfect? Nope. We all developed internal working maps and a shared understanding of emotions informed by relationships, especially with early caregivers. Disappointments and disruptions in relationships, as well as harm, neglect, or trauma, can affect so many things, including biological and behavioral set points, emotional resilience, coping, and relationships. The science of attachment (sometimes called interpersonal neurobiology) has illuminated the potential biological, social, psychological, and relational consequences of insecure versus secure attachment that develop in response to stress[25].

In simple terms, a secure attachment style (or way of relating) arises in early relationships with adults who demonstrate calm, caring, consistency. Even when upsetting things or disruptions occur, as they do, the securely attached child can recover more easily. An overall sense of safeness develops that allows a child to reset, explore, play, and problem solve. The children with secure attachment relationships integrate this sense of safety and belonging. They are also able to self-soothe and trust that caring others are available. People with secure attachment relationships can meet feeling stressed, making a mistake, or experiencing upsetting life events with a sense of connection, coping, and resilience. A secure attachment style is the bucket most of us would want to be in or move toward—and that can change based on the kinds of relationships you encounter over life.

On the other hand, an insecure attachment style results in anxiety or disconnection when faced with interpersonal challenges. There are various subtypes, including *preoccupied* on one end of the attachment spectrum and an *avoidant* on the other. These insecure styles of relating can arise from early interactions in which caregivers were inconsistent, unable to soothe, overprotective, critical, or punishing, making relationships unpredictable. Other factors, such as how stressed your mother was when she was pregnant with you can also influence your baseline levels of neurochemicals, such as cortisol, once you are born. It's a complicated relational picture because many factors are at play.

It's important to note that these various patterns of relating were *adaptive survival strategies*. Babies and children can't help their involuntary stress responses, and so they will seek stability and predictability. They may hold on tight to others or they may shut down. In other words, these styles are effective coping mechanisms to help a child stay protected or connected to those they are attached to. Considering the predictive brain, the attachment behavior becomes a default setting for relating, especially when stressed by people you care about.

It's also important to note that this is not about blaming your parents. They were very likely limited in their abilities to be attuned to your needs for one reason or another. They had factors in their lives, personalities, health, and histories that likely contributed to quirks in their parenting. And while these things could have negatively affected your sense of safety, belonging, and self-worth, at this point there's nothing you can do to go back in time and change the parenting you received. But you can learn to re-parent yourself—which is a key piece of the process that I outline in this book.

Adverse childhood experiences (such as alcoholism, domestic violence, divorce, and other crises) can also be disruptive if other caring adults are not present or able to restore a sense of safety, predictability, trust, and love. Intergenerational and systemic trauma also impacts sensitivities to stress.[26] Experiences with siblings and peers can be brutal. Over the course of a life these formative internal and external experiences shape how your nervous system responds to the things you encounter now.

What does this mean for you if you think you might travel the insecure attachment route? Well, you may have entered into the world inheriting a genetic sensitivity, such as a vulnerability to perfectionism, and were exposed to adverse life circumstances and conditions. The combination of these and other factors impacted your sense of security and how your brain wired itself in response to getting your needs met by others (or not) when you were small and vulnerable. These factors likely continue to influence your automatic stress sensitivity to cues of threat as well as your trust thermometer about other people. Naturally, even a label of insecure attachment style plays right into your inner algorithms about love and belonging, and can play out in your adult relationships in a host of ways, including distrust, coldness, clinginess, jealousy, rejection sensitivity, being overly attuned to others' emotions or behaviors, misreading interpersonal cues, and having low self-esteem.

Taking a look at your attachment pattern and relationship history can be illuminating if you repeatedly encounter interpersonal challenges, keeping in mind that labels are not a life sentence. Doing so can help you understand the unique complexity and situations that were beyond your control in the past. It also can foster self-compassion for the strategies you figured out as a little kid to help thrive as best as you could. Once you see how your inner algorithms are playing out, you have the chance to rewrite them and approach your life with a new set of tools that are more effective and that take less of a toll. Instead of seeing yourself as unworthy, bad at relationships, or a difficult employee, for example, you can begin to see the conditions, patterns, and parts of yourself that have contributed to your current situations. Your attachment responses can change. With the support of people you trust—such as reliable and kind friends, spiritual mentors, and/or counselors—you can heal the negative script you may have about your unlovability.

When he was a kid, Luis, the neuroscientist whom you met in the introduction, had to repeatedly defend himself from a harsh and critical father. He also lived in a dangerous neighborhood where he always had to watch his back. It was no wonder he had cultivated a thick skin and a tough demeanor. A part of him, stuck in his past, was responding from this childhood pattern. Once he realized this, he could befriend this part and discover more adaptive ways to cope with fears.

As in Luis's story, difficult emotions like fear and shame are often at the root of unhealthy perfectionist characteristics, as are hostility or need for control. Oftentimes, you might not even be aware of what you are feeling because expressing emotions was not acceptable, was limited to a narrow range of expressions, or was punished. So be curious.

How do I feel when I am not measuring up? What part of me is activated when I'm with others? What happens when I allow myself to be vulnerable in relationships?

Spiritual Factors

Perhaps one of the most common challenges for humans is the one only our species has—a crisis of faith. Whether we doubt our own basic goodness, or whether the world is a loving place, we get caught up in unnecessary suffering. Mostly we get trapped thinking about what is wrong with *us* rather than what's wonderful. We forget we are part of a collective, a spark in the universe, and that our presence matters in the human chain of connection. As a PhD candidate in psychology, I remember hearing a mind-body medicine lecture about the root of anxiety. The speaker said anxiety basically comes down to two primal fears: the fear of rejection or the fear of death. At the time,

I thought that was a bit simplistic. But she went on to teach a classic cognitive behavior technique called the downward arrow exercise to drive the point home. For example, you name the fear or the negative core belief you are struggling with. (*I will make a fool of myself at the presentation. She won't say yes to a date. I won't make partner at the firm. We'll never have a child of our own.*) Then ask, *And if that happens, then what?* And repeat the question again and again after each response. Sure enough, just about every example shared in the class ended up either not feeling worthy to exist or being rejected from your community. Very primal.

The inquiry usually illuminates a distortion in thinking or a core belief. (*I am a bad person! It will be the end of me! I am nothing. I will die.*) Eventually, you realize there is a lack of evidence about the fear. (*Hmm, come to think of it, that fear never comes true.*) Or there may be a more likely scenario on the upside. (*It may take longer to create a family. Someday I'll be a partner or boss.*) The arrow questions also can spark an insight about your resilience when you realize that you share the very human tendency to *overestimate* the perceived threat and *underestimate* your coping skills. You may eventually realize that others are actually on your side, especially when you have the courage to ask for help, feedback, or another perspective.

Perfectionists struggle with a pervasive inner doubt because they have yet to cultivate an experience of inner safeness or well-being. When you can connect within, you may discover a sacred knowing that deep down, you are essentially OK—you are cared for, part of the miracle of life, and a bright light—but that gets mucked over with fears of failure, faulty beliefs about your lack of worthiness, and societal narratives that make it easy to believe that you are unworthy. It can be hard to see the bigger picture and remember your connection to humanity.

Perhaps ironically, pondering the end of life can help you live more fully.

> *If I knew I had limited time on the planet, what would I change about my life?*
>
> It's another way of asking yourself, *What truly matters to me?*

Almost always the answer comes down to loving others and yourself more: Having fun. Taking more risks. Appreciating the good. Savoring the moment. Saying thank you. Forgiving others. Letting go of regrets. Helping more. Taking a stand.

Patterns of Perfectionism

While no two perfectionists are alike, in general, perfectionists develop strategies to protect themselves from rejection and shame that arise from unmet needs for acceptance and sense of worth. These strategies tend to fall into three broad categories, as defined by leading perfectionism researchers Paul Hewitt and Gordon Flett: *socially prescribed perfectionism, self-oriented perfectionism,* and *other-oriented perfectionism.*[27]

- *Socially prescribed perfectionism* is when a person is fixated on what others—parents, teachers, coaches, friends, commenters on social media—think about them. It can also present as a fascination with celebrity news, keeping up with the next cool gadget or trend, or doom scrolling. It's all about comparing yourself to others, a pursuit that can be all-consuming and a blow to your sense of self. And as the phrase "compare and despair" implies, it's a trap. In particular, socially prescribed perfectionism can be unrelenting. Studies show that people who score higher in socially prescribed perfectionism experience higher levels of distress and are associated with mental suffering and psychological turmoil, such as eating disorders, depression, anger, hostility, shame, and suicidal ideation.[28]

- *Self-oriented perfectionism* is an unrealistic desire to be perfect in anything that is considered important to the perfectionist. It is more than a wish for perfection—it's an irrational *need* for perfection. These perfectionists are their own worst critics: they are highly judgmental of themselves and feel they are always falling short. There is no settling for good enough or mere excellence. Even uncomfortable feelings are not allowed. Common human experiences like anger and shame are considered a weakness. This causes them to feel trapped by their need for success and their aversion to failure. They may be seen as nitpickers who desire to have everything just right (and often have beautiful living spaces, attire, and accessories), but never feel satisfied with their results.
- *Other-oriented perfectionism* is an unrealistic expectation that others must be flawless. While there can be overlap with self-oriented perfectionism, an other-oriented perfectionist makes unreasonable demands on others, especially those they are close to, like family members or coworkers. They can also be demeaning of strangers. No matter who is the object of their scrutiny, they can be demanding and blaming in an effort to bolster their own self-esteem or status. There may be an inner boss who demands loyalty and excellence from others at all costs and an outer bully who may critique and show contempt toward others who don't meet their expectations.

In addition, other researchers who study perfectionists in a business setting have identified two subtypes of perfectionism that show up at work[29]:

- *Excellence-seeking perfectionists* are compulsive and have exceedingly high standards at work, for themselves and others.
- *Failure-avoiding perfectionists* fixate on a fear that their work may not be quite good enough and that their reputation would suffer as a result.

If anything, you might imagine the suffering that comes with perfectionism can affect many areas of life. Gordon and Flett frame perfectionism as "a problem in living." Why such a sobering statement? They write, "One reason is that the ultimate goal for many is the perfect life, or at least to portray the perfect life to others, and this, in and of itself, is fraught with difficulty . . . Another reason . . . is that without a doubt, a central challenge is that people must learn to live with their failures and mistakes along with the consequences of these failures and mistakes. Thus, in some sense, perfectionism poses a problem in living with oneself."[30] They go on to point out that interpersonally "perfectionists are a problem for other people and other people are a problem for perfectionists." Sadly, this can lead to a creeping isolation and loneliness, which is a significant contributor to poor health outcomes over time.[31] Daria, a lawyer in an Overcoming Perfectionism workshop, labeled her perfectionism as being "miserably productive," often neglecting social connections. Luis came to therapy due to his conflicts in the workplace and hostility toward coworkers. For both, perfectionism was a fragile shield of self-protection stemming from earlier life experiences.

Can you relate to any of these descriptions or elements of perfectionism in your current life? Ask yourself, *Are there younger parts of me that learned that being perfect in some way was adaptive or helpful? Even if those challenging childhood circumstances are long gone, could I still be holding on to perfectionism to protect me now?*

Keep these reflection questions in mind as you read this book, holding them lightly and with compassion. After all, awareness is a first step in the quest for evolving inner algorithms.

Sneaky Ways Perfectionism Shows Up

No doubt that perfectionism is a messy ball of tightly wound twine—one that you likely haven't been able to tease apart or even look at all that closely, since so many of the thoughts and drives happen beneath the level of your conscious awareness. As you read through the various ways that perfectionism can manifest in your life, you may notice that your critical inner voice starts to chime in and assure you that you are just fine the way you are and this information isn't relevant to you. Or what you read may feel 100 percent true for you and a quiet, kinder voice invites you to look closer. Stay curious and be honest with yourself, because this is how you start to unwind the knots and change the code.

Here is a short list of some of the ways perfectionism shows up.

Underground Emotions

You may be trying to protect yourself from difficult emotions like anger, shame, and regret through perfectionism. Instead of reckoning with questions such as *Do I matter? Will anyone love me? If I do things perfectly then everything will be OK, right?*, you might busy yourself with avoiding mistakes or being flawless. And if you do, it could be an understandable response to ambivalent experiences in early caregiving relationships. A child may strive for acceptance by being the best, or dutiful, or compliant, as a motivator for a sense of safeness and security. When your basic needs for attention, reassurance, and connection are not met, you may develop a tenuous sense of self. This is not to say that your parents are to blame, even if you have checked out the latest #narcissisticparentquiz or #emotionallyimmatureparent videos on social media. It's more complicated.

Chloe described her parents as caring and attentive. Yet she also felt she had to compete with her brothers and sisters for attention from her highly productive parents. Chloe was never sure where she fit in the bustle of family life. Accomplishments? Expected, rather than celebrated. Feelings? Not talked about or tended to so much. So she buried them under her straight As and savvy veneer. She relied on cues from fashion magazines and the media.

What are the uncomfortable emotions that arise when I worry about being accepted and fitting in? What feelings do I avoid with distractions or by disconnecting?

Bodily Tweaks, Tension, and Pain

You can't utter the word perfectionist without also conjuring up words like pressure, stress, strain, stiff, tense, or tight. All the perfectionists I have worked with feel significant tension in their bodies. It may show up as chronic pain and illness, such as TMJ, headaches, migraines, irritable bowel syndrome and other GI issues, fatigue, heart palpitations, hypertension, insomnia, and almost any kind of pain, especially back and neck pain. Justin, the college football player, felt a constant tightness in his chest which he described as "metal armor three sizes too small." Kayla, the environmental designer, bit her nails raw. Luis, the neuroscientist, landed at the emergency department because he was convinced his splitting headache was a brain aneurysm.

This doesn't mean that you are doomed to a life of aches and pains. Physical tension is often the result of stuck energy. As you learn ways to get your energy flowing again and to listen to your body (and you will, starting in chapter 4), you can evolve toward healing.

What is my body communicating to me?

Negative Beliefs and Headspins

Because our brains are biased toward negativity, it's no wonder that fears about potential damage, worst-case scenarios, and imagined disasters recycle in the mind of a perfectionist. This headspin keeps the amygdala and the emotional networks in the brain primed for fight, flight, and freeze reactions. A worried mind can easily lead to bouts of insomnia. Core negative beliefs and automatic perfectionistic thoughts have the nasty habit of perpetuating themselves. *See, I'm never good enough. I'm not cut out for this. I'm a fraud. If anyone finds out about the real me, I'm screwed. If I don't nail this, then it's over.* All or none, black and white, and "what if" thinking patterns persist. It's that bad mental math Chloe described. Assumptions that things have to be a certain way, or should (or should not) occur, can lead to inefficiency, anxiety, lack of spontaneity or creativity, and underperformance, the exact opposite of what you desire.

What rabbit holes do my thoughts go down, and are they helping or harming me?

Harmful Behaviors and Unhappy Addictions

Sometimes perfectionism can lead to such distress that people seek relief in all the wrong places. When they land on something that gives them a small measure of peace, their body/brain's reward system emits neurochemical signals that send them in search of more. Some of the most common include Netflix numbing (my pet name for my go-to habit), doom scrolling, retail therapy, and comfort foods. Certain coping strategies can be physically dangerous, such as self-harm behaviors like cutting or disordered eating, self-medication through alcohol or substance abuse, misuse of prescription meds, and other risky behaviors that serve as a quick fix. Extreme procrastination can also cause harm to your self-esteem and standing at school or work. Avoidance is the body's way of dealing with overwhelm, dread, and a perfectionistic self-presentation that often stem from extreme fears of judgment or anxiety about imperfections. In contrast, workaholism is another kind of addiction feeding a need for control. It's what researcher Brené Brown calls "hustling for worthiness," a treadmill of busyness and productivity that can wreak havoc on physical and emotional well-being.

> *What are my methods for easing pain or increasing pleasure that can lead to unhealthy habits?*

Posers, Imposters, and Insecure Friendships

There is a self-defeating element that arises for many perfectionists, who can appear to others as untouchable, distant, cold, or disapproving, causing potential troubles with friends, partners, and coworkers. The irony is that at the core of perfectionist traits is the profound human need for connection and belonging, yet perfectionists may find themselves socially disconnected or removed. Also, in the popular vernacular, "imposter syndrome" is well recognized by many people who feel they don't measure up in some way, minimize their talents or efforts, or chock up any successes to mere luck or even a mistake. Who doesn't feel this way from time to time? Those with perfectionism, who feel the need to hide any shortcomings, chronically feel like imposters and are afraid they will be found out as fakes. Moreover, the pressures of modern culture, societal structures, and economic forces reinforce perfectionist habits such that any relief or self-care feels fleeting at best. As psychologist Thomas Curran notes, "We're more squeezed than ever by the grip of a growth-at-all-costs economy, which inundates us with perfectionistic fantasies, never allows us to feel enough, and keeps us always craving and yearning for more."[32] Instead, we blame ourselves for being inadequate.

What if my self-worth didn't rely on the perceived judgment of others?

Illusions and Misconceptions

Because many perfectionists tend to spend more time in their heads than their hearts, they rely on the material world for evidence of success or self-worth, rather than trusting the intuition of their heart, which is the seat of the spirit. For perfectionists, what is tangible feels real, while what is subtle feels unreal. In truth, you can't reliably judge a book by its cover (e.g., ability, appearance, awards, financial portfolio, partner, résumé, status, etc.). This overreliance on your intellect and social ideals can cause confusion, comparison, negative emotions, and low vitality and motivation. Quiet the noise and have a healthy skepticism. Trusting your vibes is an inquiry skill that can be honed over time by paying close attention to your sensory experiences and your unique energy—and of those around you. This is especially so when it comes to awareness of what brings you a sense of nurturance and vitality.

What am I sensing? What brings me joy? What does my spirit want?

A Perfectionism Self-Inquiry

Take a look at the following list of perfectionistic qualities or inner algorithms, which loosely fall into four themes of perfecting, performing, pleasing, and producing, derived from working with participants in my workshops. (There are clinically validated measures of perfectionism; if you are a curious reader, I refer you to the reference section, page 272).[33] Rate how often each habit, algorithm, or type of negative self-talk shows up for you in your current life. Just keep in mind, none of these algorithms is "bad" or even that unusual. On their own they are not harmful. Some are important core values. The list is simply meant to help raise awareness about your typical thought patterns and inner dialogue that might be keeping you tied to perfectionism. You may even have your own quality to add to the list.

Read the following list of items and rate on a 1 to 5 scale how often you experienced the habit, algorithm, or negative self-talk in the last month.

1 = At no time
2 = Some of the time
3 = Less than half the time
4 = More than half the time
5 = Most of the time

Perfectionist Habits and Traits	
Perfecting	
Afraid to look at results, grades, feedback, ratings	
Black/white, all-or-none thinking	
Irritability or impatience with others	
Make sure things are orderly or neat	
Fixation on flaws	
Rumination on possible negative outcomes	
Self-critical	
Unrealistic expectations for others	
Performing	
Being an imposter	
Blaming others when something goes wrong	
Disapproving and judging my own mistakes	
Fear of failure	
Purposeful/goal directed	
Small setbacks cause shame	
Self-doubt and double-checking	
Unrealistic ideals	
Pleasing	
Comparing self to others	
Dependable	
Feeling alone, isolated, and self-blaming when mistakes happen	
Fragile self-esteem	
Little patience with other people's perceived inadequacies	
Rejection sensitive	
Socially attuned	
Very attuned to interpersonal cues	
Producing	
Driven	
High aesthetic sensibility	
Highly motivated and focused	
Procrastination	
Rigid focus on outcomes, not learning or processes	
Stopping/starting projects	
Visionary	
Workaholism	

Algorithms/Self-talk	1	2	3	4	5
Perfecting					
"I won't look at my results unless it is an A."					
"If things aren't on track, then I might as well give up or move on."					
"I find others irritating when they don't understand me."					
"I don't like it when things are out of place or are messy."					
"I can only see what is wrong rather than what's right."					
"I mull over negative stories over and over in my mind."					
"There is always room for improvement."					
"If you can't get it right, you're out."					
Performing					
"People will find out I'm a fake."					
"You're the problem, not me."					
"I'm flawed/damaged."					
"Failure is not an option for me."					
"I work hard to be a good person."					
"I should have known better. I can't get anything right."					
"I have to make sure I don't make a mistake."					
"I have to be awesome, brilliant, exceptional."					
Pleasing					
"I can't ever be like others. I don't have what it takes."					
"People look to me to get things done well."					
"It's my fault."					
"My self-worth is based on what others think of me."					
"It's your fault."					
"I'm not good enough."					
"I find time for others and enjoy connecting."					
"I notice other people's gestures more than most."					
Producing					
"I have a fierce work ethic."					
"I surround myself with quality and excellence."					
"I get things done."					
"I leave things to the last minute. I'll wing it."					
"Getting outstanding results is the only thing that matters to me."					
"I repeat things over and over until I get it right."					
"I can clearly picture the best approach in creating meaningful change."					
"If I'm busy and productive, then I'm OK/worthy."					

How many of these manifestations are you experiencing? Most people can identify at least a handful of these algorithms, just by nature of being human. Since you're reading this book, it's completely understandable if you highly rated quite a number! This tool is not diagnostic. Yet, if you notice that you are rating 4s and 5s on more than a handful of items, well, the negative effects of perfectionism may be consuming a lot of your energy. Can you start to detect a pattern of how your particular brand of perfectionism is showing up for you? Take some time with this and save your answers—you'll be referring to them in later chapters as you begin the EVOLVE steps.

Perfectionism Can Evolve

For many, perfectionism is a way of being that's not easy to let go of and is often worn like a badge of honor. I've heard many of the perfectionists I've worked with over the years say, "But this is just how I am. It got me this far." While there is no simple code switch here, you *can* evolve your inner algorithms to allow for more acceptance, ease, and connection. It *is* possible to loosen the grip of the negative effects of perfectionism and find your way to being both happy and productive. Even the consummate perfectionist Kobe Bryant evolved over time.

After Kobe retired from the Lakers, he began to transform his drive for basketball excellence to other creative endeavors in the film industry and philanthropy. He went from a young and intimidating player to a beloved celebrity, an attentive partner and dad, and a motivational thought leader. His example was inspiring and gave many people hope, meaning, and encouragement. His tragic death still sears the heart. My daughter Sophie and her former teammates remain grief-stricken when they think of Kobe Bryant.

Kobe himself knew that perfectionism wasn't sustainable. Eventually, he learned that he didn't have to dominate every play and every game. In his book *The Mamba Mentality: How I Play*, he wrote:

There's a fine balance between obsessing about your craft and being there for your family. It's akin to walking a tightrope. Your legs are shaky and you are trying to find your center. Whenever you lean too far in one direction, you correct your course and end up overleaning in the other direction. So you correct by leaning the other way again. That's the dance. You can't achieve greatness by walking a straight line.[34]

In the chapters ahead, your legs may feel a little wobbly underneath you as you learn new ways of thinking and being that help you enjoy the dance and have less fear of falling off the tightrope. Where we're headed is a state I call being a happy achiever: where you can strive for excellence and seek a sense of belonging without mental suffering. Happy achievers uphold a value of excellence, yet also have psychological flexibility and heart intelligence that enable them to enjoy learning, see setbacks and struggles as part of achieving goals, and manage difficult emotions. They feel comfortable in sharing their imperfections with others and have healthy relationships. In other words, happy achievers don't care so much about what others think about them or their results. While they care deeply about others and want to feel safe and secure like any human being on the planet, they can roll with the punches, are conscientious of individual differences, and can have fun. Happy achievers have a balanced view of life, are self-aware, and see themselves as a catalyst for change or improvement. They are aspirational and often are perceived by friends and coworkers as inspirational. It's not that happy achievers are happy all the time. In fact, I have found that the happy achievers can get super stressed out and be afraid of failure—but they also call on inner resources of self-compassion, curiosity, and courage. They can walk the tightrope with confidence and ease.

Cultivating healthy striving doesn't mean you have to banish the perfectionistic parts of yourself or that you won't be able to achieve great things. Actually, getting to know the inner algorithms of management, innovation, entrepreneurship, global business, and even the salsa club. There wasn't much he couldn't do in the eyes of his peers. But this approach backfired. By the time Reed landed his first job at a consulting firm, he was a shell of himself. He was depleted, gaunt, and haggard—and others could sense it.

What do these people have in common? They're all tormented by the same trap: perfectionism. A desire to be the best, achieve recognition, and have a clear path to success. It stems from an understandable desire that can get twisted because it is stoked by a fear of failure. Not being good enough. Being left out of the group to wither and die.

Depending on the stakes, these folks are prone to suffering from the near sisters of perfectionism: procrastination and workaholism. They are suffering in the pursuit of excellence and missing out on the joy of life.

But it's not their fault. And it's not yours either.

There are two main sources of unhealthy perfectionism. The most obvious is *society*. We are pummeled with media extolling the ideal appearance, body, job, education, partner, material possessions, and lifestyle. We seek the constant applause of countless others who add their ratings and rankings to our social media posts and stories. In the United States, we are constantly fed a fable of individualism, exceptionalism, determination, power, and ingenuity. We are taught a mythology of *grin and bear it*, *no pain no gain*, and *hard work pays off*, despite the fact that the conditions for success are unpredictable and ever changing. Coupled with the unique cultural expectations of our specific heritages (whether that heritage is based on race, ethnicity, religion, or class) and any biases we may encounter (such as racism, sexism, ableism, ageism, or heterosexism), it can be quite a confusing and toxic stew.[1] Perfectionism researcher Thomas Curran builds a compelling case that perfectionism is the defining social characteristic of our time, fed by advertising, social media, supply-side economics, and a consumer culture that promotes the fallacy that having ever more—beauty, status, wealth—is necessary for health and happiness.[2] In this modern context, there is no end in sight when it comes to perfectionism and the purpose they have served until now can help free your energy to enjoy life, savor your accomplishments, and love all of yourself—even those parts that feel unlovable. The shackles of perfectionism will unlock. In their place you can cultivate inner worth, inner leadership, and inner humanity.

Now that you are getting clear on how perfectionism is showing up for you, you are ready to EVOLVE. Perhaps another way of looking at this personal evolution is learning to not hold on so tightly to the inner algorithms that no longer serve you and releasing whatever you are holding on to so tightly—like dropping a rope you've been clinging to or taking off a heavy backpack and gently placing it down.

It is true that your perfectionist ways helped you survive to this point. It's also true that they are holding you back from progressing further.

Now it's time to take the inner algorithms and survival strategies you still need, leaving the rest behind.

2

What's Energy Got to Do With It?

A New Lens for Understanding Perfectionism

*Our bodies live in the present moment, but our minds
time travel. When the body and mind are in the same place
at the same time, we discover the creative presence
that animates our Being.*

— *Tara Brach*

After working with countless high achievers, the majority of whom would identify themselves as perfectionists, I began to see a pattern of behavior. Almost all my perfectionistic clients blamed themselves for their malaise. They judged themselves for a garden variety of personal flaws that amounted to never feeling good enough. Traditional talk therapy, and even skills-based approaches such as cognitive behavior therapy and mindfulness, missed the mark. Everything felt *blah, blah, blah*.

Clearly, my high achieving clients were discombobulated and depleted. They were stuck, and they needed a way to jump-start their inner spark, but they couldn't just talk or think their way into it. They needed to get their bodies involved and to connect their heads and their hearts.

A great example is Daria, a newly minted lawyer, who was relieved to have more than two decades of academics behind her. Yet her identity as the perfect student trailed her into a first job at a law firm. She was terrified of messing up. Imprisoned by algorithms of *People will find out I'm a fake*, and *I can only see what is wrong rather than what's right*, among others, Daria was in a mental gridlock that kept her in a constant state of anxiety. One way to get her out of her head was to help her get moving. And she didn't have to go very far. The mini-exercises I suggested included gentle tapping on certain acupressure points on her body, belly breathing, and stepping outside for fresh air. Trained as a skeptic and to look for evidence, Daria didn't believe it at first.

Yet Daria agreed that these activities did no harm, and she conceded that she had a few minutes to try them out in a long workday. She committed to two weeks of daily practice before our next meeting. Over time, Daria began to *feel* some subtle shifts. A better night's sleep. Less irritability. Once on board with this idea of moving stuck energy and soothing the nervous system, we practiced an emotional freedom technique or EFT (described in detail in chapter 9). EFT is one approach in energy psychology, a relatively new field of mind-body practices for psychological healing and well-being. Energy psychology, as psychologist and leading EFT expert David Feinstein, PhD, describes it, "draws upon a variety of techniques derived from ancient healing and spiritual traditions and combines them with contemporary methods for psychological change."[1] EFT is sometimes referred to as emotional acupuncture, since no needles are involved, or simply as "tapping." EFT blends emotional exposure, acupressure stimulation, and self-acceptance in a basic recipe that is ideal for stress management.[2] Armed with scientific evidence that EFT is clinically effective, Daria practiced tapping on various locations on her hand, head, and torso while speaking aloud a self-compassion statement such as, "Even though I'm scared to death of botching up my presentation, and my heart is jumping out of my chest imagining it, I completely and deeply love and accept myself."

Tending to Your Nervous System

Why is it so helpful to find ways to connect with your body? As we started to unpack in chapter 1, so much of perfectionism is rooted in the patterns of your nervous system. The brain is a wildly complex system of neural networks simulating potential experiences below your level of awareness, which happens so fast it's hard to wrap your head around it (no pun intended). To put it more simply, you are exquisitely wired to continually monitor and adapt to your environment (what's known as allostasis) and maintain stable conditions in the body (otherwise known as homeostasis). As such, the brain continually monitors a host of internal and external signals and makes guesses about how whatever you're experiencing will affect your well-being. All the while, it is simultaneously adjusting chemical and electrical activity to recalibrate your metabolic energy in the service of survival—or to keep your "body budget" in balance, as coined by neuroscientist Lisa Feldman Barrett, developer of the theory of constructed emotion.[3]

The body budget metaphor is very useful in understanding the cost of perfectionism, as its negative effects accrue over time. Let's expand on this idea. How we think, feel, and perceive our world intimately influences the body's budget. You are likely familiar with the notion of *perception*, your ability to make sense of the world via the five senses: sight, hearing, smell, taste, and touch, which are associated with sense organs such as the eyes, ears, nose, tongue, and skin. We also have other senses that involve movement and balance and help us navigate our bodies in space—this is known as *proprioception*. We also have *interoception*, your brain's perception of the state of your body. Interoceptive awareness involves an intentional mental tuning in to your body sensations, like noticing a racing heart or the rhythm of your breathing. Cultivating interoception can influence changes in autonomic states, the flow of energy, and body budgeting.

Think of balancing your body budget as you would a bank account. You make deposits in effort to optimize your finances. Getting a good night's sleep and eating healthy food are good deposits of nutrients, oxygen, and overall cellular repair. They replenish resources. On the other hand, pulling an all-nighter or skipping breakfast is like making a withdrawal. Things that are expensive because they require some spending include studying for a test, facing uncertainty, or endlessly weighing your options. Same for a physical workout, which requires using up some metabolic resources but is ultimately a good investment over time. Chronic stress and burnout are akin to bankruptcy. Which means your pleasing, perfecting, performing, and producing habits—and the negative effects of perfectionism—eventually accrue a high cost. This may be especially so for real or perceived social cues of exclusion. Whereas cues for inclusion and belonging, being comforted by others, and engaging in regular self-care are akin to compounding interest over time.

To efficiently make sense of the signals your body experiences in any given moment, the brain scans and summarizes experiences you had while growing up or even in the near past to find something that compares to your current experience. The brain draws on many bits of sensory and neuronal data and lands on the best possible guess—all in a millisecond. But here's the kicker: the predictions your brain makes may be wrong!

For example, Daria had learned that being a straight A student kept her out of trouble and out of the scrutiny of parents and teachers. If Daria scored a 95 on a quiz, her parents said, "What happened to the other 5 points?" Then she felt a red-hot sensation throughout body, a flushed face, and perspiration—a very uncomfortable state that she experienced as embarrassment or shame. Now whenever Daria receives a critique or demand by another legal team member, her brain rapidly culls all the past little instances of disappointments, manages the energy expenditure, and anticipates what she needs to do to cope. And it often serves up a somatic experience of intense shame that is out of proportion to what is actually happening in the moment.

When you experience any threat—even an emotional threat that makes you feel as if you might be judged, shunned, and kicked out of the group—those old inner algorithms kick in. *Still not good enough! Try harder!* It could be as minor as a look someone gives you, and, boom, your desire and need for belonging are threatened and your nervous system triggers a cascade of responses. It's like a self-fulfilling prophesy where past experiences inform current ones. As Barrett describes it: "It's your brain that keeps the score and your body is the scorecard."[4]

For Daria, the simulation in her head—*I've disappointed my team*—is more real to her than what occurs in her work meeting. What she sees, hears, and feels is an interpretation of her world in that moment. Daria sees what she believes.

Understanding that the brain is using its predictive abilities to keep you alive by regulating your body budget can be profoundly helpful in coping with stress, rejection, uncertainty, or any challenge in life.

What feels like a "trigger" is really your brain being proactive—assessing volumes of sensory data from both past and present experiences in order to anticipate your energy needs. Sometimes the prediction is a good match and sometimes it's not.

Think of it like your favorite streaming TV service. Watch a few comedy specials, and the next thing you know most of your recommendations are for more stand-up comedians—even though today you'd rather watch a drama. As neuroscience offers increasingly advanced ways to study the human condition, we are learning how we can actively shape our experiences in beneficial ways. The exciting opportunity is that you can change the brain's prediction error by proactively engaging in experiences that support you.

All this is to say, don't be so hard on yourself. While this sentiment may be easier said than done, you *can* reroute those algorithms once you have a better sense of *how* to go about it. You can cultivate a kinder mind. British psychologist and compassion researcher Paul Gilbert teaches that humans have a "tricky brain" that is intimately tied into our emotions and thoughts, especially the mind loops and mental gymnastics we all too often find ourselves in.[5] Gilbert offers a model of the emotional brain that is easy to picture and can help guide you toward intentional self-care remedies. He describes three interconnected emotion-regulation or motivational "zones" that represent simplified descriptions of the intricate neural networks and cortical brain regions:

1. **The threat system** directs attention to any threat or potential danger, shapes the negativity bias, and helps you ward off harm. Experiences like touching a hot stove or getting punished for taking your sister's doll reinforce such threat detection, as does ruminating on past failures or rejections. It's associated with the fight/flight responses and with emotion concepts such as fear, anxiety, or disgust. This system mobilizes the body and mind for action and releases a cascade of neurochemicals and hormones to help with the body's energy needs. While the upside is a quick reaction time when necessary, the downside is that it's

unsustainable over time. Chronic stress affects nearly all of the body's systems. This state is referred to as the Red Zone, or the "alarm bell" in popular psychology.

2. **The drive system** is engaged when you experience elevated emotions or states such as awe, compassion, excitement, joy, love, and pride. Its function is to pursue adaptive resources for living such as food, sexual partners, social affiliations, status, security, and wealth. In a healthy state of striving, these drives are related to purpose, inspiration, and overall well-being. The downside is addictive tendencies, social comparison, and burnout. The drive system is associated with dopamine, a neurochemical that our brains naturally crave because it provides a pleasurable mood and happiness boost. Like getting a blue ribbon, the drive system is sometimes referred to as the Blue Zone.

3. **The soothe system** is a wholly underrated and underutilized system. Related to the parasympathetic nervous system or "rest and digest" functions, the soothe system evokes a sense of calm and feeling cared about. It is essential for bringing the Red and Blue Zones into harmony—to a more balanced body budget—as both threat and excitement require recovery. The downside of the soothe system is an extreme state of complete shutdown, like numbing, fainting, or freezing. Yet, it generally serves as an R&R (rest and relaxation) function. The soothe system is associated with the neurochemical oxytocin, which induces states of love, bonding, and connection and is crucial for heart coherence and mental well-being. Like the nourishment of water and sun needed to grow a garden, this system supports vitality and regeneration. It is sometimes referred to as the Green Zone, lush and sustaining, and feeling in a state of flow.

Perfectionists struggling with unrelenting mind loops of imposterism, rejection sensitivity, or failure anxiety tend to waffle between the threat and drive systems, ping-ponging between the Red and Blue Zones. There's typically little time spent actively engaging your soothe system in the Green Zone for a physiological reset.

Thinking of your nervous system as a conduit for metabolic regulation can be a helpful lens for healing the negative effects of perfectionism. For example, if you get emotionally hijacked into the Red Zone (*My boss thinks I'm totally inept! I'm going to get fired!*), it's as if your nervous system tripped a wire. Just like you might need to flip a switch on the electrical panel in the basement of a home or jump-start a battery in a car, you can reset your overall state by using coping skills that ignite the Green Zone of calm and connection. But if you try to push through your upset and launch instead into a bustle of doing, doing, and more doing in the Blue Zone of striving, you may easily find yourself back in the Red Zone, fritzed out from a depleted body budget, and feeling down or depressed.

It's not that any of the zones is good or bad—they are merely patterns of neural activity and prediction. You needn't stay stuck in any one zone. Through practice, you can change zones by taking a pause, redirecting your attention, and choosing your next action. This calls for a flexible and holistic view of your mind and body. Over time Daria noticed how often she felt in the Red Zone, and purposely engaged in skills and actions that moved her into Green Zone episodes of calm. In this way she can change the predictions her brain makes in future high stress work situations.

There are many beautiful ways to understand the human experience that can complement the social and neuroscience lenses we've explored thus far. Now let's take a look at energy from a metaphysical perspective, so that you can deepen your understanding of your own vibes and find more ease and balance.

Your Subtle Energy

Energy is a life force that exists within and around all things. It is an innate intelligence that travels through the nervous system and bodily organs and seeks harmony within and around you. Like water, your energy needs to move in order to stay healthy, but often it gets stuck with wear and tear. Life circumstances, traumas, and various stressors can cause an imbalance in the natural flow of energy. Negative emotions, for example, are a disruption in the flow of information and energy in the mind-body system.[6] Emotional blocks may pool energy in one area of the body, and this may also affect other areas: circulation, body temperature, hormones, the immune system, neurotransmitters, and so much more.[7] Imagine an elaborate water fountain in a botanical garden. The plumbing can get stopped up by grit, leaves, and debris. What is beautiful and symmetrical when everything is flowing can become obstructed, backed up, or sputter out of control.

Another useful metaphor is to consider energy pathways like an inner GPS system that tries to navigate speed bumps, potholes, barriers, dead ends, and U-turns in your emotional life. Sometimes this means your energy pathways get blocked or weakened, which is a state of being underenergized. At other times the pathways ramp up and are overenergized or overactivated. Yet, all the while your energetic system is trying to find that sweet spot of cruise control.

For better or worse, your subtle energy will adapt to whatever challenges and conditions you are facing, and influence your habits, inner algorithms, and heart coherence (described in chapter 6). Stress, trauma, the environment, other people, and your own mind (especially the inner critic—a character you'll get to know much more about in the next chapter) can interfere with the flow of energy, making it constricted and rigid or excessive and chaotic. Subtle energy, similar to the autonomic nervous system and interoceptive sensory network, prioritizes survival, and can send you into the classic fight, flight, or freeze responses to real or perceived danger. One moment you may be like a cougar ready to pounce and irrationally yell at a family member (being overenergized in a Red Zone, ready to fight). In the next moment you may be pulling an all-nighter to get your project completed (in an overenergized, workaholic state in the Blue Zone). Or you may be like a deer in the headlights, unable make a clear choice about a career move or afraid to ask someone out on a date (frozen and underenergized in a more extreme Green Zone of inactivity). These reactions can occur in the course of daily living and yet when frequent can drain your inner resources. Any of these energetic, survival states can keep you spinning in place.

Stuck energy can also manifest as aches, pains, and tension. At other times an imbalance in energy can be tied to a dip in immunity that makes you more likely catch a cold or swirling thoughts that make it challenging to get a good night's sleep. In essence, much of our distress is related to an impairment in the flow of energy, akin to a deficit in the body budget.

The good news is that energy is changeable, and, like water, seeks a natural balance. Energy flow is enhanced by healthy emotion regulation, the ability to have perspective, being present, and self-compassion—in other words, spending some time in the nourishing Green Zone. With a little awareness and loving care, you can clear some of your own energetic blockages and bring your nervous system back into equilibrium—and that helps you find greater ease and balance too, by calming the fears of rejection and failure that can cause perfectionistic tendencies to surge.

I have been delighted and amazed to discover energy psychology's treasure trove of self-care practices—many that have been around for thousands of years and others that have been developed over the last half century—that have been demonstrated to be effective in clinical populations with anxiety, depression, pain, and trauma.[8] In my clinical experience, energy psychology practices are also incredibly effective at helping perfectionists release unhelpful inner algorithms and find their way to happy achieving, especially perfectionists who tend to fixate, be compulsive, and have nagging inner voices.

The school of energy psychology teaches simple tools that help you bring yourself back into balance. It builds on the many traditions that seek to augment the flow of subtle energies in order to support health and healing. In Traditional Chinese Medicine, energy is *qi* (or *chi*) that travels along fourteen distinct pathways or meridians.[9] Ayurveda—the Indian school of medicine that is a sister science to yoga—calls energy *prana* and teaches that there are centers where prana coalesces in the body called *chakras*. In Japan, energy is known as *ki* and it is rebalanced through the healing modality *reiki*. Energy psychology combines many tools from these and other practices, including Native American shamanic healing and more recent modalities such as EFT (emotional freedom technique), to nourish and balance your own flow of energy for healing and harmony.[10] Breathing practices that enhance "heart intelligence"—by strengthening heart rate variability and vagal tone—as assessed by modern biofeedback technologies, are proving what ancient wisdom has handed down over millennia. These methods are gentle, noninvasive techniques and can be practiced as a self-help approach. I will share a sampling of them in the chapters to follow.

If anything, simple energy medicine tools can offer you something tangible to do when your perfectionism is flaring, whether you are staring into space, unable to get out of bed, or burning the candle at both ends. Not only that, but they may also well serve to recalibrate your body budget as well as adding a new repertoire of data for the brain to include when creating future predictions.

The Perfectionism Matrix

There is a delicate balance between our evolutionary blueprint for belonging and safety and the flow of energy in any given moment. Tuning into this dynamic with curiosity and compassion can help you find your footing when perfectionistic tendencies arise. Why does this even matter? Because every perfectionist I know struggles with some internal conflict related to the need for belonging and expenditure of energy—the push and pull of wanting assurance or taking risks, feeling vulnerable or feeling confident, desiring connection or being independent, having a beginner's mind or needing to be certain, and more.

Since I spend so much time with perfectionists, among whom there is a robust cohort of skeptics, I created a visual framework that addresses how energy and the need for belonging interact and contribute to the negative effects of perfectionism, as well as how they can sync up and help you find your way to a realm of happy achieving.

This tool creates a matrix of perfectionism. The x-axis of the matrix represents the state of subtle energy in a given moment, with *low energy* on the left side of the spectrum and *high energy* on the right side. Keep in mind, energy is a state, not a trait, meaning it moves constantly and can get stuck in either an over- or underenergized state. The negative effects of perfectionism can move you in either direction along the energy axis.

The y-axis represents belongingness as a felt sense of acceptance, connection, kinship, security, and wholeness, with *balanced* and *stable* at the top and *unbalanced* and *unstable* at the bottom. Think of the tightrope metaphor Kobe Bryant described in the last chapter, a delicate balancing act of connecting to family, friends, and fans in the pursuit of excellence. Belonging is not only how secure you feel with others or welcomed in your community but also how attuned to yourself you feel in any given moment, whether that is feeling connected or disconnected. This can also change in response to people and circumstances, but in general, a stable sense of belonging forms in mutually responsive relationships over the course of your life.

A stable sense of belonging is enhanced by caring, compassion, and community. It also requires continual bravery in the face of vulnerability in order to stay open to connection. And it offers an internal sense of safeness and a secure relational base from which to thrive.

The intersection of these two axes forms four quadrants. Moving counterclockwise from the top left, they are:

- *Low energy, high belonging* is a longing for acceptance and validation coupled with the pressure to prove worthiness; a tendency to avoid situations that could result in embarrassment; a struggle with imposter feelings; and a vulnerability to giving up or opting out of the very opportunities you desire to engage in.
- *Low energy, low belonging* is the tendency to avoid taking needed action or asking for support; low motivation, which can lead to a sense of futility, shame, or isolation and a fragile sense of purpose; and a risk of mental health challenges or unhelpful strategies to alleviate distress and pain.
- *High energy, low belonging* is a propensity for constant striving, workaholism, and vulnerability for burnout; high need for independence; feeling competitive, combative, or controlling; risk for hypervigilance and obsessiveness; unable to let things go; at risk for unintended mistakes; and loneliness.
- *High energy, high belonging* is an ability to feel secure in relationships and to cultivate qualities of confidence, collaboration, and connection; self-compassion; heart coherence; having a balance of ease and effort, healthy striving, and productivity; feeling proud and having purpose. This is the sweet spot of happy achieving, where the negative effects of perfectionism transform into a beneficial energy of excellence.

These quadrants are not about a judgment of good or bad, better or worse. They are just helpful information—a lens into your experience of current patterns of belonging and of energy. They are also dynamic, meaning you can flow from one to the other at different times in your life—even during different times of day. While this means that you can't attain happy achiever status and stay there forever and ever, amen, you can cultivate an orientation toward happy achievement that negates the overall negative effects of perfectionism.

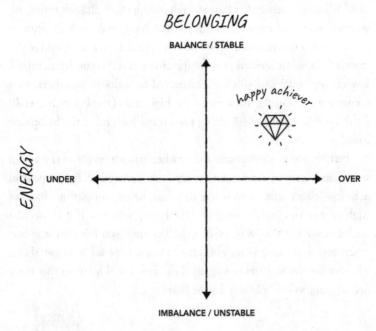

There are a couple of different ways to use the Perfectionism Matrix. The first is to think back to a specific moment in time and see if you can locate where on the matrix you were in an effort to get some insight into some of the driving forces behind you at that time. The second is to look at the statements you resonated with in the Perfectionism Self-Inquiry at the end of chapter 1 and find the quadrant that those feelings align with.

To try the first way, look back and reflect on various phases in your life.
In which quadrant do I spend the majority of my time?

Was there a phase where you didn't fit in or people around you were dismissive or frustrating or unkind? Or can you recall a time when you didn't feel confident or have any sense of direction? Or an "oh, shit" moment where you realized how far behind you were on a project or a task? When you remember how you felt during those difficult times, ask yourself, was your energy driving you too hard, making it difficult to rest and relax (putting you in the overenergized, high energy end of the matrix)? Or was it frazzled or weak (placing you on the underenergized, low energy end)? Did you feel connected to yourself, to others, to a community (meaning you were on the high end of the belonging axis)? Or did you feel isolated (situating you on the low end of the belonging axis)?

Perhaps you can remember a time when you felt on top of the world, in a good spot in your relationships, and energized by purposeful activity—that's what it feels like to be in the upper-right quadrant of high energy and high belonging—the happy achiever. If it seems like you've never felt that way, or like the last time you felt that way was when you were nine years old, know that it is possible to get there, whether for the first time or again. The tools you'll learn in this book are all designed to help you do just that.

The second way to use the Perfectionism Matrix can help you get a glimpse of where your energy and your belonging currently are. Check in with your vibes. Ask yourself:

How does that inner algorithm or belief influence my energy now?

How does my body feel when I consider this statement?

How does this statement relate to my desire for belonging?

You can also refer back to the statements you identified with in the Perfectionism Self-Inquiry in the previous chapter and consider where these items might locate you in one of the quadrants on the grid.

For example, say you rated a 4 of 5 on "Failure is not an option for me." If you notice that your fear of failure causes you to go into overdrive by overworking and that then causes you to feel disconnected from other people, you might place yourself into the "high energy, low belonging" quadrant.

Let's say you rated a 5 of 5 on "I can't ever be like others. I don't have what it takes." Ask yourself the same questions. Maybe you realize you have a need to fit in or be recognized, but opt out of doing things that might help you make new friends. Your energy feels stuck in place. That puts you in the "low energy, low belonging" quadrant in the lower-left corner of the matrix.

Or perhaps you have a high need to connect with people, and so you sign up for every opportunity to meet people because you want to cover all your bases, as Reed, whom you met in the introduction, did. You put in a lot of time and effort yet run on empty. You start out in high energy, high belonging, but either exhaustion or disconnection (or both) ensues. You might be operating on fumes to meet obligations, but authentic relationships suffer. That puts you in the lower-right quadrant—high energy, low belonging.

While you can fall in different quadrants at different points in your life—Mariah was in the lower-right quadrant (competitive) in high school and then switched over the lower-left (avoidant) once she got to college—and you can hopscotch between all of them in the course of a day or a week, knowing where you currently are on the matrix helps you understand what you need to shift in order to make your way back to happy achieving.

In this discovery process, be curious and kind with yourself—and have some fun. As you follow a new roadmap toward unseen adventures, you will be amazed when you begin the EVOLVE process in part 2. Even if it feels like an obstacle course, you can arrive at a place in your life where living with balance, ease, and joy is your new default. You can bring your best to whatever you pursue that energizes rather than depletes you. Before we begin this journey, let's meet your inner critic, who is definitely coming along for the ride.

3

Discover Your Inner Critic

When you can love all your parts, you can love all people.

— *Richard C. Schwartz*

Hopefully by now you are getting a sense that perfectionism is the result of an ancient need for belonging and acceptance, and that our brains and bodies have a basic blueprint for survival that can trap us in a constant search for personal security. As a species, we haven't evolved to catch up to the relative safety of living. We also haven't caught up to the mad pace of our modern world, with the constant flow of information, demands, and expectations. Today's threats look much different than that of living in forests or deserts. Yet, a performance review, email from a boss, or snide message on social media can catapult you into the Red Zone.

Now that you understand the evolutionary nuances from the past and the dynamic need for belonging and energy flow in the present, let's gain some insight into your particular algorithms of perfectionism and have a little fun along the way. We're going to do an exercise that always raises the energy in the room when I teach it in my workshops. We're going to meet your inner critic.

Face to Face with a Frenemy

An inner critic is an internal voice (or voices) that typically arises early in life in response to difficult circumstances, stress, or trauma, or is an internalized message from other people, family, or societal pressures. Drawing from Barrett's theory of constructed emotion, the inner critic could be considered a "concept" you create to make sense of the world, derived from mental categories—thoughts, emotions, sensations, perceptions—based on a lifetime of experiences.[1] Personifying an inner critic by giving it a label or a name is a profound way to acknowledge your inner frenemy and develop a new way of relating to yourself and the world. While the circumstances that serve as the origin story for an inner critic are as varied as there are people, the basic human need for love, belonging, acceptance, and validation are universal.

The inner critic is behind the patterns that so many people who experience the negative effects of perfectionism share: feeling like an imposter, being paralyzed with procrastination, feeling disappointed that nothing is working out the way they expected, or judging themselves for not being good enough or other people for being way better. These thought patterns are, perhaps ironically, protective strategies that the inner critic uses to manage deep survival fears.

Perfectionists are in fact very attached to their inner critics, often without realizing it. Like a little frenemy, you maintain a friendship despite feeling an internal rivalry. Think of your inner life teaming with a bunch of characters, each with a role to play.[2] Some are in cahoots with you while others are battling, and still others may be frozen in time. Typically, an inner manager is trying to maintain control, avoid catastrophe, and block difficult emotions, experiences, or memories—and it drives a hard bargain. There's a constant struggle between your desire for acceptance and belonging, and your inner critic's twisted strategies to protect you from rejection. Go back to any bundle of items you rated on the Perfectionist Self-Inquiry in chapter 1—those phrases are some of the go-to scripts that the inner critic uses to get your attention and potentially lead you into a habit of perfecting, performing, pleasing, and producing at the expense of compassion, play, peace, or rest.

Reading all this, you might think that the answer is to banish or eradicate your inner critic—*if it's a problem, let's get rid of it!* There are a few caveats when doing inner critic work. First, inner critical voices are not to be shunned, shut out, or kicked to the side. Your inner critic is sort of like one of the minions in *Despicable Me*, trying to solve problems, seek power, and defend your borders. It's running reconnaissance, predicting potential outcomes and calamities. And it needs to be seen for its important role in trying to motivate you to be the best and protect you from the unpredictability of life, social humiliation, or shame. You want to befriend the inner critic, not banish it.

Second caveat: As you begin to identify your inner critic, you may realize that you have a few distinct voices chattering inside your mind and acting out scenes and conversations. That's typical. These inner critics each have a role to play in managing your life or protecting you from danger. But there's likely one inner critic that takes center stage, which I affectionately refer to as your *Plus One*. Your Plus One comes along to every situation where you may feel on display or vulnerable in some way, as if you were walking arm in arm down a red carpet. It helps you to put on a good face and keeps up your perfectionistic habits. It's this Plus One that you want to try to give a name to by the end of this chapter, because this Plus One will come along for the ride as you embark on the EVOLVE steps. Eventually, you will notice other parts reveal themselves as you acknowledge and appreciate them despite the trouble they may cause.

Third caveat: As we do the work to raise your awareness of your inner critic, be kind to yourself. Every exercise I share in this book works best when you take a self-compassionate approach—which can be hard at first for many perfectionists. Compassion is typically defined as an understanding of the suffering of others and the motivation to relieve or prevent suffering. *Self*-compassion is directing this caring sensitivity toward oneself. Know that as you become aware of your inner critical narratives, you can make different choices and cultivate new habits. You can flip the script. Just as the human blueprint is geared toward survival, it is also geared toward caring and cooperation—yet sometimes we forget to tap into our own inner resources of compassion and collaboration. It's these inner resources that we'll lean into from here on out, as we embark on a journey of befriending yourself.

Naming an inner critic serves two purposes. First, identifying it helps to *externalize* it from your mental movies. This allows you to cultivate some distance from it instead of feeling fused with it. You are not your inner critic. Second, it helps you begin to develop a relationship with your inner critic. Once you are aware that the inner critic has shown up, you can greet it, even if the inner critic feels like an unwelcome guest. It always has some message, warning or offering for you. As transformation coach Debbie Ford stated, "Even the darkest subpersonalities come bearing gifts. We just have to be willing to spend some time with each of them in order to hear their voices of wisdom."[3] You can decide whether to take it seriously or not, or accept that it always shows up at inopportune times, or decide if this is just the perfect opportunity to take a new approach (like one of the EVOLVE steps).

Five Common Inner Critics

In meeting many people who are experiencing the negative effects of perfectionism, I've categorized the most common critics into five basic types of managerial inner critics. Let's look closely at each one so that you can start to discern which type you might be dealing with. You'll also see the power and potential associated with each inner critic as they transform and heal. You will also see how some of the perfectionists you met earlier came to notice and name their Plus Ones.

Inner Critic Archetype 1: The Judge

Remember Chloe, whom you met in chapter 1, who felt dissed by the lead when she appeared on *The Bachelor*? Her inner critic was a very loud *judge*. As its name suggests, the judge is highly self-critical and, well, judgy: imagine in your mind the TV reality court character Judge Judy, with her no-nonsense sarcasm and pointed finger.

The misguided belief the judge holds on to is that being perfect will protect you from failure or rejection. People with an inner judge are typically high in socially prescribed perfectionism (refer back to page 23 for a definition), very sensitive to rejection, and caught in the "compare and despair" trap. An inner judge can also be high in self-oriented perfectionism, by being highly critical of oneself and on a constant search for excellence.

If you notice an inner judge, your flavor of perfectionism may be driven by an inner algorithm of rating and ranking. And who could blame you? After all, we live in a culture that puts a premium on acquisition, accolades, and accomplishments.

Having a need for approval is understandable. But a habit of fault-finding in yourself or others can diminish your bright light. Imagine your inner judge as just a part of you (typically younger) that believes that being perfect will save you from criticism, exclusion, or reputation damage. That's a totally understandable fear! There are likely many good reasons why you have that belief. It's protective. It's served you well for a long time. So long, in fact, that you've likely outgrown it. Instead of being critical, that judgy voice can be put to good use by helping you map out a plan and offer guidance when needed.

If your inner critic is the judge, your inner strengths are clarity and wisdom. You are confident. A natural teacher. You love fair and decisive answers. You exude calm and dependability. Others count on your wisdom and ability to do the right thing. People want you on their side!

Inner Judge Character Sketch

The judge is characterized by being rigid and critical.

Driven by a need for approval or rewards, the judge's attention is easily hijacked by social media, the news, and other people's opinions.

If your inner critic is the judge, your kryptonite is fault finding—in yourself and others.

When you want to achieve something, you avoid getting help.

Your biggest strengths are wisdom and clarity.

MARIAH'S STORY

Now that Mariah was in college she had to write twenty-page papers on a near-weekly basis, grapple with computer problem sets, and go to labs. What also was achingly clear to Mariah was that she lacked some basic writing and studying skills. She was embarrassed. But instead of seeing this as a learning opportunity, Mariah was crippled with fear and was afraid to ask questions at professors' office hours. She felt it was rude to intrude on their time. At the end of the first semester Mariah refused to look at any of her grades.

Mariah finally showed up at my office when stricken with insomnia and barely able to function. She was in the low energy, low belonging quadrant. As Mariah learned some coping skills to manage the physiological symptoms of anxiety and agreed to meet with an academic coach, she was ready to name an inner critic. Given her childhood experiences playing softball, Mariah finally landed on Grumpire, or Grump for short. "It's my grumpy umpire who calls the shots. Bad. Good. Nothing I can do about it." Mariah would soon learn that she could do something about it

Inner Critic Archetype 2: The Drill Sergeant

Most of us have a good sense of the domineering boss. You may even have had an experience with a punitive parent or a mean coach, or have been witness to one. Some famous embodiments of the drill sergeant archetype include the sadistic Colonel Nathan Jessup in the courtroom thriller *A Few Good Men*, played by actor Jack Nicholson, shouting, "You can't handle the truth!" Or cold-hearted Felonius Gru, the main protagonist of *Despicable Me*, whom we love to hate. (Although it's important to note that even Gru's heart melted over time once he began caring for his little adoptees Margo, Edith, and Agnes).

As an inner critic, the drill sergeant is that mean boss with a compulsive need for efficiency and productivity. If you have a drill sergeant prowling among the recesses of your mind, your perfectionism may be driven by an inner narrative that being in control is necessary at all times. Your motivation may be about striving to be the best, or like Kobe Bryant, to be at the top of your game. Of course, the desire for social or professional status, mastery, or craftsmanship is completely natural and not necessarily bad. But if the drill sergeant is running the show, once you set your mind to something, you go from zero to 100— and there's nothing in between! It's like being squeezed by both self-oriented and other-oriented perfectionism. There's no room for failure by anyone. This habit of mind can be taxing over time, resulting in physical and emotional tension, which you may hardly notice until you land at a doctor's or therapist's office.

Whether you are in a position of authority or more of a worker bee, people around you know you can get any job done. But beware of a habit of going into overdrive or workaholism, which can rob you of pleasure, relaxation, and authentic connections with others.

The drill sergeant's inner strengths are charisma and vision. You're a champion for ideas, innovation, and ingenuity. You expect others to step up to the plate, and you draw them in with your magnetism and courage.

Inner Drill Sergeant Character Sketch

The drill sergeant is characterized by being inflexible and cold-hearted.

Driven by a need for control, your attention is easily hijacked by setbacks, challenges, or drama at work.

Your kryptonite is workaholism.

When you want to achieve something, you go into overdrive.

Your biggest strengths include courage, charisma, leadership, and vision.

LUIS'S STORY

Luis, the scientist you met in the introduction, had a difficult adjustment to managing people. He had a high standard for excellence—a quality that helped him make some early career achievements—but he also had a mean streak that he wasn't even aware of. High in other-oriented perfectionism, he was quick to ridicule those around him. He repudiated a need for belonging, preferring to go it alone, and he was driven to succeed at work (his low sense of belonging and overly amped energy put him in the lower-right quadrant of the Perfectionism Matrix).

It wasn't until a courageous employee filed a formal complaint that Luis was forced to get curious and question his ways. "I got pushed against a wall. I had no choice but to hear the feedback and agree to make some changes. That or lose everything I've worked so hard for."

As Luis explored his own inner critic, he realized that the drill sergeant also created problems in dating relationships. His last girlfriend broke up with him and accused him of being arrogant, selfish, and uncompromising. She was tired of him blaming others for minor offenses or things out of anyone's control: the traffic, a snow storm, the future. He turned out to be no fun. He felt genuinely sad about this and other bitter romantic endings. He worried that he might never find a partner.

When Luis began to connect the dots all the way back to his childhood, when he had to fight for his life in the streets, he started to soften a bit. He realized life didn't have to be a constant battle in the Red Zone. He named his drill sergeant "Tiny Terror." He envisioned this persona as a younger self with oversized boxing gloves, always prepared to fight, yet unable to hold someone's hand. For Luis, simply naming this part helped him diffuse some intense interpersonal situations by dropping his armor and learning to listen.

Inner Critic Archetype 3: The Sleuth

Are you the kind of person who constantly double-checks things? Or when it comes to a plan or a problem, are you the one who says, "Let me research it"? Maybe you play Dr. Google to a fault, or keep numerous spreadsheets or sticky notes. When you set your mind to something, you leave no stone unturned. If this sounds like you, your perfectionism may be driven by an inner narrative of constant evaluation and reevaluation. You imagine all the possibilities and try to predict the outcome. Your tunnel vision may cause you to miss seeing the forest for the trees. You aren't very comfortable with uncertainty and "what if" scenarios. In fact, not knowing the future kind of freaks you out.

You certainly aren't alone. Modern culture puts a premium on data, information, and innovation. The need to be on top of things or prevent calamity is understandable. But beware of a habit of falling into rabbit holes, getting distracted, or doom scrolling, which can lead you on unnecessary detours. The law of parsimony may serve you better at times (in other words, keep it simple).

Your inner strengths are curiosity and determination. You love a good adventure: treasure hunts, unsolved mysteries, escape rooms, ancestry searches, crypto investing, unusual collectables, Eye Spy, road trips, and other odysseys. You like to look at all angles and see many possibilities. People can count on you to never give up.

The Sleuth Character Sketch

The sleuth can get lost by tunnel vision and uncertainty.

Driven by fear of making a mistake or missing some crucial detail, your attention is easily hijacked by a worried mind.

Your kryptonite is distraction.

When you want to achieve something you leave no stone unturned.

Your biggest strengths include curiosity, exploration, and determination.

REED'S STORY

Taking to heart investor Porter Gale's prescription, "Your network is your net worth," Reed was relentless in building his contact list. But by his graduation from B-school, Reed described himself as "totally spent." Having over-subscribed to many clubs and obligations to organize events, he realized that the very thing he wanted to gain—a robust business network—was tenuous. He lacked authentic connections. His research, planning, and overthinking of his events took him away from personally engaging with keynote speakers, special guests, and alumni and forming the values-based connections he so desired. While his philosophy was that it's all about the handshake and small talk, he had little time for it.

Reed's energy was totally off balance too. He even joked that he was getting clumsy—spilling drinks, tripping on sidewalks, and losing his apartment keys. Brain fog settled in. He was in cognitive overload. It was as if the right and left sides of his brain weren't communicating. The pressure to land a six-figure job was too much—and when he finally did, he felt no relief whatsoever. It was on to the next goal post. His was the Blue Zone to Red Zone conundrum. He was exhausted, putting him in the low energy, high belonging quadrant. In his mind, Reed felt he had to uphold a standard from his hardworking parents. Whether it was a message from his family or a self-imposed precept, he felt it was up to him to lead the family into a next generation of success. No pressure! He called his inner critic FOMO, for "fear of missing an *opportunity*."

Inner Critic Archetype 4: The Nitpicker

Are you the type of person who likes things to be nice and neat? Does how you dress, organize your social media feed, or design your living space represent your unique sensibility and attention to detail? This is hardly a bad thing. Being trendy, owning a look that speaks to your truth, and having your own personal brand is great. Yet, when paired with an inner narrative of "not good enough," such perfectionism can be harmful to your spirit. So many of us grapple with self-worth and inner doubt. We can't help it. We are marinating in society that douses us with unrealistic ideals in every aspect of life: achievement, appearance, career, romance, and wealth, to name a few. Who's the next Internet influencer? Who made the latest list of *Forbes*'s 30 under 30 or *Fortune*'s 40 under 40?

Even if you like things to be just right and are a connoisseur of excellence, constant vigilance about every selfie, text, paper, or presentation can backfire. Sometimes, perfectionism can even stop you in your tracks. Procrastination may arise: Start. Question. Stop. Start. Compare. Stop. This can feel frustrating when your intention is noble and productive, but the result is feeling indecisive, inept, or imperfect. Your nervous energy may show up as tension as you flitter about trying to perfect every detail of your life. Worry may turn into fear or performance anxiety and then your body takes over and says, "Freeze!" Procrastination is a deer-in-the-headlights kind of move. It's an automatic survival response to protect you by being motionless in order to deter a predator—even though the only predator is the one in your own mind. It's flatlining into the extreme Green Zone of stagnation.

Your inner strengths are hospitality and orderliness. You value beauty and aesthetics. You have a knack for making people feel at home, cozy, and cared for. People can count on you to be an excellent host as you tend to unexpected details and delights.

Inner Nitpicker Character Sketch

The nitpicker is fraught with impatience and indecision.
Driven by fear of never being/doing enough, your attention is
easily hijacked by fear of the future.
Your kryptonite is procrastination.
When you want to achieve something, you dawdle over details.
Your biggest strengths include conscientiousness, orderliness,
and hospitality.

KAYLA'S STORY

Being a neatnik by nature bodes well for a future architect. "Attention
to detail, being organized, having excellent spatial sensibility" are the
phrases that Kayla, the environmental design student, used to describe
herself. But whenever she became overly focused on achieving the perfect solution without the trial and error needed in the creative process,
Kayla got really stuck. She was terrified by criticism and imagined herself being publicly shamed. Every step turned into an obstacle to the
point that Kayla could not get started until the project was due in less
than twenty-four hours. This kind of fixed mindset trapped Kayla into
a procrastination habit, and she would end up submitting inferior work.
It was like a self-fulfilling prophecy. With fits and starts she skated the
x-axis on the bottom half of the Perfectionism Matrix: between the low
energy, low belonging quadrant and the high energy, low belonging
quadrant. Emotionally, she was cycling between the Red Zone of alarm
and Blue Zone of striving until she kerplunked into inaction.

When Kayla began to reflect on the part of her that stopped her in
her tracks, she recalled some episodes in high school where she was
humiliated by a stern drama teacher. *Chin up! Elocute! Don't stand there
like a robot!* Looking back, she saw these as minor infractions, but the

shame she had felt in the moment was carved in her memory. She could still feel the other kids staring at her. Her fourteen-year-old self dreamed of being an actor, and this teacher squashed it. Kayla realized that she still carried this painful experience. No wonder she had presentation anxiety. On a deep emotional level, design school mattered just as much to her as being in the drama club had. But the stakes were much higher now.

Kayla loved the idea of naming her inner critic. She totally got into a role play on her mental stage. She decided to call it her "Inner Monica" after the famed roommate on the TV series *Friends* portrayed by actress Courteney Cox. Monica was known for her obsessive tidiness and being a control freak. "Next time my Inner Monica shows up, I'll know why."

Inner Critic Archetype 5: The Joy Thief

While most inner critical narratives will rob people of playfulness, spontaneity, and creative flow, the inner joy thief has a mistrust of feeling good and will go to great lengths to prevent you from enjoying yourself, experiencing pleasure, or having fun.

Do you find yourself unable to feel satisfied with life? Have a hard time being in the moment? Wonder how everyone else is having a good time? You may be driven by an inner narrative of scarcity mixed with constant fretting that something will go wrong. You just want to be seen as a good person. You agonize about the "what ifs." Unlike the inner sleuth, looking for clues and solutions, you wonder what catastrophe may strike. You seek preparedness.

Past mistakes or experiences from childhood may have encouraged a habit of playing it safe. You may be a highly sensitive person. Even if you make careful plans, you wonder when the other shoe will drop. Also, you care not just about what others think but also about how they feel. You worry about them. You are ready to rescue those in need without thinking twice.

The desire for security is a basic human need. But beware of a habit of ruminating over imagined disasters. Our minds are stress-producing machines. They are creative to be sure, but the joy thief harps on the worst-case scenarios and relational melodrama. It's all too easy to replay a mental horror movie again and again. Don't get caught in a headspin!

Your inner strengths are compassion and friendship. You embrace life with open arms. You have a heart of gold and only want the best for others. Patience and understanding come naturally to you, and people know they can trust you.

Inner Joy Thief Character Sketch

The joy thief may suffer from codependency and compassion fatigue.

Driven by fear of past mistakes and future catastrophes, your attention is easily hijacked by social drama or suffering in the world.

Your kryptonite is self-doubt.

When you want to achieve something, you ruminate or obsess.

Your biggest strengths include compassion, friendship, patience, and an open heart.

JUSTIN'S STORY

Justin is the football player who suffered from homesickness and anxiety. He had a soft heart and felt everything. He wanted to show up for his teammates, his parents, and the community he left behind who had cheered him on since peewee football. Of course, they were all following his college football career. Some hometown fans made trips to see him play, tailgating at games, and held up fan signs. Disappointing others was Justin's worst nightmare.

Yet being a Division 1 athlete was a full-time job. Justin realized he didn't it like very much. He struggled to divide his energies between practice and academics. Justin didn't know he could change his mind about it, feeling too deep in. He was trapped by socially prescribed perfectionism, wanting to be seen as the all-American good guy. He knew his heart wasn't in football anymore, but he wouldn't dare tell anyone. He was afraid of copping out. It was no wonder his heart spoke for him. Moments of panic, with a racing heart and shortness of breath, became more frequent. College was just no fun.

When sports came to a screeching halt due a torn ACL, Justin was secretly relieved. He was in the low energy, high belonging quadrant. He went home on a leave of absence. His anxiety symptoms went away. He took time to reflect on what happened. When it came to his inner critic, he realized that the "people pleasing part of me sucked out all the joy in my life." Tellingly, he called his inner critic "Leech."

Naming Your Inner Critic

Now it's your turn. Now that you have an idea what an inner critic is, we are going to see if you can personify your inner critic, as if you were choosing an actor to portray it in a movie.

In the spirit of play, I invite you to get your notebook or journal and a pen. Colored pencils or markers can also help you bring some creativity to the page. (Seriously, give this a try.) Once you have your supplies and you're ready to start figuring out what name to give your inner critic, follow these steps.

Step 1: Notice the Inner Critic

Think about a recent situation that caused you some distress or where you beat yourself up. Imagine you are looking back at the scene as if you were watching it on a movie screen. Imagine that this voice is a character in a movie, and then spend 10–15 minutes writing your answers to the following questions in your notebook or journal.

1. Set the scene: Who were you with? What were you doing? Where were you? What time of day and year was it?
2. What were you thinking? What did you say to yourself?
3. Describe in detail the words, tone, attitude, and feelings you experienced when you judged or criticized yourself.
4. Get inside the mind of your inner voice for a minute and be curious. How is this inner critic protecting you? What might be its positive intention or role from its point of view?

If you can't identify a primary inner voice, or Plus One, it's OK. Try again in a day or two. Over time, something will come to you. (And you can repeat this exercise to name any of your other inner algorithms another time.)

Step 2: Name This Part of Yourself

Now let's flesh this character out a bit more. Continuing to write in your notebook, answer the following questions:

1. Give your Plus One some characteristics and qualities. Does it have a gender? Something distinctive about its look? A particular way of acting, moving, or speaking?
2. What emotional charge does this part of yourself bring up for you? What uncomfortable feelings, thoughts, or labels come to mind? Any disowned aspects of your personality?
3. Does it have an age or phase in development?
4. What name fits its personality?

With naming, be creative. Maybe you want to name your inner critic after a character in a movie, TV show, or novel. Avoid giving it the name or role of a family member or foe, since it brings in unnecessary complexities, and refrain from using profanities or being too deprecating, because over time you will cultivate a healing relationship with this part of you. However, one of my clients in her 70s named her inner critic Ms. Fuck It and could trace being able to hear this voice back to her teenage years. It made her laugh affectionately every time she mentioned this part of herself. Use whatever works.

Keep in mind that some inner critics are terribly harsh, and it can be very uncomfortable to face that. It's not uncommon for people to internalize the voice of a tyrant or a tormentor as a survival strategy: you'll beat yourself up before anyone else gets a chance to. It's a sort of "If you can't beat 'em, join 'em" approach. You may even wonder, *How in the world is this inner critic trying to help me?* Suspend any judgment, and just try to remain curious—which can require a huge dose of self-compassion and courage.

Write down the name of your inner critic on a note card or sticky note. Use it like a bookmark as you read this book, so you can jot your observations about it as you go. You may even want to find an image of it, which is what Kayla did. She found a photo of the character Monica from *Friends* and talked to it. You'll learn more about tending to the inner critic in chapter 5. For now, just play with the idea of this Plus One and notice when and where it shows up.

No matter what nickname you give your inner critic, or which of the archetypes it aligns with, you can learn to let your inner critic know that you see them and that you care for them. When you notice your Plus One show up from here on out, you'll have an opportunity to tend to the triggers that roused it. Take it as a signal to pay attention: "Oh, hello, inner critic! What message are you trying to convey? How are you trying to protect, warn, or encourage me in this situation?" Be curious: What emotion zone are you experiencing? In what state is your energy? What about your sense of belonging? What kind of perfectionism may be at play?

Now instead of automatically reacting out of habit, you can respond in a conscious, beneficial manner. You can also learn to ask for help, find collaborators, and take a rest. Eventually, your inner critic won't have to work so hard for you in sorting out all the possibilities, and it can relax, play, create, connect, and inspire. In doing so, you can transform your energy—and your inner critic—to discover greater balance, well-being, and happiness.

An Inner Evolution

Throughout my years of clinical practice and study, I have distilled this journey to happy achieving into a six-step process. In essence, these steps help you evolve your nervous system, rewrite your perfectionist inner algorithms, and transform your inner critics so that you can create, play, and live the life you desire. The six steps spell out EVOLVE, and that is precisely what we are aiming to do—to bring about your own personal evolution with kindness. The steps are:

1. **E: Embody the Present Moment.** This step helps you increase your body awareness, get out of your head, and listen to the wisdom that your body is trying to share with you. It also teaches you to start considering your energy—the metaphysical and the metabolic—and discover simple but powerful ways to get it unstuck and flowing. In this step, you will learn to recruit your physiology to have your back.

2. **V: Validate Your Experience.** As you recognize thoughts, emotions, and sensations as normal responses to stress and perfectionism, you liberate yourself from harsh algorithms, accept yourself, and begin to unblock stuck energies for lasting change.

3. **O: Open Your Heart.** When you befriend the negative voices in your head, you begin a deep process of self-compassion and cultivating heart coherence, the ultimate antidote to perfectionism, shame, and unhelpful survival strategies.

4. **L: Love Your Inner Critic.** Because self-love often—and sadly—feels so foreign to so many of us perfectionists, resistance to self-compassion will undoubtedly arise. Welcome the challenge as you continually practice courage, compassion, and connection.

5. **V: Make a Vow.** By committing to change and putting in joyful effort, you will learn to identify values, clarify your purpose, and discover new possibilities you can't even imagine right now. Trust and believe.

6. **E: Spark the Energy of Excellence.** Through daily practice of self-care and kindsight, you will become fluent in directing your attention to the sweet spot of belonging and energy flow. The negative effects of perfectionism will readily dissolve the moment you recognize the pattern, and the happy achiever in you will thrive.

Each step has a clear goal, with each one building upon the previous step. Like scaffolding or training wheels, the first two steps are foundational. E and V involve being present and understanding your emotions. You will come back to them over and over again in life—and on a daily basis, for that matter. The two next steps, O and L, involve walking alongside your inner critics to truly understand, appreciate, and care for them, so they can transform into inner allies. For better and worse, your inner critics are your companions and you will learn to grow with them. Opening your heart and caring for all parts of your inner life requires vulnerability and courage. That's why the V, making a vow, is necessary. E, the energy of excellence, is finding yourself in a balance of effort and ease, connection and self-sufficiency, and compassion and courage to be a happy achiever.

I encourage you to share your intentions to evolve your perfectionistic quirks with a trustworthy friend and even work together on befriending your inner critics. It helps to have allies because, while evolution is absolutely possible, it takes a commitment. Accountability helps you keep taking action, and action is curative.

As you read on, you will begin to direct tenderness and kindness to yourself, and most certainly toward your inner critic. I call this a practice of *kindfulness*, being aware of the present moment, whatever arises, with heart. Along the way, you will learn how to make peace with your Plus One and any other inner critic you begin to notice, and to transform their energies into lasting inner resources for well-being. Just imagine the possibilities when you can harness the algorithms that keep you in the trapped mind loops and turn them into something beautiful. Gather your minions and let's keep going. You're about to EVOLVE.

PART 2

The New Solution

(That Actually Helps)

When you're not fixed, or fixated, on one part or one idea
of yourself, you're free to shift and change, and to discover
new things about the world and yourself, which is one of the
most exciting things about being alive.

— Terri Trespicio

So far you've discovered that perfectionism arises to help you meet your needs for acceptance, belonging, and love. And that there are costs to perfectionism that accrue over time. You've also identified how perfectionism shows up for you, and you've named your inner critic. This next section spells out the EVOLVE method, a recipe for overcoming the negative effects of perfectionism that hold you back from fully investing in your life. This begs a question: what does it mean to evolve?

Evolving is a gradual process of development or change. To evolve as a person means to adapt, grow, and refine. It doesn't mean to leave behind or trash what doesn't work. Evolving may mean moving from the simplistic to the more complex, or it may require simplifying what is too complicated. Charles Darwin, in his classic *The Origin of Species*, wrote, "It is not the strongest of the species that survives, nor the most intelligent that survives. It is the one that is most adaptable to change."

No matter what, evolving takes time and energy. In my quest to help people heal from the harmful effects of perfectionism, many are worried that they are asked to give up the value of excellence or the tenacity that got them to reach their goal or status. They worry they will lose their edge, dampen their motivation, or be seen as weak. When it comes to evolving perfectionism, there is no need to give up important values of success or achievement. The invitation is to release the suffering. The hope is to find harmony.

Everything is changing all the time. Just like the brain and nervous system developed over millions of years, you too are evolving in response to your experiences inside and out. The EVOLVE process offers step-by-step instructions on befriending your inner critic, bringing you into balance, and experimenting with new, lighter ways of being. With each new EVOLVE step you will hear stories of real people, some of whom you've already met, who have already walked this path and freed themselves from the negative effects of perfectionism. You will see how their inner critics were influencing their lives and how they changed too. Reflection questions are sprinkled throughout. Each step ends with Happy Achiever Tools. Consider these mini-activities as "playwork" as they will help you to Get Grounded, Get Energized, and Get Connected.

I'm excited for you. The more you become aware of how perfectionism influences your mind, your body, and your spirit, the better able you are to evolve—not over millennia, or even over generations, but in your own lifetime. You are now about to embark on an adventure to happy achieving—a journey that begins with being present to your life.

4

Step 1

E, Embody the Present Moment

What if you started out exactly where you are?
Not where you were, or where you want to be, but right
here, right now, with the best of what you carry with you?

— *Jacqui Bonwell and Andy Cahill*

No two perfectionists are alike, even if certain ways of thinking, feeling, or behaving get distilled down to a caricature—the snobby, know-it-all, controlling, and uptight made-for-TV persona such as Aubrey in *Pitch Perfect*, Sheldon in *The Big Bang Theory*, Miranda Priestly in *The Devil Wears Prada*, and Dr. Frasier Crane in *Frasier*. Rather than a fixed identity, perfectionism is more like a kaleidoscope comprised of intelligence, idiosyncrasies, beauty, longing, and mystery, peppered with core beliefs about worthiness, lovability, and belonging. The image can shift with moment to moment changes that happen in response to conversations with others, the demands of getting through a day, or your own expectations.

When I meet with a perfectionist, it's as if I see an abstract Picasso portrait. There is a blend of complexities that by turns obscure and illuminate subtle qualities about their needs and desires for a meaningful life. They are also often all "neck up."

If you have perfectionist tendencies, you likely use a lot of brain power on overthinking and analyzing. As a result, you are not quite embodied, by which I simply mean connected to your body. If I were to take a conventional therapeutic approach and start talking to you about your struggles with perfectionism, we would likely only reinforce the ruminating mind. So my approach is to nudge perfectionists back into their bodies. This means creating a connection, or an energetic conduit, from the head, the heart, and all the way down to the tippy toes. When this connection is established and energy is flowing, you can enjoy the stability that comes from being grounded. You can unlock stuck energy and experience a range of emotions and sensations—the most important one being trusting yourself.

Becoming embodied is a wonderful development. But it can be very challenging.

Daria, the young lawyer you met in chapter 2, lingered after a perfectionism workshop. "How do you know when it's your inner critic that is causing your stress, or if it's your stress that's spiking your inner critic?" she asked me. "Do I just breathe or do I recite some affirmation?" she added, somewhat sarcastically. Daria had attended other perfectionism workshops and to her credit was trying to make some shifts in her life. Yet she was looking for nice, neat categories, or a kind of map that could tell her which direction to go. She was trying to find all the intellectual possibilities but avoiding paying attention to her current physical state.

Asher, in a wheelchair, also lingered afterward. He had introduced himself as having chronic back pain after a near-fatal biking accident that prolonged his studies. In his seventh year of a PhD in astrophysics, he wasn't sure he'd ever finish. He had fallen behind because he'd spent so much time becoming his own medical advocate and searching for solutions. He felt very supported by his advisors, who perhaps gave too much leeway rather than a firm deadline. Still, Asher felt overwhelmed. He told me, "My head is saying, 'Just get up! Keep going!' but sometimes I just can't. I mean, I have to finish, but my body says 'Hell, no.' I feel that others see me as some wimp. Now I feel like an imposter."

Reed, the overextended master of the Blue Zone, recent MBA graduate student starting his first finance job, was listening intently. He slid into the conversation. "I learned today about burnout. I checked everything on the list. I mean *everything*. Exhaustion, depersonalization, no motivation, lack of meaning. I didn't even know that's what it was. All those B-school trips and conferences I organized left me feeling totally disconnected. It seems like all that effort was wasted. Now I wake up knowing a fourteen-hour day is ahead of me and ask myself, *Why bother?*"

All three in one way or another were in a nervous system collapse. Stuck in place. In freeze mode. Emotionally flatlined. A bankrupt body budget. In a depleted, stagnant Green Zone. And they were just starting to realize it. This may sound like bad news, but it's actually great news, because awareness of a problem means change has already begun.

The Goal of Step 1: Being Aware of the Present Moment

The first step in any desire for change is noticing. No judging. Just being aware. This may sound easy enough, but it can be quite challenging to move from criticism to curiosity. Yet when you begin to be curious, you tap your inner humanity. You begin to understand that those inner critical voices beating you up are thought patterns, memories, or old beliefs. Sometimes they cut, like carving your name into a tree. Sometimes that cut disturbs the flow of nutrients the tree needs to flourish. Eventually bark grows over the initial wound. Similarly, inner algorithms of judgment are well-worn incisions. They can hold a very deep groove in the nervous system. These wounds block energy flow. When blocked energy is released it transforms into healing. Noticing those cuts, then, is the first step toward freedom.

As you learned in chapter 1, perfectionism predictably shows up as physical tension. Tension is a disruption in the flow of energy. Once you start to identify these signals, you are making strides, because it means you are beginning to understand that your head is connected to your body. This bodily awareness is not some sort of in-depth investigation of aches or ailments or hypochondria. It's more of a little check-in and quick body scan. Let's try it now.

Find a moment to pause and notice your body from head to toe. Take a few deep, cleansing breaths. Ask yourself:

- *What is my body telling me right now?*
- *Where do I notice my breathing to be flowing most freely?*
- *What's the quality of my breathing?*
- *Where do I sense my heartbeat?*
- *Where is there a sense of strain or tightness?*
- *Where is there lightness and ease?*

This kind of nonjudgmental awareness is the premise of basic mindfulness practices, and it's a very powerful and necessary life skill. It's a gentle tuning into the present moment and paying attention as things unfold. Many people think mindfulness is overrated and marketed as a quick fix. Daria's tiresome quip, "Do I just breathe?" speaks to this. No doubt McMindfulness consumerism is alive and well. But one thing is true: a mindfulness practice *is* effective when you actually do it consistently. Commonly, people try mindfulness meditation on an app and quickly conclude it is not for them or they aren't good at it. It's a disappointing experience. *My mind is too busy. I can't empty my thoughts. It's scary inside my brain. It's just not for me. I don't have time.*

These common resistances are all valid. Your mind *is* busy. You *can't* empty your thoughts. Your narratives *will* time travel to the past and project into the future. It can be a nightmare when you actually peek into the latest mind movie that's playing, especially if you've also been experiencing a dip in mood. And mindfulness meditation is not for everyone— although it definitely can help a wide swath of people. The reason it might not have worked for you is that you likely paired an expectation with the first attempt of practice. That's the predictive brain for you. Maybe it felt sort of blah. Or your mind went into a rabbit hole after thirty seconds. And then you judged yourself. How perfectionistic of you!

Decades of research studies show that mindfulness and meditation have positive benefits—and potentially lasting ones when you lead your daily life with the compassionate awareness that these practices help you foster.[1] Think of being *mindful* as you might think about *fitness*, and *meditation* like *exercise*. One is the ability, the other is the method. In order to get fit, it helps to do repetitions of specific kinds of physical activities. Similarly, in order to become mindful it helps to have a routine, like following along a meditation script. And short reps are perfectly fine to start out. So is a variety of practices to keep things interesting and fun too.

The neuroscientist Amisha Jha, PhD, and her research team at the University of Miami have demonstrated that mindfulness training has clear benefits among some of the most pressured types of people, like the marines, special operation forces, and football players.[2] Jha's skeptical study subjects followed a certain routine of weekly mindfulness classes over eight weeks with homework practices prescribed for thirty minutes a day.

Of course, like most humans, these professionals weren't consistent, and they didn't follow all the instructions. Some practiced their mindfulness reps consistently and others did not. So after crunching the numbers, the researchers established a minimum effective dose for mindfulness practice: twelve minutes a day.

In the end, these elite professional groups showed improvements in attention and working memory, even though they did their practices imperfectly. There were changes in the cortical layers of their brains that are associated with attention networks, which Jha likens to the brain's version of better muscle tone. The mindfulness groups also reported greater well-being and improved relationships, suggesting that they became more present and patient in their own personal lives too.

You might think you don't have twelve extra minutes. I get it. If so, start with three minutes a day and work your way up. Or try three minutes approximately four times a day. Find a little smidge of time when a few minutes of focused breathing or a body scan or savoring can happen naturally. Think of all the possibilities: When boiling water for tea or pasta. In the shower. Waiting in the carpool line. Sitting on the subway. Walking the dog. The bottom line is: start small, and don't give up before you really try.

Types of Mindful Meditation Practices

There are many types of mindfulness practices. The following list is just some of the variations you might find in a mindfulness program, on YouTube, or in meditation apps. It's fun to experiment to see what suits you and when. Choose one or a small handful from the list below that you will try out so that you can start raising your awareness of the present moment.

Body scan
Breath focus
Compassion meditations
Gentle yoga
Gratitude practice
Kirtan Kriya mantra (sound)
Loving-kindness meditation
Mantra meditation
Mindful eating
Mindful walking
Object awareness
Open awareness
Shifting focus to awareness

A Dose of Kindfulness

The psychologist and meditation teacher Tara Brach talks about the two wings of mindfulness. Like a bird in flight, one wing is wisdom (or understanding) and the other wing is love (or compassion).[3] Both are needed to soar. After all, a focused sniper with calm breathing and intense focus might be very aware of the present moment but may shut out empathy. And compassion without wisdom—such as repeatedly giving money to a family member with an addiction—may lead to poor boundaries, martyrdom, compassion fatigue, and burnout. Tellingly, the Chinese character for heart also embeds the symbol for the mind. They are inseparable. The practice of mindfulness without compassion ignores the resonance of the heart and our innate kindness. That's why my favorite term is *kindfulness*, or being aware of the present moment with heart.

A basic kindfulness practice is simply pairing each inhale and exhale with a word that evokes comfort and care. Your word choice represents an anchor for your attention, so when you notice your mind wandering—as it naturally does—you can gather your attention around the word or phrase. This is sometimes referred to as a mantra, and it's a nice way to begin training your mind to be present. (I walk you through just such a practice at the end of this chapter—if you want to jump ahead to the Happy Achiever Tools and give it a shot now, you'll see it listed under the "Get Grounded" header.)

It's useful that you know that the mind wanders 50 percent of the time. It's just what it does. So don't get mad at yourself when you lose focus or get distracted. A mindfulness routine will serve you well, especially as we are about to embark on another lesson about the nervous system. To drive the point home, the benefits of mindfulness are multidimensional. Mindfulness practices positively influence the following areas:

- *Personal well-being*, such as reductions in stress, not getting stuck in a mind loop (less rumination), decreased negative emotions (like with anxiety, depression, or PTSD), ability to effectively manage emotions, and helps with better focus, attention and working memory.
- *Interpersonal well-being*, including enhanced relationships as well as increases in empathy, compassion, prosocial skills, and workplace satisfaction.
- *Physical well-being*, as measured by improved symptom management among people with heart disease, diabetes, eating disorders,

chronic pain, digestive disorders, and autoimmune conditions, among others.

Mindfulness is correlated with healthy heart rate variability and vagal tone, which are physiological indicators of well-being and resilience. Resilience is the capacity to flexibly navigate life's challenges. Resilience, like mindfulness, is one of those buzzwords that people love to hate. The US Department of Health and Human Services defines individual resilience as the ability to withstand, adapt to, and recover from adversity and stress.[4] In other words, resilience can manifest as bouncing back to one's original state of well-being or bouncing forward to an emerging or more well-developed state of well-being by using effective coping strategies.

The heart and the vagus nerve appear to have significant roles to play, as I describe below. Moreover, practices that emphasize compassion such as loving-kindness meditation or briefly placing a hand over the heart, are correlated with release of oxytocin and vasopressin, which are the warm and fuzzy neurochemicals that evoke sensations of care and comfort and alleviate stress.[5]

Despite its documented beneficial outcomes, you may dismiss mindfulness as either too trendy, too hard, or too *something*—especially if you haven't yet given it a good college try. What if you replace the word *mindful* with *attentive, awake, aware, curious, kindful, observant, openminded, present,* or *receptive*? Which of these options (or other words that you come up with) resonates with you? Whatever word you choose, you now have a new trick to flex your mindfulness muscle.

Embodiment Reflection #1: What's Your Brand of Stress?

Especially now, in Step 1, *Embodying the Present Moment*, I want you to key into your body's sensations when feeling stressed.

To do that, see if you can bring to mind a recent stressful moment, mild to moderate. Try to select a specific unpleasant sensation that lasted for a few minutes and might be in the 3 to 6 range on a 1 to 10 stress scale (from least to most intensity). You can read how Daria reflected on her brand of stress below to guide you. Be your own friendly detective and take an outside observer stance. Or imagine being a fly on the wall. Have an attitude of curiosity and playfulness, and then fill in the following prompts:

My stress intensity rating (on a scale of 1–10) during this
    event was:
The stressful event was:
The trigger was:
The body's sensations included:
The emotional reactions were:
The inner dialogue was:
Inner critic type:

Here's Daria's observation about a stressful moment:

My stress intensity rating (1–10) was: 6
The stressful event was: First-year dinner with law firm
The trigger was: A partner commented on a project delay
The body's sensations included: Racing heart, perspiration
The emotional reactions were: Fear, embarrassment
The inner dialogue was: *Boss thinks I'm incompetent. I'll prob-
    ably get fired. Why did I even bother to come?*
Inner critic type: Judge

As Daria sketched out her stress reactions, she described an event with her peers and the partners in the law firm. Reflecting on the scene, Daria recalled how her heart was hammering away and she had a hard time paying attention to casual conversation. She broke into a sweat. Daria interpreted one of the partners' comments personally, she noted, when there was no evidence for this. The project delay had to do with government regulations, not her performance. "I don't know why I always assume things are my fault! Or take responsibility for things when I don't need to. Am I that much of a control freak?" Great noticing. Daria was now curious about her reaction—or shall we say, overreaction. She was ready to correct her brain's predictions by doing something different.

How about you? Noticing how your body feels when you're feeling anxious or stressed offers important clues. Because these stress symptoms are uncomfortable you likely want to get rid of them quickly or ignore them altogether, missing an important opportunity to understand your own personal brand of stress. As you get to know your unique brand of stress, you can begin to more accurately interpret the sensations, triggers, and responses.

You've Got Some Nerve

Previously, you learned a bit about the emotional motivation zones described in compassion-focused therapy—the Red, Blue, and Green Zones that broadly correspond to experiences of threat, drive, and soothe. Maybe you already got curious about which emotional zones you most often find yourself in. Now we are going to dig into the nervous system to understand how it ties into these emotion motivation zones. (Here's a preview: everything is connected.) Once you see how the brain is in the service of regulating your body budget and aims to protect you, you will also come to understand how to better provide a sense of safety and protection for yourself without having to spend a lot of time in the Red Zone, in particular. Because this is nerdy information, I'll use images and metaphors along the way that various experts have translated for people like me who need simple tools. But remember, metaphors are just metaphors, and your experience is your experience.

To get started, let's look at what stresses you out. There's no denying it: life can be hard. It's easy to get stressed, and naturally, most of us get stressed out on a daily basis. There are many ordinary irritants and challenges—you can experience stress from your environment, your body, and your thoughts. There are also extraordinary events such as trauma, grief, and setbacks. Whatever their source, the body reacts to these changes with physical, mental, and emotional responses.

Stress is simply the body's reaction to any change that requires an adjustment or response. It originates from your body's highly sensitive surveillance system—what's known as the autonomic nervous system (ANS). The ANS is always operating, even when you are asleep. Some stress is positive and keeps you alert, motivated, and safe—the pleasant qualities of the Red, Blue and Green Zones. Some stress is unpleasant and keeps you in states of reactivity, compulsion, or numbing—the negative qualities of these zones. Sometimes life hits you with a lot of punches. Or your best laid plans don't work out. Or you get stuck in a mental mind loop of worry or fear. Daily hassles can turn into a thousand little nicks. That can lead to chronic stress and inflammation, wreaking havoc in your body.[6] It's often a matter of the intensity, duration, and perception of stress that eats at you, making it easier or harder to recover. Though stress also offers plenty of opportunities to notice and be curious.

Raising your awareness of your stress response will help you expand your "window of distress tolerance." This is psychology lingo for your capacity to face and withstand unpleasant experiences without getting hijacked by them.[7] The *Merriam-Webster Dictionary* defines *tolerate* as "to endure without serious side effects or discomfort." In other words, being within your window of tolerance allows you to maintain a sense of safety and connection even when you dip into the emotional Red Zone and freak out from time to time.

Expanding your window of tolerance implies a kind of acceptance and flexibility—knowing when to open and close your window. It is very hard to learn something new, progress on a goal, or change your habits if you have to put up with something that is uncomfortable and painful for too long. That can eventually lead to a shutdown or walling off, the downside of Green Zone depletion. In other words, there's no learning in a state of overwhelm; you have to feel safe yet challenged enough to take in new information and grow. Therefore, it helps to stretch that window from a narrow sliver to a generous opening that allows a fresh breeze to pass through.

As we begin to EVOLVE, having a deeper understanding of the nervous system will help—especially for the skeptical inner managers who resist change. It's not just tricky brains and the central nervous system we have to contend with, as I covered in chapter 2. The nervous system has two main parts that work in tandem: the central nervous system (CNS) in the brain and spinal cord, and the peripheral nervous system (PNS) throughout the body. As described by Lisa Feldman Barrett's theory of constructed emotion, the CNS builds a predictive internal model of your own body in an ever-changing world and serves to reduce uncertainty and regulate your body budget.[8] It constructs emotions and other mental concepts based on your unique neural system, which is continually shaped by your life experiences and culture. The PNS contains the nerves and ganglia (synaptic relay stations) outside of the central nervous system and reaches to the outermost boundaries of the body. It communicates between the brain and the body's organs, skin, and limbs and sends information from most of your senses. Some signals, such as your breathing and beating heart, are automatic and governed by the ANS, while others, like movement, are under your control.

The PNS has two branches: the somatic nervous system (SNS), which transmits sensory information and controls voluntary movement, and the autonomic nervous system (ANS), that regulates the automatic processes that we don't need to think about, like breathing, blood flow, heartbeat, and digestion. The ANS has three systems that work to achieve homeostasis or balance: the sympathetic (SNS), parasympathetic (PSNS), and enteric (ENS) systems. These are sometimes referred to as "fight or flight," "rest and digest," and "the second brain," respectively.[9]

The PSNS connects the head and the heart through an intricate tapestry of neurons. In fact, the brain and the heart are connected by both descending and ascending neural pathways. The heart has its own beautiful intelligence and sends signals to the brain via the right and left vagal nerves, which together constitute the longest cranial nerve in the body, stretching from the brainstem to the gut.[10] Vagus means "wander" in Latin, as it travels between the brain and the body's organs (the viscera), like the heart, lungs, stomach, and intestines, through a bidirectional network of sensory, spatial, and motor neurons.[11] There is a constant conversation between the brain and the body—an important one being the information communicated from the body to the brain via the winding path of the vagus nerve. Imagine the heart and the vagus nerve are entwined like a pair of lovers to create harmony in the body. Healthy cardiac "vagal tone" is an indicator of resilience as well as better mental and physical well-being as measured indirectly by heart rate variability.[12] Stronger vagal tone helps you "reset" from stress with more agility and positive emotions, which put you squarely in the healthy Green Zone of vitality.

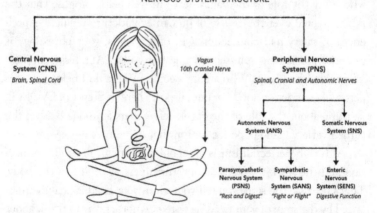

NERVOUS SYSTEM STRUCTURE

Central Nervous System (CNS)
Brain, Spinal Cord

Vagus
10th Cranial Nerve

Peripheral Nervous System (PNS)
Spinal, Cranial and Autonomic Nerves

Autonomic Nervous System (ANS)

Somatic Nervous System (SNS)

Parasympathetic Nervous System (PSNS)
"Rest and Digest"

Sympathetic Nervous System (SANS)
"Fight or Flight"

Enteric Nervous System (SENS)
Digestive Function

When Daria, Asher, and Reed began to learn some general basics about the nervous system in the perfectionism workshop, they began to interpret their experiences of stress in entirely new ways. Instead of blaming themselves for their thoughts and behaviors, like procrastination or workaholism, they got curious about their seemingly automatic reactions to life's challenges. With some mindfulness (which by now hopefully you've tried) and grounding practices (which we'll get to shortly), they could recognize these fluctuations in their body as passing states and their mind as a simulator of past and current experiences. By being more heart centered, they began to widen their windows of tolerance for the triggers of stress as well as those pesky inner critical voices that magically appeared to condemn them. As they began to understand the lingo of the nervous system, they grasped a new way to understand why they reacted the way they did—like beating oneself up or minimizing accomplishments or feeling like an imposter. Now you will too.

Finding Balance from the Inside Out

Noticing the dynamic relationship between your nervous system and your perfectionism may just help you recognize opportunities to *respond* to stress rather than *react* to it. Scientists and mental health experts who study the role of the vagus nerve in well-being propose that the ANS adapted over the course of human evolution to regulate experiences of safety *and* connection.[13] In other words, your physiology is essentially assessing split-second questions like "Am I safe or not? Where do I find help? Who are my people? Where do I belong? Is this person dangerous or not?" For our purposes here in Step 1 of EVOLVE, learning about the role of the vagus nerve offers a unique lens on the garden variety blend of perfectionism that so many of us experience.

Although perfectionism is all about the human need for connection and the stories we have about worthiness, it begins in the body. That's because the story you tell yourself in your head is heavily influenced by the state of your nervous system. Another way to think about this is that your mind narrates what your body senses from cues of safety or danger. Therapist Deb Dana, author of *Befriending the Nervous System*, refers to this as "story follows state."[14]

Our minds are always trying to create meaning out of every experience. For example, recall a time you were teased and didn't like it. You probably felt a rush of heat to your face or butterflies in the belly—like an alarm got triggered in your nervous system, even if subtle. Whether the comment was meant in friendly jest or as a purposeful slight, where did your mind go? Most likely you felt embarrassed, exposed, or began to doubt yourself. A story formed: *I'm so uncool. I'm boring. I don't fit in.* Red Zone. Or maybe you see posts on social media of people living the good life and suddenly you feel a pang in your chest followed by a thought: *Oh, I'll show them what I'm capable of.* Blue Zone.

Think of this as a "bottom up" approach to understanding how the nervous system shapes our experiences—or seeking to influence the mental state by addressing the body first. It is different from the "top down" approach you might learn in certain kinds of mental health interventions, like cognitive behavioral therapy, where the focus is on changing mental conditions or habits first. Both approaches are useful. But since so much of human behavior is automatic and habitual, it's important to have a good understanding of how the nervous system is continually adapting to your ever-changing experiences to keep you regulated and alive. Besides, sometimes we just have to get outside of our heads and into our bodies.

Coregulation: Borrowing From Others

As humans we "are faced with the dilemma of balancing the drive to survive and the longing to connect," as therapist Deb Dana puts it.[15] Or as neuroscientist Barrett notes, we are faced with the human problem of getting ahead versus getting along.[16] This is so apt for perfectionism, which is the struggle between survival fears and the need for belonging. Remember, the drive to be perfect is the nervous system responding to a perceived threat, primarily a fear of rejection by others. One of the reasons we are wired to seek connection to others and avoid rejection is that our nervous system seeks attunement with other people's nervous systems, and vice versa.

Whenever you are around another person, imagine that your nervous system is asking that person's nervous system "Is it safe to connect?" There is a constant interplay of connection and disconnection, like a tango dance—moments of disruption and disconnection, followed by moments of connection and repair. As we've covered, the ANS and vagus nerve are like a highly sensitive radar system with bidirectional pathways in the body. You can think of this like brain-body cross talk that formed unconscious patterns, culled from early interactions of caregiving that communicated cues of safety or danger. These early templates continue to shape your physiology through moment-to-moment experiences of coregulation with other people, which is an essential human need for feeling safe in the presence of others.

What this all means is that we need caring people around us. Not only are relationships an evolutionary imperative to pass genes down from one generation to the next, healthy relationships allow you to flourish. We coregulate in relationship to others through interpersonal cues and gestures that communicate safeness and care. A kind tone of voice, an expression of love, a friendly hug. That's like borrowing the benefits of other people's mojo. Your nervous system connects to another person's nervous system even if you're not consciously aware of it. I used to say to my teenage daughters, your friends can bring you up or they can bring you down. Choose wisely. (Hint: Look for connecting with people who have well-regulated nervous systems!)

Intuitively, you probably know this too. You may pick up on positive or negative vibes from someone else. Sometimes you may be right on the mark or you may miss the clues, depending on how your whole nervous system has been shaped by experiences of safety or danger with other people. Some of the earliest experiences of rejection come not from family but from peers. Playgrounds, social media, school bus rides, and middle school cafeterias the world over are breeding grounds for the struggle of acceptance and rejection. Your nervous system may also be influenced by intergenerational transmission of stress or trauma that shaped your parents and ancestors' nervous systems.

Because law student Daria had childhood experiences of being reprimanded, for example, she was inclined to take her boss's benign comment as a criticism. As she grew up she became hypervigilant about making mistakes. Now she may misread a neutral comment as negative. Reed was the scrawny player on the baseball team and compensated by being the affable kid. Hosting parties when his parents were away ensured his popularity in high school. Asher, known for being an intrepid trailblazer who people looked up to, felt crushed by his sudden disability and ensuing loneliness. He lost his social tribe by virtue of an accident and now felt left out.

So it makes sense that when there are disruptions in body budgeting, an imbalance results, and we try to make meaning of it. The window of tolerance closes or is inflexible, and like Daria and the others, you may be unable to see a bigger picture or other perspectives in a moment of stress. Over time, a dysregulated nervous system can lead to physical and mental health problems. Luckily, you can learn to bring these body sensations into awareness with interoceptive awareness and begin to readjust for greater well-being and healing.

Embodiment Reflection #2: Making New Guesses

Let's go back to the original question about your brand of stress as you reflect on moments of upset and self-berating. Think about the items you identified on the Perfectionism Self-Inquiry and your various habits, like leaving deadlines to the last minute, compulsive work hours, getting lost in a rabbit hole of details, doovers, or presenting an impeccable self. Which behaviors might be triggered by the survival states in the nervous system? Are there other ways to look at the situation? Can you recategorize the stressful moment as: A normal case of nerves? The metabolic effort needed to do something hard? Low blood sugar? Irritation from lack of sleep? Another person's bad day? Something else?

Correcting the Predictions of Perfectionism

As you may be gleaning, your procrastination may not be a personal failing, but rather your body's response to a fear of making a mistake. These responses can vary widely: You may experience being underenergized (affective states of malaise, fatigue, or unpleasantness). Remember Asher, who is worried if he'll ever get his degree and feeling hopeless—*If I don't finish this dissertation I'm done for! Why bother?* He's the perfect example of being plunked into a depleted body budget and feeling hijacked by a fear of failure and imposter feelings. Feeling ashamed and behind in his work relative to his peers, his survival response was like a battery losing its charge. No wonder "sleep" mode felt safer for Asher, the downside of the Green Zone.

Recall Reed, who drove himself to the Blue Zone height of activity. Viewed through a predictive brain lens, workaholism may seem less like a character flaw and more like a strategic gamble to optimize achievement. Sure, Reed harbored an underlying positive intention to strive for excellence but didn't have the best execution. There's an experience of overenergy, but Reed couldn't keep up with the heroics despite the financial incentives. Over time his body budget was in the red as burnout ensued. *I'm spent. Why do I equate worthiness with wealth and success? Is this the golden handcuffs trap? Maybe I'm not cut out for this.*

Daria, whose inner judge never allowed her to see her own gifts or enjoy life even a little bit, found herself in fight/flight—the energy of the Red Zone—and out of sync with other people. Her survival strategy was to flee by opting out of social settings or situations where she felt put on the spot. *Why do I take things personally when there are other explanations? Why do I think it is my responsibility when things don't go as planned?* Daria began to see that there's a difference between "striving" and comparing herself to others, and that of feeling happy, satisfied, or passionate about her life's work.

Many anxious perfectionists like Daria, Reed, and Asher ping-pong between the states of fight/flight (activation and overenergy) and freeze (shutdown and underenergy)—and have a hard time moving into the healthy Green Zone of calm and connection. But once they learn that they have the natural resources to get there, along with new strategies and support from others, they can more skillfully land squarely into the upper-right quadrant of the Perfectionism Matrix of a happy achiever.

As you may surmise, happy achievers can notice where they are—being mindful of the possibility of prediction error—and then decide what action to take. In other words, happy achievers can notice the state of their nervous system and then create a new predictive model in their mind. This is what some might call having a growth (versus fixed) mindset.

How might Reed, Asher, and Daria create new algorithms to evoke states of ease, empowerment, and fulfillment? Instead of being vulnerable to stress and addicted to unhealthy perfectionism, they can purposely develop a positivity bias. When you can interrupt the inner algorithm, you can begin to switch the code. Exercises to encourage this transformation toward happy achieving are at the end of this and the rest of the chapters.

You too can discover what helps you have greater flexibility, perspective, and emotion regulation. After all, your inner critic, that judge, sergeant, nitpicker, sleuth, and joy thief arise from narratives, scripts, and stories born out of signals of danger or safety. Once you tune in to what's implicit and make it explicit, you can rewrite the story your life. You can identify your little inner critics and see where they are hanging out. You can learn to befriend the minions in ways that bring calm, kindness, courage, and compassion to what feels threatening, compulsive, and out of control.

It all begins with awareness.

Mariah's Story

Once Mariah "survived" freshman year and had time to reflect, she hardly recognized her old self. Once the cool smart student, Mariah yearned for the kind of friends she once could count on and the comfort of a tight-knit community. Instead, it became cool to suffer the excess of studying and producing papers. Mariah had no channel for the anxiety and didn't even have a name for it. Instead, it came out as snide comments and frustration with roommates. Eventually the stress turned inward. Another symptom surfaced. Mariah began twisting her hair. It felt good—small instances of pain followed by relief. But when the bald patches appeared, she was horrified. Mariah started wearing headbands and eventually invested in hair extensions. Sometimes referred to as body-focused repetitive behaviors, Mariah's hair-pulling habit was a kind of nervous system relief.

Mariah totally related to the idea of an inner nitpicker. "Like that is exactly what I do to myself!" On the Perfectionism Self-Inquiry she resonated with the item *I don't like it when things are out of place or are messy.* While Mariah had little patience with other people's perceived inadequacies, this inner narrative was about self-doubt and double-checking. Mariah had flavors of self- and other-oriented perfectionism—an inner nitpicker alongside her judgmental Grumpire. When Mariah began to see how her autonomic nervous system was responding, another aha moment arose. "Whoa. I'm totally revved up in the Red Zone. I get it. My body senses that everything is doomed and I'm trying to control it. But my brain is telling me that someone is to blame, either myself or everyone else. No wonder I'm pulling my hair out!" Mariah began to see that the stress of college kept her in chronic fight/flight mode, followed by a plunge into shutdown and self-soothing with the hair twizzling. With humor and humility Mariah eventually named this inner nitpicker Twisted Sister.

Mariah also began to see all the fun things she gave up. When home on summer break Mariah decided to sing every day with a karaoke mic, something she loved to do with high school besties. What song did Mariah have in mind? A goodie but oldie, "Wildest Dreams," Taylor's version, of course. Just the thought of it brought Mariah's nervous system into a state of sweet relief.

Happy Achiever Tools: Embody the Present Moment

Now it's time to give yourself the experience of feeling more embodied and discover some new practices that can become part of your Happy Achiever Tool kit. These tools are identified with a diamond icon to signify ways to build self-worth. Here and in the rest of the book, these closing activities will help you get grounded, energized, and connected so that you can continue to EVOLVE.

GET GROUNDED: 3X4 MINDFUL MINUTES

Remember, a minimum dose of mindfulness can go a long way and move you into the Green Zone of calm and connection and recalibrate your body budget. No matter how busy you may find yourself, can you find four natural mini-breaks in your day to practice three minutes of quiet time? Or three breaks of four minutes? For example, when making a cup of coffee. On the train. Waiting in the car to pick up kids. In the shower. Between meetings. Before bed. During those few minutes, bring an attitude of kindfulness by simply being aware of the present moment with heart. This means releasing the impulse to judge or fix or change whatever is arising. When your mind wanders (which it does naturally) redirect your attention to the rhythm of your breathing, placing a hand on your heart or belly, or focus attention on your feet being supported by the earth or floor. This is particularly useful if you feel a constant urgency in life or trapped by the to-do list, swerving into the fast lane of the Red Zone. I'm including the instructions for a particular exercise in the box at page 95 below. If you need guidance or more variety, look up the many types of practices or scroll in a meditation app library. You will find something for everyone: belly breathing, box breathing, loving-kindness meditation, smile meditation, sleep meditation, and more. (You can check out my website for audios and other resources.) The key is consistency as you build up your endurance. Mindfulness can become a stable trait of awareness rather than a fleeting moment. Make a pinkie promise to practice some form of mindfulness for a few minutes every day for a month and see what happens.

Find a quiet place to settle in. Begin by noticing where you sense your breath the most easily. Alternatively, notice your body supported by the chair or sense your feet solid on the ground. Relax.

> *Breathe in and silently say the word peace.*
> *Breathe out and silently say the word calm.*
> *Breathe in peace, breathe out calm.*
> *Peace. Calm.*

Repeat a few times.
Now with a caring attitude and tone,

> *Breathe in as you silently say the word accept,*
> *Breathe out as you silently say the word love.*
> *Breathe in accept, breathe out love.*
> *Accept. Love.*

Repeat the pairs a few times with each inhale and exhale.

> *Peace/calm, accept/love.*
> *Peace/calm, accept/love.*

You can choose your own words or count a number sequence or use another kind of anchor for your attention, like holding a smooth stone in one or both hands, resting a hand on your heart, or focusing on an object in nature. Play around with a focal point for attention. It gets easier over time. (For real.)

GET ENERGIZED: A QUICK RESET

If you find yourself in procrastination, burnout, or total exhaustion, you may need to do a total reset. That could be a decent night's sleep, of course. But if you are chronically underenergized you may need to recharge your human battery, literally. Doing some physical movement is often the best hack to shift energy. Donna Eden, a master energy medicine practitioner, developed the Daily Energy Routine (DER). It's a simple series of postures with light tapping on acupressure points and movement designed to help you develop a balanced energetic core. I'm including three exercises from DER below, although there are more exercises in the full version (see Appendix C for a link to the full routine). I like to think of it like jump-starting the battery and then keeping it humming with ongoing maintenance. We'll just focus on a few that connect your head and your heart—and take less than three minutes!

1. **Four thumps (1 minute):** Tap the following four areas with your fingers for about ten to fifteen seconds each: below the eyes (lightly), under the collarbone (moderately), over the heart area (Tarzan thumps), and under arms at the lower ribs (moderately).

2. **Hook-up (30 seconds):** Bring the first two fingers of one hand to your belly button and the fingers of your other hand to the center of your forehead. Lift your torso slightly as you inhale a deep breath. Take three full breaths as you gently hold both points, like you are charging the +/− terminals on a car battery.

3. **Zip-up (30 seconds):** Bring a positive thought or affirmation to mind. You can use a mini-script (in the next exercise) or an affirmation that feels true to you in the moment, such as "All is well," "You've got this," or "It's all good." Trace your fingers from your pubic bone up the front line of your body to below your lips, like a jacket zipper. Repeat this zipping gesture three times as you recite your affirmation and zip in the good.

GET CONNECTED: CODE SWITCH

Just like the energy exercise above can help you recalibrate, you can also begin to make an internal code switch by creating a set of instructions you can easily remember. As you become familiar with your color-coded emotional zones, you can readily connect your head and your heart by applying the concepts you learned in this chapter to a simple script. Such a script is also the basis for the Emotional Freedom

Technique or tapping. But for now we are simply naming an experience by acknowledging the stress and holding it kindfully. If you like tapping, you can gently tap the pinky finger side of your hand with the other hand, or place one hand over your heart. It's a way to address the question: *What can I say to myself when my survival response is activated?* Here is a mini script to get you started:

Even though I am _____,
[hurried, tired, angry, scared, frustrated, critical, fill in the blank],
and the intensity level is a _____*[number on a scale of 0/none to 10/most intense],*

I choose to _____*[honor, accept, appreciate, love, fill in the blank]* myself/my nervous system. I will do one beneficial thing to reset and balance my energy, such as _____
_____
[name a skill or activity].

Optional: I will share this practice with _____,
who I can count on for support.

As with all these closing exercises, try something out of your comfort zone. It may feel weird at first. That's OK. In the next step, you'll learn how to better cope with unpleasant sensations such as awkwardness—and many more.

5

Step 2

V, *Validate Your Experience*

> *I want to still have a sharp pen and a thin*
> *skin and an open heart.*
>
> — *Taylor Swift*, Miss Americana

T aylor Swift is a great role model for believing in the value of your own story. Because she did not own the copyright to the music she recorded early in her career, when the COVID pandemic hit and concert halls closed their doors, Swift methodically began rerecording the songs on her early albums and releasing them as "Taylor's version." It was a savvy business effort to reclaim her work, shake up the music industry, and encourage musicians to maintain ownership of the rights to their songs.[1] But it was also an inspiring example of owning the things that have happened to you and having your own back.

Inspired by Swift's example, Mariah became all about validating her own lived experience, which she dubbed "Mariah's version." And it was this self-acceptance that helped Mariah begin to understand that inner nitpicker and realize that she didn't have to give up fun, friends, or sleep in order to have success. The more Mariah made time to soothe her nervous system, the more she thrived. That's what embracing your experience—instead of questioning it, ignoring it, or judging it as bad—can do for you too. And that's the goal of this step of the EVOLVE process. As you'll discover, validating your experience is an essential precursor in opening your heart to all your imperfections.

The Goal of Step 2: Validate Your Experience

Your focus now is to have empathy for yourself as a unique human living in a physical body with automatic systems in place to survive and thrive. In other words, to validate your own experience.

In psychology, validation means acknowledging and accepting your thoughts, feelings, and experiences. It's a basic tenet of friendship, mentoring, therapy, and other meaningful connections. Some of the synonyms for *validation* include *confirmation*, *corroboration*, *testimony*, and *witness*. Self-validation is also a coping skill that can lead to self-acceptance, reaching out for comfort, and emotional healing. When you find yourself in a tender or scary moment of vulnerability, such recognition can lead to greater trust in yourself. You allow yourself the validation in your present life that you may not have received in the past. In mindfulness trainings, this process of acknowledging your own feelings is sometimes referred to as spiritual re-parenting. Whatever you call it, it takes courage to witness your vulnerability without judgment and to go against the scripts you may have learned as a child. Therefore, validating your inner algorithms is nothing short of a bold move.

Compassion-focused therapist Russell Kolts describes emotional courage as "an aspect of compassion, the willingness to approach and connect with difficult feelings, in the service of helping yourself work with these experiences."[2] With compassion and emotional courage, you can know yourself better, accept yourself more, and treat yourself better. Ultimately, this work of honoring your personal experience is how you cultivate inner worth.

The previous chapter focused on the autonomic nervous system that is so intimately tied to heart energy, because noticing signals of safety and danger without being hijacked by extreme reactions fosters resilience. And yet, while the body is an exquisite radar system and many clues reside in physiological sensations, the thoughts, emotions, and interpretations of lived experience are formulated in the mind. You can't just feel your way to happy achieving—you need to think differently too. So let's turn our attention toward cultivating a kinder mind.

Why It's So Hard to Think Clearly When You're Stressed

The thing is, we aren't naturally skilled at interpreting our lived experiences. Because we have these tricky brains, we tend to overestimate potential danger and underestimate our ability to cope. "Neuroscientists like to say that your day-to-day experience is a carefully controlled hallucination, constrained by the world and your body, but ultimately constructed by your brain," writes Lisa Feldman Barrett in *Seven and a Half Lessons About the Brain*.[3] When perceiving an emergency, including criticism and comparison, all hands are on deck. Your brain compresses past experiences of being judged into mental simulations to land on the best guess of how to respond, even if imperfect or inaccurate.

The problem happens when the stress response exceeds your ability to cope—or taxes your body budget at a great metabolic expense. Whether real (a snake in your path), imagined (an email from your boss in your inbox you avoid opening), or even a common nuisance (a social media post showcasing another's good life), you can temporarily lose access to your brain's higher executive functions, just when you need them the most. Instead, you may have brain fog, poor mood, discomfort, irritation, or other kinds of dysregulation affecting your sleep, motivation, or social connections. Maybe you find yourself having a temper tantrum or acting out in some unflattering way or shutting down from overwhelm or not-good-enoughness. In that moment, you can't really help it. You're human.

When your metabolic and metaphysical energies are burdened, your mind is typically churning out fake news, like a news screen with a broadcast ticker running below it. There may be times when you feel that your mind could explode from too much nutty information combined with all the mean things your Plus One says: *You're such a loser. Why did you say that? Could you be more awkward? Seriously. WTF.*

Ouch.

You might experience self-criticism in the mind, as a thought, words, or images. Or you could have a felt sense of being unworthy or incompetent. Or you could experience a feeling of disconnection—you might disengage the millisecond self-criticism shows up so you aren't even aware of it.

Findings in neuroscience and brain imaging show that self-criticism inhibits important neural networks and can carve neural interstate highways of shame and blame.[4] Many factors contribute to this shaping of the mind and body. For example, anxiety or depression could run in your family, encouraging the mental habit of a worried mind and catastrophizing. Or you might have had a brutal coach who pointed out your mistakes. Or you were bullied by peers, unwittingly internalizing a harsh critical narrative about yourself. A trauma or unexpected event could have upended your sense of safety in the world, making you hypersensitive to cues of danger. Attachment wounds stemming from childhood experiences can make it hard to trust others. One way or another, these inner algorithms, scripts, or stories become a "voice" in your head. You may come to believe that all the inner badgering is what will motivate you.

And here's the irony. Psychology studies show that people with harsh self-criticism take longer to progress toward their life goals and are less likely to achieve them.[5] Remember, perfectionistic habits do *not* get you any further along the success track.[6] In fact, brain imaging studies reveal that networks in the prefrontal cortex in the brain are inhibited by self-criticism and cause people to *disengage* from their goals.[7] Criticizing yourself is like putting the brakes on.

It's helpful to imagine self-criticism patterns like roadblocks and detours in the central nervous system that lead to dead ends, fatigue, and resignation. These patterns can lead to an out of whack body budget and create a looping of rumination about how you are not good enough. The mind struggles to make sense of what the body feels. A key part of overcoming perfectionism, then, is to learn how to bring your body budget back into some balance.

How Self-Criticism Becomes a Habit

There's something else going on too. By now you probably get that your brain is complicated, right? Well, we also have what is referred to as *a negativity bias*, as I introduced in chapter 1.

The negativity bias is not about being a pessimist or a Debbie Downer. It's a component of your inner surveillance system—like a baby cam over a crib or a wireless home security camera. The negativity bias alerts you to potential danger and communicates warnings to the nervous system. It's operating all the time. Just like the heart beats and the lungs breathe, the brain/body is continually scanning the environment for danger, and most of this happens below our awareness. The negativity bias is trying to warn us, tell us when to get out of harm's way. While that's not necessarily a bad thing, our tricky brains can take it too far.

Psychologist Rick Hanson describes five ways the negativity bias can manifest:[8]

1. We scan for bad news, including what we say to ourselves. Remember, we've got a lot of fake news inside our heads.
2. We get tunnel vision. We focus on the bad news and narrow in on negative storylines.
3. We overreact to it. It becomes associated with unpleasant emotions and squirts out the hormone cortisol for needed energy. You're in Red Zone territory.
4. We remember it. In other words, the experience or sensations fast-tracks into our memory banks and affects the natural flow of energy landing you in the extreme states of any the color zones: overreaction (Red), overactivity (Blue), or overwhelm (Green).
5. We dwell on the experience, creating a negative feedback loop. When we're in a negative feedback loop, the neural networks associated with motivation, caring, and perspective taking deactivate.

Why do we do this to ourselves? After all, the most common triggers most of us face in day-to-day interactions are typically not life threatening. The usual suspects are fears about being liked (or not), performance, friendships and relationships, money, news, and the future—and the stories we tell ourselves about these situations. It's our changes in *interoception* (sensory awareness of the state of the body) of threat that readily ignites the physiological stress responses described in chapter 2, like motion or window detectors. The mind jumps in with *perception* to create a seemingly coherent explanation, like security cameras. (Because as we covered in the last chapter, in EVOLVE Step 1, story follows state.) And then, bam! We're beating ourselves up.

Validation Reflection #1: Attention Grabbers

Let's see how the negativity bias might be manifesting in your life. This is not about being a negative person, mind you, but rather, what grabs hold of your attention? What do you experience as threatening to your sense of self? Pause now and take a moment to reflect:

1. Thinking back on the last twenty-four hours, what stories or situations or inner drama caught your attention?
2. How did you react to those stories (sensations, emotions, behaviors)?
3. What did you tell yourself about those stories? Notice any assumptions, beliefs, or biases.
4. Is there a flavor of perfectionism (look at the self-inquiry on page 31)?
5. What did you do next?
6. Without judgment, how do you view your reaction now?
7. Do you notice any habits of mind or body?
8. How might you respond differently the next time a similar situation arises?

Mind Loops and Headspins

It's another human foible that we tend to overemphasize the perceived threat as if it's "do or die," and we discount our ability to meet the challenge. Once your inner alarm switch is stuck ON, and you're in the Red Zone of threat, unpleasant feelings of anger, contempt, or disgust arise. Your body can't easily recover. And because the brain loves a good pattern, it recycles the make-believe stories. These mind loops are self-perpetuating patterns and become an unconscious working model for your sense of self.

What you pay attention to grows stronger in the recesses of your mind. So if you find yourself in a headspin, you are strengthening the neural and energetic patterns indicating you are a failure or are never enough or will be dumped. Recycling these thoughts both reinforces the physiological threat response in the body and allows the corresponding mental habit to flourish.

A common distortion is *what if* thinking, which on the whole is not necessarily bad and can help with planning, but can easily slide into rabbit holes of anxiety.[9] For example, you might imagine some life-like scenes that get conjured up with the following *what ifs*:

> *What if I don't land that job?*
> *What if my partner dumps me?*
> *What if I end up all alone?*
> *What if I made a big mistake going to grad school?*
> *What if I can't speak well in the interview?*
> *What if this cough means I have lung cancer?*

Fortune telling is another common cognitive distortion that just about every perfectionist I have ever met has described at some point. Fortune telling is when you predict some negative outcome without considering the odds of that outcome actually happening. You think you have the answer, but you really don't. There's no genie in the bottle. Yet you assume that something will end badly in the future rather than clearly looking at a situation right now. Your assumptions sound like truths:

> *I'm not going to land that job.*
> *My partner will eventually dump me.*
> *I will end up all alone.*
> *I made a big mistake going to grad school.*
> *I don't speak well in interviews.*
> *This cough means I have lung cancer.*

A good acronym to remind you of this trap is FEAR, False Evidence Appearing Real. It's helpful to look for quality evidence in your day-to-day life and reality check with a trusted friend. You can ask yourself: are there possible *positive outcomes* I haven't even considered? It's also practical to ask yourself about the underlying fear, notice the state of your body budget, and tune into your vibes (interoception). In other words, where do you notice the threat experience in your body? Do you plummet into a state of overwhelm or ready yourself for action? Or are you able to notice the self-criticism and yet also reassure yourself?

And *catastrophizing* is exactly what it sounds like: imagining and magnifying the worst-case scenarios in vivid detail. We all do this from time to time. Catastrophizing can arise from some distressing experience in the past, like loss or trauma, that primes you to be cautious. Or it can freely arise when you feel uncertain about the future. While anxiety is useful as a momentary signal of the nervous system, catastrophizing and being preoccupied by imagined danger lead to unpleasant emotions, avoidance, and unnecessary suffering.

There are other familiar cognitive distortion traps perfectionists can fall into, like "black and white" or "all or none" thinking, minimizing the positives, "shoulding" on yourself, and taking things personally.[10] These algorithms can lead to worry, panic and self-sabotage, disrupting the flow of information and energy.

So while we are pretty good at internal scriptwriting worthy of a Golden Globe best drama award, it is possible to use this ability in positive ways for mental well-being.

How?

You can nudge yourself into a Green Zone of feeling safe and connected. For example, if you find yourself catastrophizing, consider the opposite. What might the *best-case scenario* look like? If that's too much of a stretch, imagine if everything worked out just fine. You can remind yourself to do the little things that bring you some measure of security, connection, and joy. You can also visualize yourself enacting helpful coping strategies and meeting a challenging moment with more confidence and ease. It may feel a lot harder than imagining how things could go wrong, but that's only because the neural pathways of the negativity bias are deep and well-traveled, while more positive imaginings require you to forge a new neuronal path. The good news is, the more you do it, the easier it gets.

You can take advantage of neuroplasticity and the ability to influence your brain by choosing to practice a different way of thinking that places your attention on something much more helpful, and thereby create new predictions for your brain to consider. In this way you can reframe FEAR as:

Face Everything And Respond
Forgetting Everything is All Right
Feeling Excited And Ready

Small tweaks in thinking can have great effect.

Cultivating Kindsight

If being present to your experience is the first call to action as covered in the previous chapter, the current step is *validating* that things can be difficult. Or distressing. Or confusing. Or boring. Acknowledge that you are having an unpleasant thought, emotion, sensation, or storyline. Accept that you just beat yourself up or got caught in a mind loop. When the inner critic shows up, acknowledge its presence. The second you do, you can pivot your point of view and be a little nicer to yourself.

One of the most profound and simple teachings I ever encountered was listening to the psychologist Jack Kornfield at a mindfulness meditation teacher training. It was a lesson in imagination, but I didn't notice it at the time. The gathering occurred not long after Hurricane Maria hit Puerto Rico, where several students were from. The US emergency response was frustratingly ineffective. Many people were suffering without electricity, shelter, food, and fresh water. When a student lamented, crying out in anger and helplessness, Kornfield explained that when such difficult emotions arise, the art and skill is not to ignore the feelings or rush to reaction. Rather, it is to see them clearly. Then he brought his hands in a prayerful position and bowed slightly. "Anger, I see you," he said. "Come sit. Have a cup of tea."

This image of inviting your unpleasant emotion to sit across from you, just like you might an upset friend or neighbor, was powerful. "Come sit. Have a cup of tea." The cognitive scientist might call this a reframing or distancing tool, whereas the spiritual master frames it as using skillful means to cultivate compassion. Either way, you're externalizing the emotion, freeing yourself from the vice grip of the threat, and "seeing" the emotion as outside of you rather than controlling you. In this way, you begin to relate to this triggering experience as being worthy of your attention and care—rather than automatically criticize yourself or someone else for your reaction or try to distract yourself from it. That's pretty radical.

This is not all that different from the simple teachings of the late Mr. Fred Rogers, a modern day mystic if there ever was one.[11] He taught millions of children and parents that feelings are mentionable and manageable. In psychology we refer to this skill as "name it to tame it" and "feel it to heal it." Easier said than done, of course. Feeling such uncomfortable emotions can catapult you into fight/flight/freeze states.

And yet you must turn toward these feelings, even if it's just a peek at first.

The invitation that masters like Kornfield and Rogers extend to us is to create a welcoming relationship with our emotional experiences, and to reimagine pain as worthy of compassion. It's what I call *kindsight*, viewing your experiences with tenderness and understanding. Kindsight is especially helpful when you notice the inner critic, which you now know is often a manifestation of a physiological reaction to a perceived threat—a story that follows a state, just like a heart palpitation or sweaty palms indicate nervousness, anxiety, or fear. When the inner critic shows up, you can quietly say to yourself, "Twisted Sister, I know you are here." "FOMO, thanks for the warning, but I've got this." If you are not sure of what is happening, you can ask yourself, "Who in me is afraid?" And then send some love to that part of you.

The reason validating your experience and extending yourself some kindsight can be so helpful is that if you are experiencing anxiety or an intense emotion, it is very hard to talk yourself out of it. You might be able to say, "STOP IT!" or shake it off, or see it as a passing cloud, and if that works, great. Yet, if you can imagine your inner critic like a small child tugging at your shirt for attention, holding on to your leg out of fear, or pounding their fists in frustration, you may be able to have more compassion for that part of yourself.

Validation Reflection #2: No Wonder!

By now you've noticed how you interpret challenges or threats, whether it's the stuff that's happening in the real world or in your own mind. That's the first step toward shifting your inner algorithms. A next step is allowing some perspective and understanding. In Validation Reflection #1, you observed what grabs your attention. Now apply your growing wisdom and self-compassion to those scenarios you identified by using a *no wonder* statement:

No wonder I felt . . .
No wonder I behaved . . .
No wonder I thought . . .

Complete each *no wonder* statement—for example, "No wonder I got mad, cried, swore, shut down, etc."

This is not about letting yourself off the hook, but rather discerning how you got hooked in the first place and recognizing the presence of your inner critic. Think of this like being a friendly detective or outside witness. Then you can begin to catch yourself in the moment and see you have a choice in how you can respond.

Reimagining Your Life

Visualization can be a very powerful skill when trying to establish new neural pathways. Visual perception, one of the five primary senses, takes up a lot of real estate in the brain networks—it's estimated at about 50 percent.[12] The visual cortex is highly networked with other brain regions and is hardwired from birth to allow you to daydream, recall memories, picture scenes, and imagine things you have never seen before.[13] It gets activated when reading fiction or in a visualization meditation, for example.[14] We can also create mental movies of situations that we've never experienced but simulate in our own minds. This is the power of imagination.

When it comes to learning new material, as we are about to do, practicing visualization is extremely effective. That's why color-coded note cards and highlighters are popular studying devices. Plus, consider that a perfectionist can readily envision potential disasters, shame storms, and rejections, and can tell you exactly how it will go down. That's a not very helpful form of visualization, but it's the same mechanism of habit that can help you create beneficial imagery. In other words, you can recruit your brain to be on its own side.

Your brain reacts to the things you visualize—especially when you purposely imagine the sights, smells, touches, and sounds of whatever scene you are imagining—as if they were real.[15] In fact, it's a common training practice for athletes to mentally rehearse the physical actions of their sport—a practice known as top-down simulation or "vision in reverse."[16]

Kobe Bryant relied on a personalized meditative process that he used in the moments before a game. With his eyes closed during the national anthem, he would imagine his teammates, the baskets in front and behind him, and picture the entire arena to feel the energy of the environment. His was a fully immersive visualization that primed Kobe mentally, physically, and emotionally for the actual experience. "I've done that as a kid sort of naturally. I never put too much thought into it," he wrote about his practice in his book *The Mamba Mentality*.[17] Exactly. This is not about thinking. It's about transporting yourself into a scene. Nor was Kobe "manifesting" a win, which only amounts to wishful thinking. Rather it was the process of becoming fully engaged in his love of the game and rehearsing the skills that could lead to a great competition.

You too can envision meaningful and beneficial scenes that enable you to be on your own side. Social scientists are beginning to study how visualization can increase compassion, described as "our ability to transport ourselves beyond our present experiences and imagine distant events in time and place."[18] It's a kind of a reversal of catastrophic thinking that I described above. Or put another way, it's mental time traveling with intention.

To do it, you imagine certain positive interactions in vivid detail, such as helping other people during a specific encounter, followed by reporting what you might imagine other people in the scene are feeling. Social scientists have guided study participants to imagine witnessing someone getting a flat tire or being affected by violence. That someone could even be a person from an "out group," such as an opposing political party (which is more likely to thwart a willingness to help.)[19] After the visualization exercise, the researchers gauge how willing the study participants are to help. So far, the research suggests that these visual simulations trigger empathy and compassion for the other person, even when that person is someone who is a member of a different group than you (whether another race, class, religion, or political party). Researchers have noted that vividly spelling out the details of the situation, including the emotions the study participants feel, seems to be a key element. Beyond empathy, this type of visualization fosters prosocial behaviors, ignites positive feelings, and reduces intergroup biases.[20]

In my clinical experience, inner critics are often like people in an out group. The tendency is to ignore, dismiss, or antagonize the inner critic—it becomes the enemy, even though it is a facet of you. By resisting the inner critic, you end up just hurting yourself. Even though there are plenty of pop-psychology headlines about banishing or silencing the inner critic, *that just never works*. What can work is creating your own visualizations of a meet and greet with the little inner critic.

Validation Reflection #3: Being in the Driver's Seat

Best-selling author Elizabeth Gilbert describes how she manages her fear about writing:[21] She imagines that she and her pal Creativity are on a road trip. She knows Fear will also come along for the ride to warn her of the unknown dangers. She recognizes that this companion is part of her inner family too. She tells Fear, "There's plenty of room in this vehicle for all of us, so make yourself at home, but understand this: Creativity and I are the only ones who will be making any decisions along the way. I recognize and respect that you are part of this family, and so I will never exclude you from our activities, but still your suggestions will never be followed . . . but above all else, my dear old, familiar friend, you are absolutely forbidden to drive."

Imagine meeting your Plus One, your inner critic who hovers about, comes along for the ride, or even stalks you at inopportune moments. Get to know it. Create a scene in your mind or on paper that evokes curiosity, empathy, and a willingness to see it for what it is. This is a variation on inviting the critic for a cup of tea.

- Assume positive intentions.
- Say hello.
- Ask it about its role, job, mission or purpose.
- How long has it been doing its job?
- How does it feel about its role?
- How does it experience the threat response?
- What emotional motivation zone does it often navigate (for example, the Red, Blue or Green zone)?
- What would it need to feel safe or supported so it didn't have to work so hard on your behalf?
- What is its main message? Is it helpful?
- Might there be other ways to be helpful? What would need to happen?
- Thank it for sharing and consider your response next time it shows up.

Daria's Plus One

When I lead perfectionism workshops, I ask the people in attendance to envision their Plus One. I ask them to answer questions about it, such as, *How old is this persona? When did it show up in your life? How is it trying to help you?*

A lot of people get stumped by this line of questioning. That's when I show some photos of kids: the boy dressed in a superhero costume, the girl with hands on her hips, or the playground bully standing with arms crossed. Typically, a Plus One is much younger than you are, and this part has no idea that the present day you is as old as you are, whether you're nineteen or twenty-three or thirty-four or fifty-one years old. When you can see that this part of you is stuck at a younger age, it helps you be gentler toward it. These images of children help transport those workshop participants who struggle with connecting their inner critic to a place of innocence. It can be a reminder of the basic goodness inherent in oneself and therefore in the part of you that you define as your Plus One.

At one particular perfectionism workshop where I showed the photos of children, Daria, the young lawyer, remarked, "Wow, that is really helpful. It *never* occurred to me that my inner joy thief is just a freaked-out kid trying to save the day."

Now, I hadn't suggested any such thing. This wasn't therapy after all. But I was glad she could see her inner critic with fresh eyes—now she was primed to invite her joy thief for some cookies and milk. By being able to see her inner critic with empathy, Daria made it more likely that she would discover the positive intention her minion had all along. Released from her perception of her inner joy thief as something that was all-knowing and all-powerful, Daria learned she could spread her wings a bit—she felt more free to play.

Switching Up Your Self-Talk

In addition to using your powers of visualization to validate your own experience, you can also unkink those mind loops and headspins by taking a new approach to the way you talk to yourself.

Distanced self-talk is the skill of taking an outsider's view of one's own situation. A slight tweak in self-talk can have a very positive impact. Instead of using first pronoun dialogue of "I" or "me," you can address yourself with your name or the pronoun "you," as in the more universal or generic "you," or third-person pronouns he/she/they.[22]

Psychologist Ethan Kross has tested this practice with young people. In one of his studies, college students who wrote about their stress and used distanced self-talk tended to view their stressful events as a *challenge* that can be addressed.[23] They coached themselves with encouragement, such as:

"Daria, you've got this."
"You've done hard things before. Take it one step at a time."
"It's OK to stop working. Better to get a decent night's sleep. Let her rest."

The students in the other study group who viewed stressful situations as a *threat* and appraised the stressful situations as out of their control tended to have what's known as self-immersive talk. Their inner dialogue might be: "I always mess things up" or "I'll look like a fool." Not surprisingly, people who step back, consider taking proactive steps, and reassure themselves have greater well-being. A subtle shift in point of view can have a big effect by moving away from the internal I/me egocentric voice that can be so disheartening.

Taking this another step, imagining what a role model or revered other might do can also foster some meaningful perspective and grit. One child development study offers a great lesson for us grown-ups. Children as young as five years old were asked to imagine what an inspirational figure would do when asked to do a repetitive task instead of playing a cool video game.[24] Called the Batman effect, the experimental question with these youngsters was *What would Batman do?* The kids who imagined the mighty Batman persevered longer on the task, demonstrating an emergent skill for problem solving. Procrastinators, take note! Insert your favorite childhood protagonists—Dora, Woody, Buzz Lightyear, Mulan, Harry Potter—and create your own hero's journey to help you write that elusive dissertation or apply for a job or ask someone out on a date. Modern-day real-life heroes and inspiring celebrities can work well too. Sometimes referred to as parasocial relationships, imagining an encouraging or benevolent mentor figure can be motivating. Just like Mariah thought, *What would Taylor Swift do?*

Turning Your Attention Toward Caring

If you can't connect to the idea of naming your thoughts, validating your own feelings and experiences, or relating to an inner critic with compassion, that's OK. Think back to Luis, the scientist from the introduction, who wasn't aware that he had a brutal inner critic and could be highly critical of others. Over his lifetime Luis emotionally armored himself against the abuse he was exposed to as a kid. His was a complex, defensive move of self-preservation. Given his harsh upbringing, it made total sense—Luis basically had to raise himself. He wasn't yet skilled at calming his threat response because he couldn't actually sense it. His was a narrow lens, limited to good/bad, black/white, and all/none. Nor could he be a witness to his self-loathing or care for his wounds, because he didn't recognize that they existed. And if he couldn't feel it, how could he heal it? If he couldn't name it, how could he tame it?

Luis had learned to shut down as a kid. So it was no wonder he had temper tantrums as an adult that seemed to come out of nowhere. He had few grown-ups who consistently modeled soothing behaviors and empathy, like hugs or kind words of reassurance. Internalizing a caring voice was difficult for Luis.

The ability to reason or infer things about the self and situations in the past, present, or future (or in Luis's case, inability), is called *mentalizing*.[25] As we grow up, we come to create mental models to make sense of our world that include the variety of thoughts, feelings, beliefs, and needs. These adaptations come to underlie our behavior. Mentalizing develops across childhood and is cultivated in relationships with others, especially during the first five years. It is also related to the ability to put yourself in another's shoes. Luis was often punished as a kid and developed insecurities in relationships. When caregivers are critical, punishing, or neglectful, or adverse childhood events take place, children are very vulnerable to a host of physical and mental consequences. Self-criticism is one such outcome and can lead to hypervigilant and persistent threat responses.

In a perfect world, we would all develop secure attachment as a result of receiving caring, responsive interactions from attentive and reliable caregivers who model and teach us about navigating the world. If mistakes happen, they get worked out. There's room for error. You are loved even when you trip up. Sadly, this is very often not the reality many of us are raised in—and the attachment wounds of our upbringing can last for a long time.

While Luis was successful with his career, he had difficulty with any sort of relationship. He had little experience with trusting himself and others, and didn't truly believe that everything might work out well. Worse yet, he didn't believe that deep down he was a good human.

Brain imaging studies suggest an intriguing relationship between self-criticism, attachment styles described in chapter 1, and the ability to visualize. One study by the Compassion Mind Research group in the UK exposed young people to self-critical thoughts to see what happened as their brains got scanned in an fMRI machine.[26] The study tracked the activity in two regions in the brain associated with emotional reactivity and visualization. The participants were primed with either neutral statements such as *I keep up with my commitments in life* or negative statements such as *I fail to keep up with my commitments in life*. Then they rated how unpleasant and intense these statements were.

The results suggested that the people identified as having secure attachment have more activity in the visual cortex when exposed to self-critical thoughts, suggesting they aren't hijacked by the emotional response and may be able to *picture* how to address the challenge or remember how to practice self-kindness. Whereas the people with avoidant attachment tended to inhibit mental visualization. It's as if they dismiss or dissociate from picturing a solution or other interpretation in a nanosecond, like Luis did. To Luis, reflecting on his bullish behaviors would be too threatening to his sense of identity and success. Luis was trapped in the Red Zone with very narrow tunnel vision, seeing only problems. Meanwhile, his body made use of the metabolic squirt of cortisol to go on the attack. *I'm right and you're wrong!*

The implication is that self-criticism is an embodied experience, often below the level of cognition. This means that creating internal maps of belonging and safety really do matter. Having insight and book smarts aren't enough. It's learning to connect the head and the heart. And a key part of doing that is to care for your inner critic as if it were a vulnerable child—picturing a little person who's just looking for protection, love, and affirmation. For Luis, this practice is spiritual reparenting he can do for himself and through reparative connections. It can be as simple as asking yourself, *Who in me is afraid?* Or, as writer Elizabeth Gilbert proposes to her *Letters from Love* online community, write a letter to yourself from the perspective of unconditional love. The prompt is *Love, what would you have me know today?*[27]

While Mariah could use Taylor Swift as an inspiration to change her mental script about the fear that she wasn't up to college life, and Daria was able to practice self-compassion by imagining her inner critic as a younger self, it took Luis more time to cultivate a gentler internal script and more accurately interpret cues of danger and safety. He needed the help of a counselor or mentor, and that's perfectly OK. One of the most validating practices can simply be to ask for help. We need other people around us with calm nervous systems, who are encouraging and authentic and who can mirror feelings. Someday, Luis will become better skilled at this with some kind and patient one-on-one coaching.

That means you need to consciously choose to be in caring circles. What you focus on grows stronger. If you let the inner critics manage your actions, the minions will get into all sorts of misadventures. Given that your attention influences your nervous system and your life, point your focus in the direction of healthy relating. Utilize the amazing capacity of your brain's neuroplasticity to jump-start or rewire your compassion neural networks. You *can* influence your brain to be kinder toward yourself.

A well-known phrase from the neuroscientist Charles Hebb is "neurons that fire together, wire together."[28] Or as Joseph Dispenza writes, "What syncs in the brain begins to link in the brain."[29] Therefore, if you want to have more experiences of happiness and contentment, you actually have to actively seek out positivity in your life.[30] Otherwise, if you ruminate on how you are a failure or not ever good enough, guess what? You are reinforcing that algorithm.

Keep in mind, your brain and its ability to predict are shaped by experience-based learning.[31] In order to get good at anything, like playing the piano, coding, painting, speaking, or being a good friend, parent, partner, or coworker, you need to actually engage those experiences. Same goes for self-care, rest, and play. You must purposely go through the motions of connecting your head and your heart. Practice makes progress.

Of course, it's not as simple as it might sound. There is the negativity bias to reckon with, after all—your memory bank files danger in the top drawer for easy access. And cognitive distortions can arise in response to perceived fears. To cultivate a positivity bias you must redirect your attention to beneficial experiences over and over again until they become second nature. This is not toxic positivity or gaslighting yourself out of acknowledging your own challenges. This is a bidirectional dance between the central and autonomic nervous systems, between head and the heart—where that amazing vagus nerve travels—that nudges you toward vitality and self-care.

Notice It. Name It. Nurture It.

Critical inner thoughts can sound like a jackhammer or nails scraping a chalkboard or muted yelling from some far-off ravine, echoing, echoing, echoing.

I should have known better. I can't get anything right. You loser. You don't have what it takes. Told you so told you so told you so.

Tuning in to that mental Metallica may cause your body to fight or shut off the sound, or else, unaware, it may play that soundtrack over and over. Neither is particularly helpful. If you numb yourself to the beat of your own dark thoughts, you also numb yourself to the sweet sound of kindness, caring, and joy. And by mindlessly ruminating on worthiness, or lack thereof, you beat yourself down with your own drumsticks.

So here's where I ask you to tune in and immerse yourself in that inner narrative—an ask that may piss you off a little bit—or a lot (it often annoys my perfectionism workshop participants). You likely aren't going to like it, until you realize you are part of a human chorus, singing the same old tunes, looking for love in all the wrong places. We all have similar lines running through our heads. The way out of letting those self-critical narratives run the show is through a daily practice of retraining your attention, of practicing kindfulness.

Here's the inspiring part. Knowing this, you can choose to create a different tune, a new movie, and identify an alternative voice, perhaps a kind voice that has been there all along too. What you pay attention to seriously matters. Remember, a self-reassuring voice activates brain networks associated with empathy, compassion, and emotional regulation. You *can* calm the threat system and soothe the judgy voices. How? First, you can notice the inner critical voice as we have been doing and accept that it is a part of your internal system. Second, you can be aware of the negativity bias and your brain's tendency to make habitual predictions, witness your tricky brain at play, and validate your lived experience. Third, you can retrain your attention to focus on beneficial images and self-talk, practice mindfulness and self-care, and find people in your life who reliably support and love you. In other words: Notice it. Name it. Nurture it. The Happy Achiever Tools I share next will help you do just that. Give each of them a try to determine your favorites.

Happy Achiever Tools: Validate Your Experience

The following skills can be helpful in cultivating curiosity, kindsight, and courage.

GET GROUNDED: RAIN TECHNIQUE

Acronyms are great shortcuts the brain to visualize and remember. (List makers, this may be a helpful skill to add to your personalized tool kit.) RAIN is a mindfulness recipe to practice in a difficult moment that allows you to notice, name, and nurture.[32] It's a practice that can be used in a variety of scenarios where compassion is called for. In particular, RAIN is helpful when you are caught in "the trance of unworthiness," as explained by psychologist and meditation teacher Tara Brach.[33] RAIN can also serve as one of your 3x4 mini-meditations (the Get Grounded exercise from Step I).

- **Recognize** means consciously noticing any strong emotions, thoughts, or sensations that arise with curiosity. Notice the shadow qualities that offend you or avoid admitting. This can be a silent nod or a mental whisper. It is essential to take a nonjudgmental attitude and move away from trying to interpret or overthink. Instead, bring your awareness to the felt sense in the body and allow direct experience or connection in the moment. It can be helpful to name the experience, such as "This is anger," "I'm feeling frustrated," "I'm just so tired," or "Oh, that's my inner bully acting up."

- **Allow** means letting the thoughts, emotions, or sensations simply be there. Instead of trying to suppress, resist, or repel the experience, you can give it airtime and soften into the experience. The life cycle of an emotion traveling through the nervous system is about sixty seconds. Because we apply stories to the states, however, emotions can recycle and thoughts can spin. This means not getting hijacked by fight/flight/freeze reactions or being harassed by mind's incessant commentary. Rather, give your inner bully a time-out. Interrupt the cycle. Accept the moment. You might say to yourself, "Yes, this is what's happening right now," "It's OK," or "This will pass."

- **Investigate** your experience with kindness. Tap your inner detective and ask yourself, "What most wants my attention right now?" "How am I experiencing this reaction in my body?" "What is my inner critic telling me or trying to warn me about? Am I believing it? Is it true?" "Is there a gift to uncover?" Avoid analysis paralysis! Instead, befriend yourself as you would care for a dear friend in need. An attitude of curiosity and care helps with a sense of safety and understanding.

• **Nurture** means to intentionally care for the vulnerable places inside. Often strong reactions result when there are unmet needs that are carried over from earlier experiences in life that felt invalidating. It can be different now. What do you need in this moment? Acknowledgment? Calm? Courage? Forgiveness? Friendship? Love? Reassurance? Respect? Rest? You can reflect: "How can I bring kindness to this moment?" N can also stand for "next best step." Ask, "What beneficial action can I take?" Adopt a sense of care, ease, and compassion.

GET ENERGIZED: ANTISTRESS SMOOTHIE

It's also important to ease overstimulation from the outside world and allow your senses to calm. In Traditional Chinese Medicine there is an energy pathway called the triple warmer meridian that governs the fight/flight/freeze survival responses (also referred to as triple heater or burner). It has the important task of keeping us out of danger and alive when the Red Zone is triggered. Like a military commander, this energy pathway is concerned with survival issues. It keeps you alert and vigilant. This meridian is engaged when you have a worried mind, suffer from insomnia, feel overwhelmed or anxious, and have a hard time relaxing. It keeps habits well entrenched, whether positive or negative. It can befriend as well as agitate.

It helps to soothe this pathway on a fairly regular basis given the onslaught of daily hassles and life stress. This is particularly nice for perfectionists, who tend to hold tension in the head and neck. You can assure the inner critic that this exercise is for their benefit too. Energy practitioner Donna Eden offers a simple way to balance this meridian, aptly called the Triple Warmer Smoothie.[34] I like to call it an antistress smoothie, much like you might drink an antioxidant smoothie. It's good for your system. Here's how you do it.

1. Rest your face in the palms of your hands as if you're playing peekaboo. Hold for a few breaths.
2. On an inhale, lift your fingers to your forehead and gently drag each hand to the temples, then smooth the skin from each temple to above the ears with gentle pressure.
3. On an exhale, trace your fingers around the back of your ears until you can rest them at the sides of your neck.
4. Allow your hands to hang from the back of your shoulders, and give yourself a nice little squeeze. Stay here for a few breaths.
5. Drag your fingers gently from each shoulder with mild pressure, and cross your hands over your heart. Breathe for a few moments.

GET CONNECTED: IMAGINE A KIND BEING

There is almost nothing else more irritating to perfectionists than being asked to be kind to themselves. In the spirit of using visualization for personal growth, I hope I can convince you otherwise. There are many effective compassion-based therapies that are the subject of innovative research.[35] These practices are highly visual and tend to evoke feelings of warmth and tenderness. Their goal is to allow you to more readily offer compassion toward yourself and others. Some practices focus on receiving compassion from an imagined benevolent person or being. This is how you do it:

1. If you're able, please close your eyes. Perhaps place your hand over your heart, or fold your arms gently across your chest, or find some other soothing gesture. Rest there for a few moments, allowing your breath to flow naturally, and your shoulders to relax.

2. Recall a situation or behavior that triggers the Red Zone, or something else you are struggling with and would like to change—not because you're unworthy or flawed in some way or made mistakes, but because there is a compassionate voice that wants the best for you.

3. Bring to mind an image of a person, a dear friend or loved one who cares deeply for you. Or perhaps there is an iconic image of love, mercy, compassion, or wisdom, such as Buddha, Jesus, Mother Mary, Kuan Yin, or a guardian angel. Or a childhood superhero, a beloved pet that evokes strength or courage, or even a color or healing light. This kind and wise being also sees clearly. It is expansive and flexible. It has a sense of how your self-critical voice might be protecting you, and how it may create challenges for you. This compassionate image also wants you to thrive and to live wholeheartedly, but for very different reasons. Visualize this being as if it is sitting next to you.

4. Imagine what this kind being is communicating to you. Perhaps there are words or phrases that are kind and caring, or it is more of a feeling. It may be as simple as:

    "I'm here for you, love."
    "I care for you."
    "I want to help you make the changes you want for yourself."
    "I don't want to see you suffer."
    "Take my hand. I'm here to support you."

5. And perhaps—with an emerging recognition of that self-critical voice and the bias to scan for danger—see if you can direct a kind awareness toward your critical self, whether it is an inner taskmaster, bully, judge, or vigilant naysayer. And in doing so, you can make some space for another aspect of yourself that is also there. It's always existed. It is a wise voice. It is a kind voice. It is a reassuring voice that loves and accepts you exactly the way you are. It makes room for all your inner minions.

This might feel strange at first. Or it may come surprisingly naturally to you. Sit with the comfort or curiosity that you are receiving. Close the meditation when you feel ready.

You may even be inspired to take some time for this wise part to write a note to the part(s) of you that wants to change or needs some healing. I highly encourage you to write down the words or images that arose and note any qualities of this kind and compassionate image.

Or your inner skeptic may kick in. If so, try telling yourself, "Even though this feels new, or weird, or foreign, I will give this kinder voice a try for a while."

As with any of these exercises, travel around the edges at first and set the intention to make room for this compassionate and wise voice. You'll see over time that new mental associations will form. In fact, I'm confident about this process, and the next step in the process will nudge you along a little bit further allowing you to open your heart to new possibilities.

6

Step 3

O, Open Your Heart

People call these things imperfections, but they're not,
that's the good stuff.
And then we get to choose who we let into
our weird little worlds.

— *Ben Affleck and Matt Damon,* Good Will Hunting

"I made this small mistake," Asher shared at an Overcome Perfectionism session. "I mean, a really stupid small thing. I was telling myself how dumb it was, and even horrible, that this one mistake symbolized how I am a total failure. That my research is doomed. This little thing turned into a total catastrophe in a nanosecond." The other students nodded in recognition. Asher continued, "But I found myself saying to myself: *Let's take some notes on this.*"

Then Daria shared, "I can't detach like that. The brutal judgy voice, I mean, that IS me. I don't see how to separate from it." Even though she was so identified with the inner judge, she observed another voice that didn't allow her to have any pleasure. She felt stuck, yet her lens was widening enough to see that there's the judgy element trying to control things and there's also an inner joy thief grinding any feelings of happiness to a halt.

Reed added, "You know, I noticed I am more aware of the voices and I'm picking up some patterns."

Asher agreed. "Before it was just this diffuse notion of being worthless. Now I can pick up on the specifics. And it's kind of shitty when you start to notice." The group members murmured in recognition. *Uh-huh. Mmm. Yep.*

Then a shy member of the group spoke up. Saanvi struggled with procrastination. They thought their inner critic was more like a detective, going down rabbit holes. "This week I was scrolling through Bollywood actors' public lives. Like, I really don't care one bit about any of them, but there I am scrolling. I realized it is more of a defense, to avoid the things I don't want to do or I am afraid to get started."

All in all a conversation like this can be downright depressing. But something was happening through the long awkward pauses. There was a stretch of space where the participants allowed their Plus Ones, these long-standing algorithms, to have some room to breathe. To speak. To be heard. I asked them, "If you could imagine a friend you cherish having these same thoughts and feelings, what would you say to them?"

Daria, ever the skeptic, wondered, "Can we see ourselves as a friend? I mean, is that even possible?" Yes, it is absolutely possible. In fact, offering yourself the same loving attention you'd give to a friend is the next step in your evolution.

The Goal of Step 3: Open Your Heart

These perfectionism group members were discovering that their inner critical voices needed their attention—not their dismissal. Learning how to turn toward these inner voices with curiosity and kindness is how you begin to develop inner worth, humanity, and leadership, and so much more. Sound like a tall order? Don't worry. It begins with uncovering compassion for yourself—and all the parts that live in your weird little world. How? By opening your heart a wee bit more than it is right now.

Let's talk about the heart. I know the title of this chapter, "Open Your Heart," may be a stretch for some skeptical Plus Ones. But when you discover the power of the heart, you'll want to know more. Indeed, the heart is an energetic organ and has its own neural network known as the intrinsic cardiac nervous system.[1] The heart is the first organ to develop in a fetus, emitting electromagnetic information even before it is fully developed. Your heart not only pumps blood to the far reaches of your body, but it has its own intelligence. The heart interacts dynamically with the brain through bidirectional communication. It has been affectionately referred to as the "little heart brain."[2] Intentionally experiencing uplifting emotions can change the information the heart sends to the brain. Purposely visualizing and creating beneficial states like calm, tenderness, play, and joy are stabilizing. The heart is an amazing guidance system that communicates with the autonomic nervous system (ANS), which you are now familiar with from Step 1. The heart is part of the hormonal system and functions to slow down the release of cortisol in the body.

The heart is also an electrical organ and is thought to be the largest source of bioelectricity in the body. It radiates an electromagnetic field that energetically affects your moods and the emotional climate of those around you. Your heart's electromagnetic field expands several feet around you like your own force field. It offers intuitive guidance that goes beyond implicit processes in the brain. Truly, the heart is always working on your behalf. One wonders why most of us don't trust our vibes more often instead of deferring to the unreliable, judgy mind!

The HeartMath Institute's Howard Martin describes how emotions change your electromagnetic field beyond the biological qualities of the heart, bringing heart intelligence into the realm of physics. Negative or difficult emotions (anger, frustration, regret, resentment) are associated with disruption or *incoherence* in the heart energy field, whereas benevolent or positive emotions (appreciation, care, kindness, patience) cultivate stability or *coherence*. Amazingly, this can be measured through biofeedback using heart rate variability analysis (HRV), which you can now track on a mobile app. HRV is simply measuring the rhythm or time intervals between heartbeats and is an indirect measurement of vagal tone, as described in Step 1.[3] Greater variability in HRV is a positive indicator for maintaining overall physical health and well-being. People with high HRV tend to have greater psychological flexibility, can adapt more easily to stress, and are happier.[4] Breathing techniques with a focus on the heart area in the center of the chest or calling on a benevolent emotion or attitude (appreciation, gratitude, warmth, etc.) foster greater heart coherence.

Consider that a harsh inner critic is telling you are a failure or not good enough. This judgment leads to feeling bad about yourself, perhaps igniting sadness or shame. (Remember, the brain is making simulations every moment to help the body run efficiently and it calls on patterns from the past, keeping your inner critic alive and well.) This disrupts your heart energy, sending signals to your brain that deactivate neural pathways in the prefrontal frontal cortex and potentially cause brain fog and confusion. Disrupted heart energy is associated with a fight/flight/freeze response (the downsides of the Red, Blue, Green Zones) and a depleted body budget. Ouch.

But here's some comforting news. You can purposely cultivate greater heart coherence by practicing self-compassion, mindful breathing, and other heart-based skills to generate a new experience and thereby new algorithms. This may be the kindest thing you can do for yourself . . . if you are willing to try.

The Superpower of Self-Compassion

Kristin Neff, PhD, a psychologist at University of Texas in Austin, operationalized the concept of self-compassion and ignited a robust field of research on what happens when people are kinder to themselves. Neff describes three components of self-compassion:[5]

- *Mindfulness* or being in the present moment without judging what you are going through, and having a balanced view of positive and negative experiences. (The skills in Step 1.)
- *Common humanity*, which means knowing that you are not alone in how you are feeling or in the experience of human suffering. After all, feeling like you are the only one in the world with a particular experience can be challenging. One reason I

enjoy running workshops so much is that members learn they can truly relate to one another. The members hold up a mirror to one another and see each other reflected back.

- *Self-kindness.* Rather than beating yourself up in your mind, you talk to yourself like you would to someone you love, care for, or respect. It's befriending yourself. Often, this is the hardest element to embrace, especially for perfectionists and those who question their worthiness. That is why these next two chapters focus on honing the muscle of self-compassion.

For many high achievers, the idea of self-compassion is like trying to squeeze into shoes that don't fit. You really want to wear them, but it just isn't working for you. Remember Justin, the Division 1 college football player burdened with anxiety and homesickness? Justin struggled with self-compassion. He felt he had to be a tough guy all the time. While he could identify one inner critic, Leech, who sucked the fun out of life, he began to see some other algorithms running in the background.

Justin began to notice certain body sensations, in particular a rapid heartbeat that seemingly arose for no particular reason. (Most likely, Justin's heart rate variability could have used some strengthening.) He also had a tendency to think that a scratchy throat or swollen lymph node meant he had cancer or a rare disease. Justin would be in class, or walking about, and boom! He'd notice his heart pounding. The more he tuned into the sensation with fear, the more his heart rate sped up. That freaked him out even more, and he began experiencing panic attacks that could last thirty minutes or three hours. He was embarrassed by it. A visit to the ER eventually prompted him to make an appointment for counseling after the medical personnel determined his heart was just fine. With some reflection, Justin discovered another inner voice, like an inner detective, that was on the prowl for any signs of illness and looked up symptoms on the Internet. This inner sleuth arose to protect him by predicting terrible outcomes. He called this voice "Dr. Google."

As a child, Justin experienced appendicitis. Even though it was taken care of, Justin's fear of what could have happened if the doctors hadn't diagnosed and treated him in time never left him. Now some years later, this inner algorithm kept him on the alert. It crept up sometimes when he was bored or not focused on anything in particular. His wandering mind would land on some bodily sensation and grab his attention, and then he'd be down a rabbit hole of worst-case scenarios.

This kind of health fixation or phobia is fairly common. The brain has learned to overemphasize the danger and dismiss any rational self-talk, assurance from a physician, or normal lab test result. Then the "what if" thinking, fortune telling, or catastrophizing we covered in Step 2 kicks into gear. This particular algorithm is like an energetic hiccup in the nervous system based on predictive patterns from the past. A misfiring of sorts.

Rather than trying to change Justin's mind or thought process around his health, we began by building grounding skills—things like feeling the soles of his feet, keeping a smooth stone in his pocket to rub, or lying on the floor with legs up the wall—in an effort to redirect his attention to feeling safe and supported in his body, and retrain his body's oversensitized surveillance system that so often trapped him in a Red Zone. These self-care skills foster greater heart coherence rather than interference and settled him into a Green Zone of peace.

Justin also noticed that this fear *never* arose when he was playing a casual pickup football game or other sports because his mind was focused on having fun with his friends and he was relaxed in a Blue Zone of inspired action. It was a completely different story, however, when he had to get up for football practice or game days when the pressure was suffocating.

Now, if there is any time your heart is racing, it's playing sports, right? So together we got curious about this. Justin began to sense that his heart rate changed quite naturally depending on what he was doing and if he was feeling emotional pressure to perform at his best. Tuning into body sensations in a curious way is called *interoception* (mentioned in Step 1). This lesser-known sense helps with understanding—and appropriately addressing—the body's signals and needs, such as feeling hungry, thirsty, hot or cool, in pain, tired, nervous, or afraid. Without being aware of his interoceptive sensing, Justin was misinterpreting his beating heart, causing him to panic.

As we developed his ability to self-regulate, Justin began to have a new experience in his body. He had tools to deal with the quivers. Justin practiced these self-compassion practices in ordinary moments too, not just when he was stressed out. And as a result, he was reshaping the story in his mind. Yet we never directly discussed self-compassion. "Self-care, compassion, whatever—is what therapists say," Justin told me. Rather, Justin drew on an encouraging coach-like tone, one very natural to him. It was his own voice and he recalled using it often when he helped little kids in peewee football summer camps. He called it a daily drill.

I often hear patients and clients say things like "I can't even begin to imagine what self-compassion means" and "I don't *do* self-compassion." I get it. In addition to potentially being sappy or soft, it's very hard let go of something—in this case, perfectionism—that's been effective for so long. Eventually, Justin began to take his daily drills seriously as he began to see the beneficial results. Whenever he felt a twinge or a tweak in his body, he would talk to himself, sometimes using his name. These breaks are modeled on the "self-compassion break" offered by Kristin Neff and addresses the three elements of mindfulness, common humanity, and self-kindness. Justin's inner dialogue went something like this:

1. "Justin, it's OK. Your body's nervous system is in a momentary survival response trying to protect you. Be curious and ride it out." Or "Justin, sometimes your heart races and it can feel uncomfortable. Breathe down to your feet." In this way Justin was being mindful rather than judgmental.

2. Then Justin would consider something like this: "Moments of distress happen for everyone. Even though I don't like this sensation right now, I know it will pass." That's an expression of common

humanity, a sense that the human body is both complex and responsive and that he is not alone with such experiences.

3. Then Justin began to be caring toward himself as if a younger part of him needed some encouragement, just like the peewee footballers: "Justin, you've got this. Breathe. Look how much you've learned. You're doing amazing."

The self-kindness element took some time to include. Justin said to me one day, "I'm being nicer to myself and that is surprisingly helpful." His was a quiet inner leadership, and he began to see this as a strength.

Over time Justin discovered that having a routine of breathing exercises and enjoyable physical activity helped him to feel steady, strong, and connected to his body in a new, healthier way. And guess what? Both his inner Leech and Dr. Google parts relaxed.

Heart Opener Reflection #1: Self-Compassion Break

Now it's your turn to practice a self-compassion break. Like Justin, you can label this reflection exercise whatever feels right to you. It involves practicing the three elements of self-compassion defined by Neff and can be done in under a minute. Because the self-kindness element is a particular challenge to many perfectionists, it's helpful to jot down your phrases ahead of time. This way you can read the phrases until they sink in as a kind of "fake it until you make it" approach. The instructions for creating these personal affirmations are simple: Be clear and conversational. Be genuine and real. Use a kind or encouraging tone. It's up to you if you want to switch up "I" for "you" depending on how you like to hear your inner voice as discussed in Step 2. Below are examples to get you started.

- *Mindfulness statement*

This is a moment of _____

   (anger, awkwardness, curiosity, courage, distress, grief, nerves, stress, suffering, etc.).

Choose your own phrase:_____

- *Common humanity statement*

I'm not alone. Others experience this too.

Everyone gets a Red Zone reaction sometimes.

I'm having a survival response. This feeling is universal.

Choose your own phrase:_____

- *Self-kindness statement*

I choose to be _____

   (accepting, bold, calm, kind, patient, understanding, etc.).

It's OK not to feel OK. You're doing the best you can right now.

Be gentle with yourself. Breathe. (Hands on heart.)

Choose your own phrase:_____

String your three statements together and repeat several times. Whenever you need bolstering, you can craft a self-compassion statement by asking yourself, "What do I need to feel steady in my body?" like Justin learned to do.

You can also locate what emotion zone you're in. Or you can craft a message by asking yourself, "In this moment, what do I need to feel worthy? Accepted? Calm? Confident? Inspired?" The answers are typically universal human needs: belonging, connection, encouragement, love, patience, protection, or respect,

> tolerance, validation, and well-being. You'll know it when you land on it. And if not, just experiment for a while or call on an "even though" statement that you created in Step 1 and tap on the acupressure point on the side of your hand. "Even though this feels awkward, I will be patient and try to be nicer to myself."

Meditation teacher Pema Chödrön said, "Compassion for others begins with kindness to ourselves." She also noted that, "Compassion isn't some kind of self-improvement project or ideal that we're trying to live up to . . . Having compassion starts and ends with having compassion for all those unwanted parts of ourselves, all those imperfections that we don't even want to look at." That means giving compassion to your inner critics too.

If Justin could do it, so can you.

Warming Up to Self-Compassion

Daria's question on whether it's possible to befriend yourself might be echoing through your mind right now. Being nice or easier on yourself might seem difficult, lame, or too touchy-feely. Plus, if you've been aiming for 110 percent on everything you do and productivity is a measure of your worthiness, then anything short of full throttle may feel very uncomfortable. The bias toward exhibiting "hard" outcome-oriented skills, like benchmarks and key performance indicators (terms often used in business settings), over "soft skills" persists in most high-achieving arenas. While there may be talk about the values of emotional intelligence, self-awareness, relationship building, compassion, or self-care, actually witnessing your bosses, coaches, instructors, managers, and leaders consciously practice and allow for such skills on their teams is usually the exception. It's not because people aren't capable, but because the organizational systems and performance mindsets often make it impossible or else give off a mixed message: Use an app, take a walk, do what you need to do, but get your work done by midnight.

As an early-career lawyer, Daria was learning the consequence of being overenergized. Intellectually, she could foresee the path toward burnout, depression, and apathy. Eventually, her battery would run out from overwork. But the idea of taking a five- or ten-minute brain break was anathema to her, just like using the term "self-compassion" was for Justin. She wanted to work hard and strive for excellence. As leadership expert Greg McKeown points out, Daria falls into an "engaged-exhausted" group of employees who are passionate about their work but also experience high levels of stress—and are at highest risk for quitting.[6] She was willing to put in the grueling hours to prove herself, and she was well aware that the organizational demands and attitudes would not change. Her job called on the very perfectionist traits that served her well throughout her academic career. Her inner judge, then, was in fine form to keep the pressure on. No slacking off. She could not conceive of an alternative inner narrative.

She literally had to warm up to it.

To learn anything new it is helpful to feel safely challenged. After all, it's very hard to take in new information, make beneficial changes, or create new habits when you're stressed or shut down. To visualize how we learn best, imagine three concentric rings as framed by the Mindful Self-Compassion program.[7] The very center ring represents *safety*, the middle ring represents *challenge*, and the outer ring represents *overwhelm*, which is being overcome by thoughts and emotions about life's difficulties. This may feel akin to the emotional motivation zones of Green, Blue, and Red that can drive your emotional reactions. Similarly, our capacity to learn thrives in optimal conditions. Daria's inner judge, which was harsh and unrelenting, orbited the outer ring of overwhelm. Round and round it went like a siren.

Most days, Daria was in the ring of challenge, navigating her cases, deadlines, commuting, eating, and the usual activities of daily living. It's where most of us spend our time. Yet all the while her inner judge

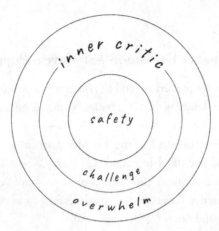

was poking, prodding, and pushing from the outside in, aiming. *Don't make a mistake. Prove yourself.*

Daria rarely dipped into the inner circle of safety, a refuge where she could truly ground and center herself. This inner sanctuary is where you experience calm, coherent heart energy, steadiness, warmth, and well-being, and is often entered via practices of quiet, mindfulness, prayer, journaling and the like. Even with mounting evidence for the health benefits of simple mindful moments in the brain, heart, and body, this ring of safety was a ring of fire for Daria, where she felt untethered and out of control. It was a paradox.

Because Daria's mind was so frantic and full, slowing down was very hard for her. But there was one mindfulness practice that finally opened her up to being kinder to herself and being even more adventurous with the EVOLVE practices described in this book. The simplicity was surprising to Daria and is described in the following Heart Opener Reflection.

Heart Opener Reflection #2: Have a Puppy Mind

Because we are primed to tend to potential threats and ward off danger, the brain is like a predictive modeling machine (as described in Step 1), churning out possible scenarios while going about the usual demands of the day. Metaphorically, inner critics swirl around like the flying monkeys in *The Wonderful Wizard of Oz*. Indeed, a common mindfulness phrase is "monkey mind" to depict the active nature of the mind, leaping from one thought to another, and rarely touching ground.

A more helpful metaphor for some is "puppy mind." Imagine having a puppy you adore—its big eyes, floppy paws, and soft fur. Just picturing a cute puppy is enough to release the calming cuddle hormone oxytocin. (Remember the benefits of visualizing benevolent images from Step 2?). So when your puppy pees on the carpet, spills the kibble, chews on socks, and yelps at the mailman, what do you do? You wouldn't get mad at a puppy and kick it out of frustration, would you? Much more likely, you'd redirect the adorable creature and then reward it for good behavior.

It takes an enormous amount of love and patience to train a puppy. That is exactly what your busy brain needs too. Here are several ways to use the principles of puppy mind on your own self:

- When you feel irritated, distracted or frustrated, redirect your attention to the present moment with an attitude of play, curiosity, and joy.
- When you notice a critical inner narrative, remind yourself that you are working on being kinder to yourself. This may be a good moment to add in a self-compassion break too.

- When you recognize an inner algorithm or old pattern of self-sabotage, begin to install a new algorithm by repeating a phrase like "I'm my own best friend."

Remember, what you pay attention to grows stronger in your nervous system. You can nudge the predictive modeling activity of your own brain toward self-compassion practices. Just like a puppy eventually settles into a new routine based on calm, consistency, and kindness, so can you.

Amplify Your Inner Tone

With puppies on the mind, it's a good moment to pay attention to how you speak to yourself. Asher noticed that he was unnecessarily mean to himself, calling himself dumb and inept. He began to take some mental notes about how he was speaking to himself. He was an unhappy achiever and feeling adrift. He was hovering, being both underenergized and isolated (in the lower-left quadrant of the Perfectionism Matrix) and needing to fit in (in the upper-left quadrant of the Perfectionism Matrix). It took enormous courage for him to be vulnerable with others in the group. But by being open with his fellow attendees, he became better able to hear his own negative self-talk, as well as connect with others who do the very same thing. He was not alone after all. That feeling of being in community helped him be safely challenged.

American psychologist and neuroscientist Stephen Porges has, through his research, proposed that the vagus nerve, which travels from the base of the skull though the throat, heart, lungs, and torso, is sensitive to vocalizations, especially tones of caring and connection. Called "motherese," these are sounds we utter when caring for a friend in need, a baby in distress, a child with a skinned knee, or a beloved pet. These vocalizations are often brief—*ahhhh, uh-huh, oohhh,* and *hmm*—and paired with an eye gaze, head tilt, hug, or a pat on the arm or back. These behaviors communicate empathy and understanding. That's what Asher was taking in from the micro moments of murmurs among the group. It calmed his nervous system, enabling him to learn new self-care skills.

In a similar fashion, you can alter the tone you use when talking to yourself, moving away from harsh banter and calling on an encouraging and empathic tone that is true and pure. It's not babying yourself. Think of this as strengthening your vagal tone, massaging your autonomic nervous system, and balancing your body budget with greater calm and connection.

If you can do it while placing your hands over your heart, you'll also foster heart coherence. In Hindu and other Eastern wisdom traditions, the chakras represent seven main energetic vortexes in the body, with the heart chakra at the center (with three chakras below and three chakras above). A gesture of a hand or fist over the heart can be soothing and stabilizing, thereby opening up energy pathways. Pairing physical touch with soothing or encouraging words strengthens the mind-body-spirit connection. It gets you in the flow.

You can even apply this kinder vocalization to countering your inner critical narratives and limiting beliefs. Essentially, befriending your inner critics helps move them into feeling safely challenged. The inner critics originated during a younger phase in your life to protect you and are rather like children and teens running amok without the coping skills and tools to manage life's ongoing challenges. Whether you experienced big traumas or little traumas as you were growing up, your body-mind did what it could to cope, your energy patterns were shaped, and your mental algorithms took root. Although you grew up and learned how to manage adult things, the inner critics are still locked in the past, on guard and ready to defend. These parts are doing what they can with the knowledge they had when they were corrected, rejected, punished, slighted, shamed, or teased. They seek to avoid a repeat.

Take, for example, the character of Will in the 1990s indie classic *Good Will Hunting*. Will, portrayed by Matt Damon, is a troubled math genius who finds himself working as a janitor at the prestigious Massachusetts Institute of Technology (MIT). Along his journey, he encounters Dr. Sean Maguire, an endearing therapist brought to life by the late Robin Williams. Will was a tough Boston kid from Southie who suffered in the foster care system and had a problematic legal record. As a young adult, he sought solace in his loyal friends and took on low-wage jobs, but struggled to form meaningful connections. His penchant for sneaking around to prove his mathematical prowess eventually caught up with him. Rather than punishment, MIT administrators offer him therapy. Once in counseling, Will's limiting beliefs about love and belonging soon become apparent. When Will begins a relationship with an intelligent and funny Harvard student, he breaks up with her before she can reject him. His modus operandi is to outsmart anyone who could harm him.

During a therapy session, Sean is looking at the case file photos of the physical abuse Will endured by the hand of his foster father. Will asks Sean if he's experienced anything like that. In a moment of self-disclosure Sean confesses that he too had his share of pain at the hands of an alcoholic father. Will, with his protective armor of sarcasm, attempts to deflect any potential psycho-babble about attachment disorders or fear of abandonment from Sean. However, instead of maintaining a distance, Sean gradually draws closer and closer while looking directly at Will. Sean's voice is persistent yet gentle as he repeatedly utters: *It's not your fault. It's not your fault.* This unwavering affirmation begins to resonate with Will, gradually softening the wounded part within, until he finally welcomes an embrace.

The scene serves as a reminder that sometimes we need another person to mirror back the truth in a way that evokes care and understanding. And yet it's important to recognize that such compassion is something we can do for ourselves too. A soft yet persistent tone, a gentle touch, and a clear gaze are antidotes to inner criticism and shame, from the little everyday traumas to the big ones.

Being on Your Own Side

Because it's natural to shut down when stressed, it's easy to deplete the body budget. The smallest of triggers can block the neural thoroughfare in your brain and disrupt the coherence of the heart. And courage is exactly what you need when learning how to befriend yourself.

Luckily, you have a very deep drive for compassion. After all, the human species would not persist if we didn't have empathy. There is a beautiful construct in psychology called *tend and befriend*. Tending and befriending is an alternative survival response to stress.[8] It is our natural need to seek safety, comfort, and support from others. This caring response is fueled by the bonding hormone oxytocin, sometimes referred to as the cuddle or love hormone. The truth is that we are wired to care. And yet, because of those loopholes in our nervous system, it can be easy to miss the essential need to *care for oneself*, to tend and befriend our own being when facing hardships. Instead, we often fight with ourselves, punish our perceived inadequacies, and insist on figuring things out alone.

You can spark your natural instinct to seek comfort and safety by reaching out to trusted and caring people. In fact, you likely do it all the time. Think about watching a football game, shopping with friends, or volunteering at a soup kitchen. Or seeking advice, consulting a doctor, and getting reassurance from a trusted friend, mentor, or expert. When you pursue helpful human connection, the stress hormones dissipate, the body recovers, and you experience a sense of renewal and energy. Often, we don't consider reaching out for help or we wait too long, but doing so is so important for overall well-being. An important question to answer for yourself, then, is how can you be on your own side when you're caught in a tough spot and find yourself alone?

Here are some ideas: You can speak to yourself just like you would to a friend. You can lower the volume on the inner critical voice or ask it to step aside to allow you to practice self-care. Doing these things activates other brain networks associated with empathy, compassion, and emotion regulation, which in turn buffers the stress response.

Saying nice things to yourself may sound quaint at best or ridiculous at worst. Daria would have none of it. At least at first. Yet research drawing on self-affirmation theory indicates that positive messages can sink in just like messages from advertisements can sink in.[9] And unlike subliminal ads shaping your beliefs about beauty, bodies, and branding, you can intentionally choose messages that can enhance your sense of self and lead to positive outcomes.

Here's the amazing part. Knowing this, you can choose to create a different soundtrack in your mind and steady the beat in your heart. The nervous system is amazingly flexible—that's the gift of neuroplasticity. You have the ability to influence your little heart brain based on what you choose to experience and practice. The key is being ready—and willing. Despite how automatic those inner critical narratives may seem, how you talk to yourself and treat yourself is entirely your choice.

Heart Opener Reflection #3: Giving Voice to Self-Compassion

Let's navigate the edge of being safely challenged and take some time to call on self-compassion to ease the inner critics enough so they can relax a bit.

It can be helpful to imagine what you'd say to a friend who was talking to themselves the same way your Plus One talks to you. (If you need help remembering some of the things your Plus One likes to say, and which of the five general archetypes it matches the best, go back and look at the Perfectionism Self-Inquiry on page 31.)

Naturally, you can relate to the struggle. Yet you respond in a compassionate way. Compassion is the ability to see the suffering in another with a desire to alleviate the pain. Think about how you would go about it—what you would say, as well as what tone or gestures you might use.

To help you envision it, below are some examples of what each archetype is likely to say to itself, and what kinds of messages and tones from a compassionate friend are best suited to address that particular inner algorithm.

The Judge

A judgmental narrative typically runs along the lines of *Who do you think you are? What makes you so special or deserving? You're not good enough.* When pushed to an extreme, the judge can be rigid, critical, and unrelenting. An underlying unmet need: Worthiness.

> Asher: *I really fucked up my PhD program. I should have turned things around much sooner.*
> Reed: *Hey, man. I know it feels hard right now, but you're rounding the corner. There are valid reasons it took you longer than others. Don't give up. It's going to work out.*
> (The tone is encouraging, yet firm.)

The Drill Sergeant

A bullying narrative that arises from a limiting belief or algorithm is that being in control is necessary, and vulnerability is to be avoided at all costs. When feeling pushed to a wall, the narrative might be: *Failure is not an option.* You only see what's wrong rather than what's right. An underlying unmet need: Acceptance.

> Luis: *I hate it when others don't pull their weight. Ultimately it reflects on me. That's just unacceptable.*

Daria: *Being good at what you do is really important to you. No wonder—after all you went through.* (The tone is soft, yet curious.)

The Sleuth

The inner algorithm for the sleuth is looking for answers, sometimes in all the wrong places. Whether hyperfocused on one line of inquiry or feeling scattershot by looking at all options, the inner narrative might be: *I leave no stone unturned! I have an answer to that!* Focusing on the present can be very hard. An underlying unmet need: Respect.

Reed: *I'm all over the place. I'm running on empty. I did it to myself and I don't even know why.*
Asher: *You put in your all and did your best. It's OK to chill out. Give yourself a break. You deserve it.* (The tone is kind and patient.)

The Nitpicker

Wanting things to look impeccable and needing things to be in place can cause so much unnecessary stress when a nitpicker is in overdrive. There may be fits and starts, doing and undoing, and unnecessary energy spent on improvements and procrastination. *Wait. There's one more thing to do! It has to be perfect.* An underlying unmet need: Validation.

Kayla: *I just can't seem to get things just right. I know it's insane to go over and over things.*
Saanvi: *Oh, girl. I know what you mean. It's cool when things go well. But mostly, I think, people just appreciate*

your effort. You're amazing just as you are. (The tone is empathic and relatable.)

The Joy Thief

Doing everything you can to avoid disappointing yourself or others is one of the hallmarks of an inner joy thief. Most of us rob ourselves of fun, play, and relaxation in the service of success. You may even entertain worst-case scenarios and people-please at your own expense. A worried mind can lead to rumination. A narrative might be: *What if something goes wrong? What if others are unhappy? I can't make a mistake.* An underlying unmet need: Love.

> Mariah: *I don't have a second to do any of the things I used to enjoy. Every second is accounted for. If I let up, something will go wrong.*
> Justin: *You really care a lot. That's so cool. But you have to care for yourself too, you know. Give yourself permission!*
> (The tone is caring and confident.)

As you can see, the compassionate responses are not fuzzy and flakey. The responses are grounded and authentic. It's not about perfection, it's about connection. Your goal now is to simply talk to yourself like you would to someone you care about. You can be your own best friend. And while you might not get the back rub, shoulder arm, hug or fist pump of a friend, you can do that for yourself with the Happy Achiever Tools included in this chapter.

Happy Achiever Tools: Open Your Heart

One of my favorite sayings is "Love is patient, love is kind." Wherever you are in the process of befriending yourself, start with finding a still, quiet place within. These tools will support you in connecting with your heart energy.

GET GROUNDED: A COMPASSIONATE VOICE

Play with the idea of using a kinder tone. Be an encouraging, patient coach that sees your potential. This inner wisdom also nudges you forward into unknown territory, orbiting the edge where you are safely challenged. Similar to the "Imagine a Kind Being" tool in the last chapter, here you will conjure your own voice, grounded and steady. You can try this quietly in your own mind, speak aloud, or write in a journal.

1. Take a few deep nourishing breaths.
2. With an emerging recognition of that self-critical voice and the bias to scan for danger, see if you can direct a kind awareness toward that aspect of your critical self, whether it is an inner boss or bully or judge or that vigilant naysayer.
3. In doing so, make some space for another aspect of yourself that is also there: a wise voice. It is a kind voice. It's your essence, a reassuring voice that loves and accepts you exactly the way you are.
4. This inner kind and wise voice also sees clearly. It is expansive and flexible. It has a sense of how your self-critical voice might be protecting you and how it may create challenges for you. This compassionate voice also wants you to thrive and to live wholeheartedly, but for very different reasons.
5. If you're able, close your eyes. Perhaps place your hand over your heart, fold your arms gently across your chest, or find some other soothing gesture. Rest there for a few moments,

allowing the compassionate aspect of yourself to emerge, bringing it into the foreground of your awareness.

6. Allow yourself to be still with this emerging voice, noticing the tone, the feeling, the sensation of being seen clearly, and the courage to face your vulnerabilities.

GET ENERGIZED: IGNITE JOY

Cultivating a new relationship with self requires a big dose of fun and play. After all, if the inner critics were relieved of their extreme roles to manage all aspects of your life and ward off pain and rejection, what would they do instead? Most of these parts would probably chill out, create something, build a fort, or play with abandon. This life force energy is essential.

In Traditional Chinese Medicine, there is an internal wellspring of energy called extraordinary vessels. Master energy practitioner Donna Eden refers to these as Radiant Circuits (described in more detail in Step 6). These are energetic circuits of joy, and it's important to ignite them on a regular basis, for they offset the fight/flight/freeze responses. Importantly, as you begin to create new algorithms through the mechanism of neuroplasticity, you can create a positivity bias with Radiant Circuit activities. Think of this as flexing your tend and befriend muscle. The capacity is already there, it's just a matter of releasing or exerting it. Here are a few ways to spark Radiant Circuit energy:

-   **Child's Pose or Happy Baby Pose:** If you are familiar with yoga, a child's pose is wonderful for the vagus nerve and heart coherence. Start by kneeling on the floor or a mat with your knees wide and toes touching. Fold forward, place your chest and head on the mat, and stretch your arms in front of you or drape them along your sides toward your feet with palms up like you are a sleeping baby. Your head can rest on one cheek or your forehead on the floor, a yoga block, or pillow. Gently breathe for a few minutes. Alternatively, the Happy Baby pose is great for playful energy: Lie on your back, face up, with legs up and out to sides and knees bent. Grab the bottom of each foot with your hands and rock gently side to side.

- **3x3 Hearts:** Trace heart shapes nine times over your body as you breathe:

  1. Begin with your fingers tracing the outline of a heart over your face three times from forehead to chin.
  2. With the palms of your hands, repeat the tracing of a heart over your torso three times (begin at the heart space at the center of the chest, fanning outward around the middle of the body, then pointing down to hips and pubic bone).
  3. Trace a full heart over the length of your entire body. Start at the top of pubic bone, trace up the center of the body to above your head, inhaling a deep breath. Then expand your hands, palms fanning out like wings. As you exhale, bring your arms down to the sides of your legs or down to your feet.
  4. Do this three times and finish off with a zip-up the front of torso (from Step 1) to seal in the good vibes. Close with both hands resting over your heart.

- **Sing and Dance:** Moving or swaying or humming or singing along to a song that makes you happy is good medicine. Tracing hearts and figure eights in the air gets your energy pathways to harmonize. Air guitar? Go for it. And if it helps, follow the sage advice of doing so as if no one is listening or watching. Be awkward and ignite your Radiant Circuit energy.

GET CONNECTED: HEART ENERGY

Doc Childre, founder of the HeartMath Institute, writes, "Our true self represents an achievable vibration within us that contains the wisdom and intelligence of our heart. In this higher vibration, we are harmoniously connected with the hearts of others and all lives."[10] In the spirit of cultivating heart resonance and higher vibration, try this simple breathing exercise:

1. Find a quiet moment or space. Begin with connecting to your own heart by contemplating a quality you would like to grow from within, such as confidence, compassion, courage, leadership, patience, worth, and so on.
2. Direct your attention around your heart area. Imagine the breath as a gentle breeze and find a comfortable rhythm of the heart and lungs. Inhale slowly for a count of four and linger on the exhale for a count of six. Repeat several times.
3. Imagine the inner quality of the heart you would like to strengthen and breathe into the heart energy. Smile.

Opening your heart to your inner critics and to your underlying resource of inner wisdom creates much more space for joyful energy and happiness. It's natural to resist such befriending of oneself. As with anything new and unfamiliar, it can take some tough love—as you will see in the next chapter.

7

Step 4

L, Love Your Inner Critic

take a moment to be grateful to your old self
for getting you this far

— *Yung Pueblo*

U p until this point, you've been noticing the limiting beliefs and algorithms you've encoded over time. You've contemplated how your life conditions and the evolutionary design of the heart, brain, and nervous system have shaped the scripts you carry in your mind and body. By doing so, you have begun to cultivate kindsight about who you are, your motivations, and the self-sabotaging habits you may have. You've named and said hello to your Plus One, allowing you to hold its hand as you continue this journey of self-acceptance. After all, it's up to you to lead the inner critic, not the other way around, as you will learn in this chapter. And then you turned your attention to another kind of voice—the voice of self-compassion that is hopefully beginning to pipe up inside you.

All these wonderful and powerful steps you've been taking are very likely to have your inner critic(s) up in arms. The parts that have been managing your life and helped you to achieve, control, grind, persist with goals, and hold your shit together aren't going to step aside easily. No, no, no. After all, perfectionist tendencies are highly rewarded in our world, and people count on you. So no wonder that the practice of self-compassion can be tricky. People feel they are letting themselves off the hook.

It's OK to feel skepticism about self-kindness. People associate self-compassion with being soft, weak, or selfish. In part, the word *self* poses a problem. We have a tendency in Western, individualistic cultures to overuse the prefix: self-absorbed, self-abuse, self-acceptance, self-actualized, self-determined, self-criticism, self-doubt, self-esteem, self-educated, self-hatred, self-involved, self-righteous, self-sabotage, and on and on. This separates you not only from others but from your inner minions.

Even the word *compassion*, which means *to suffer with*, can feel like an aspirational virtue relegated to a select or saintly few, like Mother Teresa or Gandhi. Compassion can feel too tall of an order—the stuff of heroes.

Because of these negative connotations to the term "self-compassion," I prefer to call it "befriending yourself." To many perfectionists I've worked with, the idea of befriending feels a bit more appealing—and doable—than exercising self-compassion.

Befriending yourself is about connecting the head and the heart when you are challenged or suffering, even at the metaphorical hands of your inner critics. And that connection is the intention of this step.

The Goal of Step 4: Love Your Inner Critic

This step of loving your inner critic is a turning point. We're in the messy middle. It is no longer just noticing what you've been doing but starting to do things differently. Of course, it's important to practice all the skills and repeat what works (over and over), as well as trying new skills and thereby letting go of those algorithms and habits that no longer serve you. This can kick up resistance. After all, it can be very hard for perfectionists to be kind to themselves. Psychologist Richard Schwartz aptly states: "You are going toward what you have spent your life avoiding. On the journey, you are likely to encounter a great deal of resistance from the parts of you that have tried so hard to prevent the very thing you are heading toward."[1]

The practice of befriending yourself—including your inner critics—fosters not only resilience and overall well-being but also encourages posttraumatic growth in the aftermath of difficult life challenges. But those inner critics can muster up so much pushback! The main reason people say they don't practice compassion toward themselves is the mistaken belief that being kind to oneself will lower their motivation. They'll slack off, it's an indulgence, feels selfish, is a kind of self-pity, it's weak—or like Asher, they feel they don't deserve it.

Asher's Story

"Doc, I need help. I don't know if I made the right decision," Asher wrote to me a year after the perfectionism workshop. In the meantime, he had successfully defended his dissertation. "On a whim," he said, Asher had applied to a prestigious postdoctoral fellowship on the other side of the country—and was completely surprised when he received the acceptance letter. We arranged a consultation session to help him sort through his concerns on whether or not he should take it.

In that meeting, I learned more about Asher's final year in his PhD program as well as how he managed the physical disability that left him in a wheelchair and prone to debilitating migraines. Against the odds, or perhaps because of these adversaries, he landed in an esteemed university for his PhD and now another for a fellowship. Still, he felt he didn't know where he belonged. He had a sense of being inherently damaged.

What struck me most about Asher was his good humor and casual attitude paired with his sharp survival instincts. He had made friends easily in his perfectionism group, yet he often felt lonely outside of organized workshops or classes. He felt the workshop had jump-started his motivation, and he was feeling less alone. Yet he still felt like an imposter. And it was true that he wasn't a typical student as his path was less academic and more entrepreneurial. Moreover, navigating the world in a wheelchair had its challenges. As such, Asher was in a constant, low-grade panic, not quite in the Red Zone. It was more like soaking in a tepid Pink Zone. He felt he was in over his head. It seemed clear that as much as he wanted to succeed on his academic path, he was equally afraid of that success.

At age thirty-one, Asher sensed that his next decade needed to be different. From an extreme sports adrenaline junkie to a serious student, he had been constantly adapting and pushing himself. It was exhausting. He had trouble seeing a way forward without struggle, and every decision felt like a cliff-hanger.

We got curious about the part of him that was leaving decisions to the very last moment.

> *How did he experience this in his body?*
> *What emotions arose? What thoughts or ideas spun in his mind?*
> *What role might this procrastinating part be serving?*
> *What would happen if he stopped using avoidance as a strategy?*
> *What was this part afraid might happen?*

As he listened to his own answers to these questions, Asher observed that the procrastinating part was trying to get him to slow down. It was making sure he didn't get hurt again. Not only that, he noticed that another part blamed him for the accident and was totally overcompensating. He was stuck.

No wonder!

Like Asher, it's not unusual for people to feel like a fraud or imposter at some point, often with good reasons. But it's like bad mental math, making calculations based on false assumptions or competing predictions negating the other. A fear of success is a type of limiting belief or unconscious block, and it's often due to two Plus Ones being in opposition or cancelling each other out. Play it safe? Take a risk? Ironically, both these aspects of Asher wanted to protect or warn him, but an internal war kept him in an unending battle of indecision.

Asher is not alone with his imposter experiences and feeling stuck in place.[2] See if you can relate to any of the following statements.

I feel I don't deserve my success.

When I get recognition for my skills or talent, I feel others don't know the real me.

Even when I get rewarded for my hard work, I still feel I haven't earned it.

I feel afraid that others will find out that I'm not very smart after all.

I chalk up my success to luck, some mistake, or that I was just at the right place at the right time.

I have a hard time accepting compliments.

I downplay my achievements because they aren't very impressive compared to others'.

I tend to remember my mistakes, flaws, or what went wrong rather than what went right.

I hate being evaluated, especially in person.

A fear of success makes no sense to high-achieving people, but it can be a tenacious algorithm. Asher's ask for help required both courage and compassion. I knew he had both. I wondered aloud what the other perfectionism group members might say if they were in the room with us.

"Nah, doc. I understand what you are saying, they'd encourage me. But it's too easy for me to be an ostrich with my head in the sand," commented Asher. His resistance was in full force.

Self-Compassion Is Good Medicine

The science of self-compassion continues to prove its benefits: making the choice to be kind to yourself in response to your suffering makes you more likely to meet your goals. In other words, your pain can be your greatest teacher. Beyond that, scientific studies are piling up that demonstrate that the more you are kind to yourself,

- The more motivated you feel
- The more personal responsibility you take

- The more agile you are in managing emotions, taking perspective, and persisting[3]

Studies looking at levels of self-compassion suggest that people who report greater self-compassion compared to those who report less have beneficial outcomes depending on what's being studied. Greater self-compassion has been shown to alleviate symptoms of PTSD in combat veterans, and in other groups to reduce symptoms of depression, anxiety, chronic pain, grief, and poor body image, to name just a few.[4] Self-compassion also appears to be a protective factor for well-being and reduces the likelihood of risky behaviors in teens. The superpower of self-compassion, if ever there is one, is that it's an antidote to the shame the inner critic has been warding off.[5]

Self-compassion pioneer Kristin Neff refers to the yin and yang aspects of self- compassion, a kind of complementary balance.[6] The yin, or receptive, elements of self-compassion lead to a more loving, connected presence and a softening into self-care. The yang, or active, aspects of self-compassion are fierce and active—having emotional courage, establishing healthy boundaries, and taking action to protect the weak and vulnerable. The bold aspects of self-compassion also encompass respect and responsibility for oneself, for one another, and the planet. Greta Thunberg, who protested outside of the Swedish parliament to address the climate crisis and ignited a global youth movement, is an apt embodiment of the yang aspects of compassion for self and others. When we tend to our own suffering with care, we also tend to the greater good.

Self-compassion is different from self-esteem, something most of us believe to be important.[7] Self-esteem is inherently an evaluation or judgment: "How am I doing compared to another or compared to my own idea of what I *should* be doing?" Whereas self-compassion is accepting yourself unconditionally. This is not always easy, but it is essential.

Importantly, the wellspring for self-compassion already exists, just like the Radiant Circuit energies I introduced in a Step 3 skill,

"Igniting Joy." It simply needs space to flourish. How do you create space for self-compassion to emerge? Well, you've been navigating your way toward this. Give your brain fresh experiential data for creating new predictions by trying something different from what you've been doing—like being kinder to yourself.

As you get to know your inner critics you can help these parts trust that it's OK to be nice to yourself and that befriending is a strength and not a weakness. It requires a little more looking under the hood, so to speak, as we've been doing, and mapping the various inner critical voices that have been working overtime.

Getting to Know Your Parts

You may guess by now that the Plus One, that tenacious inner critic who can go overboard with managing your life (or other's lives), has some company. It's time to take your curiosity about your inner algorithms a little deeper by examining your behaviors and habits, as they are often helpful clues about what form your resistance takes. For starters: What ticks you off? What do others say about your habits (whether you believe them or not)? What characteristics would you never want anyone to say about you? What traits (your own or others') do you find unacceptable? What do you feel or believe with great intensity? Answering these questions requires some mindfulness and a curiosity about what's going on in your mind. What are the familiar mental algorithms, movies, and scripts that capture your imagination? The Internal Family Systems (IFS) model, developed by Richard C. Schwartz, offers a compelling method for understanding our mental and emotional lives.[8] He posits that we embody different parts of our psyches. Parts are essentially subpersonalities that imbue your life. As you seek to deepen your understanding of your inner life, the tenets of IFS can offer a very helpful language: After all, we've been talking about your parts all along.[9]

It's helpful to see that your parts are normal. Parts are natural states of the mind and emerge during the course of development and when needed. Most parts are young and use coping skills they had at the time to manage difficulties. You may recall noticing part of yourself and saying something along the lines of "A part of me said, *Hold on!* But another part said, *Oh, I'll just wing it!*" Or perhaps you've noticed that when you visit a family member, you revert back to an adolescent version of you when you know it's out of line. Or you feel compelled to binge-watch a streaming TV series even though another part calls you lazy. Parts have unique characteristics, beliefs, emotional reactions, energetic patterns, and survival responses to triggers. Some parts may be in chronically stressed or freeze states.

It's also important to remember that your parts are trying to help you survive. According to Schwartz, "[Parts] are little inner beings who are trying their best to keep you safe and to keep each other safe and to keep it together in there." They are also quite colorful. "They have full-range personalities: each of them have different desires, different ages, different opinions, different talents, and different resources," Schwartz explains.[10] Each part's true nature may be adventurous, passionate, persistent, smart, successful, and so on. Some parts can dominate your life, just like the perfectionistic part that we've been referring to as a Plus One. And some can be forced into extreme roles such as rigid, uncompromising, avoidant, or combative. These parts may only be partially aware of their impact of their strategies on other parts on the inside and people on the outside. Yet they are still, ultimately, well-intentioned.

Maybe the most challenging aspect to wrap your head around is that there are no bad parts. "Instead of just being annoyances or afflictions (which they can be while in their extreme roles) they are wonderful inner beings," Schwartz writes.[11] Each part has resources and valuable qualities and can be enrolled in helping you move toward happy achieving.

With so many parts, you can imagine that there can be some clashes. A tug-of-war can result, for example, when your procrastinator and workaholic parts duke it out for who will control your behavior at any given moment.

Luckily, the parts system has a basic organization in IFS. Each of your wonderfully distinct part falls into one of three categories:

- *Manager* parts. Managers try to control circumstances and avoid calamity. Perfectionist parts are most often inner managers driven by the Blue Zone motivations of accumulating resources and accomplishments. They never stop doing and have a hard time just being, resting, or allowing access to any emotions (even the positive experiences, like rest, joy, and play). Manager parts are akin to parentified children, taking on responsibilities they shouldn't have to. They have a hard time with self-care or self-compassion—they may say it's because they have no time, but it's often because they hate tuning into their inner lives. When managers aren't perfecting, performing, pleasing, or producing, they are great planners, organizers, innovators, coaches, teachers, leaders, and mentors. IFS therapist Karen Grayson refers to unburdened and healthy parts as "actualizers."[12] Many perfectionists can't imagine separating from their inner managing parts, but when they do, they free up so much energy. For example, consider the five archetypes of perfectionists and imagine the possibilities when they are free to explore their innate qualities.

    o The Judge, who can be rigid and critical, transforms into a Teacher or Guru with strengths of wisdom and clarity.
    o The Drill Sergeant, who can be inflexible and even heartless, transforms into a Coach or Captain with strengths of courage and leadership.
    o The Sleuth, who can get mired in tunnel vision and uncertainty, transforms into a Pioneer or Pathfinder, an intrepid adventurer with curiosity and innovation.
    o The Nitpicker, who can be impatient and indecisive, transforms into a Host or Maker with strengths of hospitality and creativity.

o The Joy Thief, who can fall into codependency or burnout, transforms into an Ally or Optimist with strengths
of compassion and generosity.

- *Firefighter* parts. These parts manage the Red Zone. They seek to
relieve any pain or distress you may be feeling in the present
moment. They look for the quick fix—something that will trigger a neural squirt of dopamine. They find ways to distract,
soothe, and numb any sort of discomfort. These firefighter parts
are drivers of the addictive tendencies common to all humans
that are typically triggered by mental and emotional distress.
Examples include comfort eating, retail therapy, Netflix numbing, online gaming—to more serious behaviors like substance
abuse, gambling, porn addiction, disordered eating, self-harm,
and suicidal behaviors. Many of our vices are firefighter behaviors and every one of us have some form of them.

  Firefighter parts can be impulsive and destructive, and they
fight against the inner managers who are trying to keep it
together. They can also trigger problematic procrastination as a
response to an unconscious fear of failure or success or get so
overwhelmed they flatline to inactivity, the downside of the
Green Zone. The good news is that when firefighter parts are
relieved of their extreme roles, they are a source of positive distractions and play, happy addictions (beneficial hobbies and
interests), and offer the internal system some balance, relaxation, fun, and spontaneity.

- *Exiles*. This is the third type of part with deep psychic wounds.
These parts get squirreled away, tucked deep into layers of the
unconscious as a survival strategy. They carry the difficult
experiences of loneliness, shame, rejection, and experiences of
terror. They are often cut off from the whole self and are
shielded by the protective managers and firefighters. They are
frozen in time and are the age they were when you were made
to feel invisible, ashamed, or traumatized. Exiled parts feel

worthless, unlovable, defective, damaged, overwhelmed, and unsafe. Working with these parts is often best facilitated in therapy. Even so, you can begin to understand your exiled parts by approaching them with curiosity through practices of kindfulness, kindsight, self-compassion, journaling, and/or meditation. Just keep in mind that working with your exiled parts requires treading lightly.

Parts carry burdens from earlier life experiences when the world felt unsafe or you were hurt or rejected. Burdens include not only past events but the meanings a child ascribes to them: *It's my fault. I'm a bad person. I'm not good enough.* Exiled parts get locked away holding the fear and shame, as if frozen in time, and have good reason not to trust you when you start to notice and tend to them. That's what happened with Daria, who didn't believe in her capability to befriend herself. She had strong protective parts who shamed and criticized her before the outside world could, building a fortress around the vulnerable exiled part. This younger part not only carried the childhood fear of punishment but also the never-ending story—a misguided prediction—that convinced her that the risk of failure was too great. For Daria's protective parts, the notion of self-compassion was initially too threatening, even though eventually she learned to see it an elixir for healing.

Parts can also be a real nuisance and can cause a lot of pain and trouble. They will do whatever they can to get your attention, such as self-sabotage in the name of self-preservation, just like Will in *Good Will Hunting* who yearned for love yet preemptively dumped his girlfriend because he was terrified of being hurt. The more these parts engage in extreme roles, the more likely that other difficulties may arise, such as stress, physical illness, addictions, troubled relationships, and mental health symptoms—bankrupting the body budget. Importantly, parts are not their burdens, rather they *carry* burdens. In other words, the strategies and behaviors that people use to cope are protective and serve to keep you safe and feelings of shame at bay. Seeking relief makes sense yet ends up causing more harm to oneself or others—and ignites the very troubling feelings you desperately want to avoid. A classic example is a person struggling with a substance use disorder who uses substances to numb feelings of abandonment, loneliness, loss, overwhelm, and so on.

Respecting the protective strategies of parts and their positive intention (even if the method is flawed and potentially lethal) is an important step in connecting with them. Your overarching aim in working with your parts is to earn their trust. You may discover that you would like to dig even deeper with a qualified professional, who has training in IFS, energy psychology, trauma-informed therapies, and/or other healing modalities.

It's also crucial that you remember that *parts are valuable and deserve your kind attention.* This knowledge is an integral piece of the goal of Step 4: to begin to love your inner critics. As we've covered—and hopefully you've begun to understand for yourself—the positive intention of a perfectionistic inner voice (or any part) is to ensure safety, love, and belonging. By tending to your parts with kindness and caring, and by listening to them, your outdated algorithms can get an upgrade and your Plus One can release its burdens. When it does, you can successfully get unstuck and heal the parts that self-sabotage. You and your part can be free to follow your passion and purpose with ease and confidence.

Another crucial IFS concept to embrace is that *you are born with basic wholeness and goodness.* Each of us has the wiring to cultivate a treasure trove of inner resources. This capacity is part of the basic blueprint of our brain and is ready to flourish in the right conditions. In IFS, this inherent goodness is known as the Self. The Self is a wellspring of inner leadership and the source of your deepest wisdom. You may think of it as the true self, highest self, divine source, or another word or group of words that refers to the essence of your soul. The inner resources that are contained within the Self include calm, clarity, compassion, confidence, connectedness, courage, creativity, curiosity, patience, and validation.[13]

Bringing the Parts into Balance

When all the parts in your unique system are in healthy relationship to one another—meaning, they can communicate with mutual respect and caring, even the disowned or troublesome parts—your Self comes into greater balance. Naturally, no one can maintain that ideal state all the time. But it is the Self's nature to seek balance, harmony, and wholeness. The more you can cultivate inner leadership and self-compassion, the more benefits you will enjoy over time.

If there are parts that you would rather not have a relationship with—the aspects of yourself you get most frustrated with or hate—consider that these parts likely carry the most meaningful lessons.

As you discover your perfectionist parts and understand how they developed to protect you, you won't perceive your inner critics to be as bothersome as they once felt. Rather, you'll begin to view them as important messengers that highlight beliefs or behaviors that need your attention—just like an alert signal on a GPS map. As your relationship to your parts evolves and becomes more loving, you can also help them to heal, play, and relax. In her book *Bittersweet: How Sorrow and Longing Make Us Whole*, the writer Susan Cain captures the upsides of the necessary work of learning to live among life's burdens:

> We're taught to think of our psychic and physical wounds as irregularities in our lives, deviations from what should have been; sometimes, as sources of stigma. But our stories of loss and separation are also the baseline state, right alongside our stories of landing our dream job, falling in love, giving birth to our miraculous children. And the very highest states—of awe and joy, wonder and love, meaning and creativity—emerge from this bittersweet nature of reality. We experience them not because life is perfect—but because it is not.[14]

Love Your Inner Critic Reflection #1: Dabble with Mind Mapping

Life is imperfect. There are good times and bad times, joyful moments and awful moments, ugly memories and beautiful ones. Looking at your internal family of parts can help you better understand the roller coaster that is your life and withstand its inevitable ups and downs. Mind mapping can help you take an objective look at all those various parts. It is a way to visualize various concepts and ideas in an organic way, without forcing a structure. Mapping your internal system is an ongoing process that evolves over time. It can be a wonderful way to get curious about emotions, energetic patterns, thoughts, beliefs, and behaviors.

This reflection exercise is adapted from Schwartz's *No Bad Parts*.[15] It simply requires some quiet time to focus on what's inside, as well as some paper and pencil or markers.

As you undertake mind mapping, think of it as you would a mindfulness practice—you merely want to observe without trying to change or fix anything.

You already identified a Plus One, a perfectionist part, or a judge or joy thief or any other inner critic. You may now be aware of other parts too. There may be a part that opposes the perfectionist part or joins forces. To begin, simply choose one part to focus on.

1. Where do you feel it in or around your body? What do you notice about it? Jot or scribble down an image or words.
2. How do you feel toward that part? Irritated? Afraid? Angry? Impatient? Dependent on it? What judgments come up? Write or draw these feelings or judgments.

3. Can you be curious about it? Can you be open to its presence? Is this part pushed to the edges of your map, or does it feel like it takes up a lot of space?

4. If so, ask the part if there is something it needs you to know about it or its role and wait for a response. Is there a positive intention behind its actions? If you get an answer, you can wonder what would happen if the part didn't do its thing. What's it afraid of? Write it down.

5. What is this part's unmet needs? Universal human needs include acceptance, belonging, empathy, love, meaning, nourishment, play, rest, safety, and so on. Be curious.

Stay with this part and the sensations that arise until you notice a shift toward another part that may be emerging. Now direct attention on this part and notice where you feel it in or around your body. When you have a sense of this second part, jot it down on your mind map. You can repeat this process with each part that reveals itself. If these parts are new to your awareness, name them like you did in chapter 3 with your Plus One.

Take some deep breaths and hold the map away from you as you survey the inner landscape.

- *How do the parts relate to each other? Are there protector parts? Are some partnering up or fighting? Are any all alone?*

Draw whatever lines or keys to represent these relationships. Then, finally, ask:

- *What does your internal system need from you?*

When you feel complete for now, thank the parts for showing up and assure them you will meet them again. Then refocus your attention back to the outside.

You may notice that some parts exist in a group or cluster, or what is referred to as a subsystem in IFS. Over time, you can use this reflection exercise to map more subsystems, particularly when you are facing a challenge—for instance, gearing up for a family gathering at a holiday, a presentation at work, attending a high school reunion, getting a flat tire, watching your kid's sports team, or creating a profile on a dating app for the first time. You will see that your inner family system is rich with parts and is a microcosm of the universe that holds all of life's experiences. Be sure to save your maps as more connections may arise.

The act of discerning your various Plus Ones, which you began to do in the mind mapping exercise, allows for more space to see them as independent beings fighting on your behalf. This kind of awareness of your inner world is called *unblending* in the Internal Family System model. It helps you disentangle your identity from a part. For example, you aren't a perfectionist in totality—only a part of you is. With this understanding, you can begin to make new choices for yourself. As poet Andrea Gibson beautifully states, "To know exactly what parts of me are comforted by other people's approval and comfort those parts myself instead."[16] This is the inquiry we'll get to next.

Facing Your Fears

Asher had no fear when it came to extreme sports, yet he was terrified about succeeding in the academic world, even with a hard-won PhD under his belt. His self-esteem had plummeted as he held certain expectations for himself about being a scientist. Challenging his assumptions, reframing cognitive beliefs, and having insight—the staples of modern psychotherapy—didn't work.

Asher had a classic struggle: to be or not to be. Lynn Mary Karjala, PhD, is a trauma therapist and past president of the Association for Comprehensive Energy Psychology. In her book *Healing Everyday Traumas*, she notes that if you could simply change your limiting belief or unhelpful habit, you would. Yet our culture reinforces personal responsibility in achieving most everything. Nike's refrain of "Just do it" falls flat for many people and often adds shame into the equation when you don't measure up. Instead, we overthink, fall prey to analysis paralysis, and minimize the positives. We get stuck.

Asher had what Karjala describes as a *psychoenergetic reversal*, a hidden block or objection to implementing a desired change—that is, a limiting belief about something you feel to be true even though you know better (for example, I don't deserve to be happy).[17] In business leadership, organizational psychologists Robert Kegan and Lisa Laskow Lahey refer to this as subconscious *competing commitments*. They write, "Resistance to change does not reflect opposition, nor is it merely a result of inertia. Instead even as they hold a sincere commitment to change, many people are unwittingly applying productive energy toward a hidden competing commitment. The resulting dynamic equilibrium stalls the effort in what looks like resistance but is in fact a kind of personal immunity to change."[18]

A fear of success is a psychoenergetic reversal. It also represents a *polarization* of two or more inner parts in survival mode. Imagine two kids playing tug-of-war. Each is afraid to let go of the rope and holds on with all their might. In looking at your inner parts with curiosity you begin to kindfully separate from the thoughts, emotions, fears, and behaviors that each part is holding. What can't they let go of? What are they trying to prove or protect?

Asher wanted to be on the leading edge in his discipline, but he was avoiding opportunities. This is because he struggled with a high need for belonging yet was afraid of social humiliation. He kept himself relatively isolated and emotionally safe, locking him in an underenergized, depleted state.

Back in Step 2 (Validate), I introduced the idea that the word *fear* can be interpreted as an acronym for "False Evidence Appearing Real." There are several other versions of what those letters can stand for that help to express how we self-sabotage when there are currently no true threats to our survival:

- *Future Events Already Ruined*
- *Finding Excuses And Reasons*
- *Frantic Efforts to Avoid Reality*

Remember, the brain constantly makes those best guesses and lands on the most efficient scenario in the moment, which isn't always helpful.

When you have a hunch that your perfectionism is getting in the way of living the life you desire, a part of you is harboring an underlying fear and predicting an unpleasant outcome. Learning to befriend yourself is the beginning of uncovering the hidden fear so that part of you can heal. It requires not only facing fears and allowing vulnerability but also loving the parts that are fiercely trying to protect you. Just imagine if you could transform fears into a new reality. It may look more like:

- *Face Everything And Respond*
- *Feeling Excited And Ready*
- *Forgetting Everything is All Right*

There's another quaint saying in personal development circles: *What you resist persists.* It takes gritty self-compassion and lots of practice to greet the inner critic, face it, and gently release it from its extreme behaviors. After all, some behaviors feel good in the moment, like escaping or numbing, and are powerful motivators to stick with the status quo. It can feel strange, ridiculous, or even frightening if you try to douse yourself with your own TLC, especially at first. As you practice this step, avoid trying to figure out *why* you are a certain way or reliving a past trauma. Instead, be mindful of *how* the brain seeds predictions based on past experiences and how you can transform old familiar patterns into new learning. If anything, be curious about the inner critic's needs and fears as they arise in your life right now.

Love Your Inner Critic Reflection #2: Deflecting the Arrows of Self-Sabotage

A useful metaphor about suffering derived from Buddhist psychology is that of the double arrows. The first arrow of distress—or the first hit of pain—is one we can't help. This is the initial wound created by everyday hassles and disappointments, as well as the small and big traumas that occur. Your nervous system will automatically spend metabolic resources to manage the discomfort or pain. It's the searing "ouch" you can't help but feel.

The second arrow of distress is the one infused with some interpretation of the wound, often an evaluation about oneself, a judgment, or attribution of blame. (It's when the protector parts will jump in.) *Why me? What am I doing wrong this time? Not again! That jerk. Who does she think she is? This is so unfair. What the heck?* You may notice that there are more than a few arrows coming at you, compounding the initial hurt with added suffering. You may fall into rumination, or your inner critics may get very reactive. By the end of the day, you may have hit yourself with a hundred arrows of distress. That's self-sabotage.

It's important to recognize that sometimes things that happen in life are random, conditioned by family or culture, out of one's control, or traumatic. There may be good reasons to feel upset. Yet we can begin to minimize the additional arrows that contribute to mental suffering or self-sabotage. Rather, you can practice being safely challenged and look at your suffering with compassion. Instead of confusion, blame, or shame, you can ask:

What have I learned about myself?

What are my human needs?

What challenges have I faced and overcome or am I still working through?

Where am I in my own story arc or hero's journey?

What parts are there?

Who do I want to become?

What allies might support me?

What gifts are hidden in the pain?

The next time you feel the arrow of distress, such as anger, disappointment, discomfort, judgment, just notice what comes next. Then apply some self-compassion and any of the Happy Achiever Tools you are learning.

Fanning the Flames of Self-Compassion

In the last chapter, Daria was learning to warm up to self-compassion, trying it on for size and practicing kindness toward herself. For many like Daria, there is trial and error with this practice. In this chapter, Asher is locked in a struggle among his protector parts. Sometimes the resistance to befriending oneself is fierce. Psychologist Christopher Germer, codeveloper with Kristin Neff of the Mindful Self Compassion method, offers a helpful analogy of a firefighter in a burning building. You don't rush in to open all the doors and windows. That would be reckless and can cause a *backdraft*. Self-compassion, he posits, is like adding oxygen to the flames of a fire.[19] The flames roar in response. The natural resistance to self-compassion—which is like an infusion of fresh emotional oxygen—draws attention to old wounds. This may stir up memories of times when you were disrespected, hurt, rejected, unloved, unseen, or it may arouse the exiled parts of you. Exiles are heavily protected by inner managers (the critics) and firefighters (the pain relievers). Too much self-compassion too soon can hurt when not enough trust and safety are established among the protector parts.

The caution here is to go gently, just like real firefighters will case the joint, scouting the walls, windows, and doors of a house on fire and determining if anyone's trapped before rushing in. You too can navigate the edges of self-compassion when it feels hard. As you create space on the inside, the natural resources for compassion, courage, and connection will arise. Germer notes, "A moment of self-compassion can change your entire day. A string of such moments can change the course of your life."

You may notice that there is a spiritual element to this step of loving your inner critics. When you connect to your inner parts and cultivate inner humanity, you also begin to extend this kind awareness to your relationships in your external life. As you become more integrated with the various parts of yourself, you may experience greater awareness of connections beyond yourself. As you feel more at ease, confident, and connected within, the quality of inner leadership will infuse your daily life and interactions with others. You see that you have choices. "In fact," writes Jack Kornfield, "the two things you are always free to do—despite the circumstances—are to be present and to be willing to love."[20] You may be more discerning of the kind of people or activities you engage with. You can let in what's good and keep out what's not. You may be able to see when other people are operating from their parts too. You may embrace your relationships with more clarity, curiosity and compassion.

Love Your Inner Critic Reflection #3: Don Your Spiritual Space Suit

It can be helpful to consider your personal well-being boundary. Like a firefighter in gear, imagine an invisible protective shield, field, orb, or aura around you. You can also visualize wearing a space suit of your own design. As you visualize this protective suit or force field, notice that it is flexible and porous, like a cell membrane. It enables you to intentionally keep in nourishing elements and keep out toxic forces. Whenever you notice some negativity lurking in your awareness, you can unzip the suit down the centerline of your body, and release it. You then can follow this up by taking in the good—a lesson learned, a positive affirmation, appreciation, or any beneficial quality that serves you in the moment—and zip that up the frontline of the body (just like the zip-up exercise in Step 1).

Asher's Growing Trust

As you become more curious about and accepting of your parts, you can learn to appreciate your inner critics and see them as warning signals or invitations to pay attention. That means you will be much less likely to be crushed by a negative comment or overwhelmed by an uncomfortable emotion or limiting belief. You may recognize an unmet need or a fear and more easily release a burden. This is what happened for Asher.

When Asher, ever the emerging scientist, began to map out his internal family system, he began to see the various parts that were trying to protect him but inevitably kept him trapped. "Doc, I get it. I'm giving myself a lot of arrows. If I really go for it, the part that likes challenges feels stoked. But there's another part that puts up a barrier, a huge wall that I can't penetrate so I don't get crushed again. Makes sense now that I see it." Once Asher focused inside and helped those parts relax and trust him, he was able to tend to a wounded part that needed to grieve his accident. That helped his protector parts release their grip so that he didn't have the same fear reaction to things that could lead to his success.

The Happy Achiever Tools for this chapter will help you do the same.

Happy Achiever Tools: Love Your Inner Critic

It's hard to befriend yourself and apply self-compassion skills when you feel stressed, skeptical, or unpracticed. The following tools drawn from Eden Energy Medicine can help you skirt the edges of your resistance to self-love until you are ready to go for it more wholeheartedly.[21]

GET GROUNDED: A SECRET SELF-HUG

The triple warmer meridian governs the fight/flight/freeze responses and is typically in opposition to the spleen meridian, which is responsible for metabolizing whatever we take in, including food, environmental toxins, and psychological stressors.[22] Often the triple warmer pathway is overenergized and sucks energy from the spleen pathway, which is then underenergized. This leads to a depleted state and fatigue. To augment well-being, the triple warmer meridian typically needs to be soothed and the spleen meridian needs to be strengthened. A simple way to tend to this energetic polarization is by holding acupressure points on each pathway in what amounts to an energetic self-hug. To do it:

1. Fold your arms in front of your torso.
2. Wrap the left hand around the right arm just above the right elbow, at the dimple (a triple warmer acupoint).
3. Wrap the right arm around the left side of torso under the armpit at the lower ribs (a spleen acupoint), like you are folding your arms in a smug gesture.
4. Hold this position as you take in three or more deep nourishing breaths.
5. Switch sides and hold for another three deep breaths.

This is a great incognito pose that you can do in a class, meeting, or family gathering when feeling stressed out. It can foster heart coherence. No one even knows what you are doing, but your inner parts may appreciate it.

GET ENERGIZED: BLOW OFF STEAM

When you're feeling stressed out, overwhelmed, irritated, or angry, this energy release exercise can help. This may be especially helpful when certain inner critics or parts are making their displeasure known.

1. Bring your elbows and clenched fists to your sides. Inhale as you reach your fists up over the top of the head. Pull down fast as you exhale. If you are feeling mad, for example, you can even call out someone's name or a situation as you pull down your fists. "Uncle Bill!" "The election!" Be in touch with the sensations. Do this fast pull-down action two times.

2. For the third blow out, reach your fist up above your head and then pull down very, very slowly as you exhale. This slow motion of control and calm helps you feel empowered. It is a stance of fierce self-compassion. You can even add a power statement to pair the energetic release with a beneficial attitude—such as "I am at ease" or "I can control my response" or "Thank you, nervous system, for your reminder to get grounded."

GET CONNECTED: REBOOT WITH CRISSCROSSING ENERGIES

As we've covered, when you are stressed, it's hard to think. Thoughts are scattered, and there is a tendency for the classic cognitive distortions to arise: all-or-none thinking, catastrophizing, discounting the positive, magnifying the negatives, fortune telling, overgeneralizations, being right, blaming, "shoulding" on yourself or others, taking things personally, and more. (Hopefully, after reading this chapter, you can view these thought patterns as aspects of your protector parts.) One result of these negative thoughts is that your energies can get scrambled—an occurrence the body naturally tries to correct via crossing patterns. If you notice kids sitting or playing, they are always crossing energies: sitting cross-legged or playing clapping games or double-Dutch jump rope games, to name a few. As adults, we forget to do this!

The following gestures can help to recalibrate your frazzled energy and rebalance the right and left sides of the brain and body. (You can find links to videos at www.perfectionistsdilemma.com.)

Cross Shoulder Pulls: Place your right hand on your left shoulder. Squeeze the back of the shoulder and then drag your right hand over the top of the shoulder and pull the hand firmly down and across your body diagonally to your opposite hip (like a sash). Do this several times. Repeat with your left hand on your right shoulder.

Crisscrossing Arms and Legs: Try this sitting in a chair.

1. Put your arms out straight in front of you, parallel to the floor. Cross your right wrist over your left wrist, bring your palms together, and clasp your hands. Pull your crossed arms under and up to rest at the chest.
2. Cross your right ankle in front of your left ankle.
3. On an inhale, lift the torso slightly as you fill your lungs with air like balloons, and then exhale slowly as relax the body. Do this for several rounds of breaths.
4. Switch: Uncross arms and repeat with left wrist over the right and the opposite cross of ankles. Pull arms under and up to chest and breathe again.
5. Now uncross your arms and legs for a new hand position at your head. Bring your fingers into a steeple position, resting your thumbs above the bridge of your nose as you breathe in and out several times.
6. On a final exhale, cup your fingers at the center of your forehead and gently drag the fingers of each hand slowly away

from each other across to your temples, stretching the skin on your forehead. Release your hands.

7. You can do this standing as well, with or without crossing your feet and ankles, depending on your balance.

Crown Pull: You can add this exercise to the previous one or do it on its own. This hand motion is like parting hair down the middle part of the skull. Shampooing your hair in the shower is a great time to try this.

1. Place your thumbs at your temples with your fingertips resting in the middle of your forehead. With mild pressure, pull your fingers apart, stretching the skin across the forehead above your eyebrows and toward the temples.

2. Then move your fingers to the beginning of the hairline (top of forehead) and repeat the stretch again away from the midline for a few inches, using mild to moderate pressure as you pull your fingers apart over the sides of the skull toward your ears.

3. Repeat this pulling pattern at the top, center, and back of your head. Continue all the way until you reach the base of your neck.

4. Finish by moving your hands down to your shoulders and hook your fingers as your arms hang from your shoulders (give a gentle squeeze) and hold there as long as it feels good. Let gravity pull the arm weight so it feels like a mini massage. Breathe.

5. Finish by resting your hands crossed over your heart. Take a final deep breath.

If you've been trying these novel tools along the way, just know that small shifts are taking place. Stick with them. Be playful. As you move through the EVOLVE method and begin to befriend yourself, your body, and your inner critics, it will take some grit to keep going. Remember that evolving requires your loving intention, caring attention, and courageous action. As you will see in the next step, having clarity and commitment will help you on your way.

8

Step 5
V, Make a Vow

*What would you do even if you knew that
you might very well fail?
What do you love so much that the words failure
and success essentially become irrelevant?*

— *Elizabeth Gilbert*

After the airing of the opening episode of *The Bachelor* when Chloe was cut from the lineup, she felt the heat of public humiliation—in her own mind and body. Her inner critic anticipated the shame and was ready to shield her. She left town for a weekend getaway with her sister. Ready to face the hecklers when she returned, Chloe was shocked by what happened. Contrary to her worst nightmare, she received an avalanche of love and admiration from friends, family, and coworkers. She didn't know how to take it in.

That's so cool. How did you get on the show?
You looked so elegant.
Well done, Chloe.
You're too good for that guy.

Red roses showed up at her doorstep.

The months of tension began to fade, and Chloe felt some emotional relief and could see her pain from a new perspective. She got curious. *Why was I so hard on myself? Why did I give this show such importance? How can I believe in myself more?* She was ready to make a change.

Chloe, who struggled with socially oriented and self-presentation elements of perfectionism, often experienced the "spotlight effect." This is a common social phenomenon where people believe that others pay more attention to their personal details and appearance than is actually the case.[1] It reflects an egocentric bias that we are the center of our universe. This makes complete sense when you realize that your Plus One emerged at a much younger age—when it was developmentally natural to be egocentric—in response to a moment of admonishment, a feeling of rejection, or a need to please or perform for coveted attention.

Chloe's friends and family remarked on her style, grace, and courage, not on her dress, French twist, or facial expression. This experience of unconditional love snapped her out of unhealthy rumination. It was time to update her inner algorithm that she had to be perfect in order to be accepted. Chloe began experimenting with the self-distancing techniques (from Step 2) and self-compassion (from Steps 3 and 4), yet largely stayed in her head trying to muscle through the self-defeating thoughts. She was clearly motivated, but motivation is a limited resource that requires constant tending. The quest for personal improvement can be tiring. There are many fits and starts. Chloe was missing one crucial ingredient to help her keep going— *trust* in her own inner capacity for healing. She started developing this trust by calling on her heart energy and gradually learned to transform her need for perfection into connection. This required a commitment to radical self-care from the inside out—not the other way around. She decided to make a vow to herself, a clear declaration of self-acceptance.

The Goal of Step 5: Make a Vow

A vow is a solemn promise or pledge to oneself or another person. It's a pledge to a value or intention that meets a deep human need. We make pinky promises, cross our hearts, wear badges, pins, rings, or tattoos to symbolize our commitment. (And yes, sometimes we offer up a rose as symbol too.) Often a vow is a phrase or set of intentions to remind ourselves of the promise made. Making—and keeping—a promise to yourself to continue to befriend yourself is the goal of Step 5.

The difficulty in making a conscious vow arises when you can't clearly name your intentions because your mind is muddled with so many expectations, thoughts, rules, and judgments. You may well have made an unconscious vow to protect a younger part or to live up to standards imposed upon you by your family or culture. We can remain very loyal to vestiges of the past that no longer serve our survival needs. You can appreciate your old self for the past efforts and choose to be authentic to who you want to be *now*. Finding that clarity requires making space in your heart for your true self to emerge. When making a new vow to yourself, you're not rushing to find an answer, reach a goal, or cure yourself. On the contrary, you're allowing yourself to be still. Martha Postelwaite's poem *Clearing* speaks to the humble process of being patient with yourself.[2] Instead of striving for the impossible ideal, she writes, "create a clearing in the dense forest of your life" and then see what unfolds.

Making a Clearing in Your Life

When you struggle with self-sabotaging thoughts, spin in place, or suffer a psychoenergetic reversal tugging you in opposite directions, you may feel confused and frustrated. You may feel like a complete mess. Learning to trust yourself is a process that asks you to be vulnerable in the face of uncertainty. No one can predict the future, but you can consciously cultivate the conditions in your life that support change, healing, and success. This means not only caring for the inner critic and company but also acknowledging your needs, desires, values, and strengths. You can intentionally exert your personal power and take leaps of faith, even when outcomes are uncertain and failure is possible. Yes, it takes effort, but it can be joyful effort, which means simply, don't make it so hard. Release the struggle. Slow down.

How? By creating space in your internal world so that you can listen to the intelligence of your heart. One way to do this is to circle back to the Perfectionism Self-Inquiry and look at the algorithms and self-talk items you rated and have them handy (see Reflection #1 below). Let's learn how to unhook from these thoughts so that you can stop overidentifying with them. This investigation will reveal elements of your true self. It requires both kindfulness, being aware of the present moment with an open heart, as well as kindsight, viewing your experiences with tenderness and understanding.

How to begin? Be curious about the hidden needs, desires, values, or strengths that your algorithms, limiting beliefs, and self-talk may be obscuring. These are not questions for the thinking mind; this is a heart-based inquiry. To help you find those answers, here's some insight on what needs, desires, values, and strengths are.

Naturally, there may be overlap between needs, desires, and values, so don't get hung up on which is which. For example, belonging, respect, or stability can be all three.

Being curious about your needs, desires, and core values gets at another essential question: *What is my "why"?* Understanding your motives is key to feeling a sense of purpose and meaning in life. Uncovering your "why" allows for conscious, intentional, and wholehearted living. It creates the energetic space you need to grow your inner strengths.

> **Needs:** Needs are thought of as universal to all humans but are shaped by family and culture. Naturally, your individual needs are influenced by your social reality and learned over the course of life. In common discourse, needs are often stated with one word, reflect a positive attribute, and they typically are powerful drivers of both feelings and behavior.[3] For example, those of us raised in the United States might agree that we have needs for achievement, autonomy, belonging, companionship, empathy, harmony, love, play, protection, subsistence, rest, respect, and so on. Other cultures will espouse other needs, like discretion, community, honor, spirituality, and so on.
>
> Marshall Rosenberg, who developed a method of nonviolent communication (aka compassionate communication), succinctly

stated the connection between needs and harsh self-talk when he wrote, "Self-judgments, like all judgments, are tragic expressions of unmet needs."[4] Remembering this connection helps you extend compassion to yourself and view the banter of your inner critic as an expression of an underlying innocent need, and any resulting behavior as a self-protective response to that need not getting met. By gaining clarity on your needs, you make it easier to not only express yourself and make requests that can enhance your life but also to dialogue with your inner parts and to make space to harmonize your heart energy. (It's worth familiarizing yourself with what human needs are. You can find lists by searching online for needs and nonviolent communication.)

Desires: Desires are your personal wants and cravings in life, a wishing and longing for a thing, feeling, or a certain state of mind. These can range from superficial desires to deep passions. Desires can be sexual, intellectual, material, status-seeking, and many others. These too can be motivational and fuel strong intentions, feelings, and behaviors.

Desires can have a dark side, feeding appetites, fetishes, and compulsions. Or they can be Blue Zone desires for connection, security, equity, and productivity, among others, such as desiring a partner, community, home, education, or better-paying or more fulfilling job (or both!). Identifying a desire answers a basic question: *What do I really want?* And that is a very practical question when you can pose it without judgment or expectation. For perfectionists, answering this question can be particularly challenging because the years of striving have largely been in the service of others' expectations (family, friends, culture, and so on) and fears of being judged.

Values: Values constitute conceptual beliefs about what matters to you personally at any given juncture in your life. In a way, they are the opposite of limiting beliefs. As with human needs, there are many good inventories of core values readily available online. Values tend to be relatively stable and shift gradually over time as new life experiences, perspectives, and wisdom accrue, whereas needs come to feel instinctual and necessary to subsist in your community, and desires can be momentary and context specific. Values tend to have a longer arc over the lifespan. With that said, the values you may have as a twentysomething may be different when you arrive at midlife or beyond. Because of these gradual inner shifts, it helps to revisit your core values at various junctures in life.

Strengths: Inner strengths, also known as character strengths, are resources you have inside, even if they are seedlings. You are born with these potentialities, and they are intrinsic to your individual architecture and spirit. They just need the conditions to grow.

In psychology, the concept of character strengths was posited by innovators of positive psychology Christopher Peterson and Martin Seligman. Over time, research homed in on twenty-four main character strengths, defined as "the positive parts of your personality that impact how you think, feel and behave."[5] A sampling includes: appreciation of beauty, bravery, creativity, curiosity, fairness, forgiveness, gratitude, hope, humility, humor, kindness, leadership, learning, perseverance, self-regulation, social intelligence, teamwork, and zest. From the Internal Family System perspective that we covered in chapter 7, the eight Cs of being self-led—curiosity, calm, clarity, compassion, courage, confidence, creativity, and connectedness—can also be viewed as inner strengths.[6]

As you get more familiar with your needs, desires, and values, you may also begin to get glimpses of your strengths—even those that have been dormant, denied, overlooked, or too uncomfortable to admit. Just like cultivating a nuanced emotional vocabulary fosters greater well-being and more choices for your predictive brain to consider, as we covered in Step 2, naming what matters to you is also essential.

This is often a wonderful discovery process, especially if striving for achievement and accomplishments have consumed your headspace and may have obscured other hidden strengths. As you radiate your heart's intelligence, insights may reveal themselves naturally and feel quite intuitive. Deborah Rozman of the HeartMath Institute states, "In our research, we found that intuitive insights occur more frequently when people are aligned with the core values of their heart. Insight often comes as a high-speed intuitive download activated by genuine feelings of appreciation, compassion, or kindness . . . Humanity will in time come to realize that the heart contains a higher intelligence software package, designed to provide intuitive guidance needed for navigating life."[7]

As you uncover these aspects of yourself, own them! Here's where an "I statement" can be very powerful. For example, over time Chloe recognized that she was attractive, capable, desirable, and sexy. She practiced saying to herself, "I am attractive. I am capable. I am desirable. I am sexy." Energetically, her confidence showed.

Kayla's Story, Part 1

When Kayla, the environmental architect, was a little girl she absorbed a belief that if you couldn't be perfect, or at least excellent, at whatever you tried right out of the gate, then it wasn't worth the bother. She remembered her mother once saying, "If you have to work hard at something, then you aren't very good at it." She admitted she wasn't sure if those were her mother's exact words, but she felt the sting when she was a seven-year-old about to perform at a music recital. It trailed her when she was in the high school drama club. Now every time she had to start a new creative project, she found her nervous tiny self on the stage at the local community center feeling utterly exposed. "I definitely have an inner doubter taunting me that I'm not up for the task. Logically, I know that's not true. It feels so stupid!" Kayla complained. Not only did she have a nitpicky Inner Monica seeking excellence, but she also had a freaked-out part that popped in from the moment she opened her eyes in the morning. She called this part Cold Feet.

Kayla lived with a paradox. She was a talented designer, yet her natural qualities were stymied by her fears. She knew it and felt she couldn't do anything about it. So we embarked on a reverse engineering activity. You might think of this like the "Curse Reverse" ritual portrayed in a captivating scene in the *Ted Lasso* television series.[8] The AFC Richmond soccer players believed that their team's treatment room was cursed, leading to AFC's notorious poor record. According to an old myth, the stadium was once used as a ploy to recruit young men for the war effort under the guise of soccer team tryouts. Few returned alive. Coach Ted Lasso, respecting the presence of "ghosts, spirit guides, and aliens" asks the players to meet at midnight and bring something of sentimental value as a sacrifice (a blanket, photo, cleats, etc.). Slowly, each player shared the meaning of their chosen item and dropped it in a barrel, which they then burned in a group bonding moment that celebrated their vulnerability and courage. It was a great example of "name to tame it" and a clear marker for change. Bad vibes turned into good ones. Of course, it turned around AFC's unlucky streak.

Television entertainment aside, creating a ritual, ceremony, or declarative statement is very powerful. First, Kayla did a grounding criss-crossing practice (the Happy Achiever Tool on page 197) to get her energies aligned. Then she looked at a list of core values and circled the ones that jumped out at her. At first Kayla noted many values, and then she whittled the list down to the top five values that felt the most meaningful to her at that moment: authenticity, creativity, learning, social impact, and sustainability. She also included her desire to be a thought leader. This surprised her at first as she hadn't yet articulated to herself that she wanted to "leave a mark." Importantly, she recognized for the first time that a vulnerable part of her needed reassurance and validation. "When I look back to that musical recital, I just wanted to feel unconditional love and acceptance, but I didn't know what that was at the time. I suppose getting a hug would have been enough." Truth bomb.

Next, on the Perfectionism Self-Inquiry Kayla referred to the top three items she rated as experiencing a 4 or a 5 more or most of the time.

1. "If you can't get it right, you're out."
2. "I have to be awesome, brilliant, exceptional."
3. "I leave things to the last minute. I'll wing it."

Kayla's goal was to install a new algorithm by creating a declarative I/me statement based on her values/needs/desires. True to form, she used a lot of colorful sticky notes on her wall to sort things out. Here's where she landed: "I commit to being authentic and true to myself. I will honor this by prioritizing my creativity, balancing my time to meet both obligations and interests, and unapologetically sharing my work without caring about the opinion of others."

Guided by these words, Kayla started living into her heart instead of living behind a mask to cover her self-doubt and fears. By addressing her current limiting beliefs about success and achievement, she could see that her personal currency was rooted in her own creativity and authenticity—not on how well she executed tasks. This is what happens when heart energy is in alignment with your true self.

This can be a tricky transition for many perfectionists. It's hard to release old, protective patterns. It's not just a shift in mindset. Yet, when you recognize that everything that arises from your inner world is reflected in your outer world (not the other way around), you elevate the vibration of your energy field and life flows more easily.

Making a Vow Reflection #1: Reverse Engineering a Limiting Belief

There are four steps in "reverse engineering" a limiting belief into a commitment statement for yourself. This is an encouraging self-talk statement or simple mantra you can practice daily.

1. **Identify the algorithm(s) and self-talk you want to change.** What's your kryptonite? If you need help thinking

of something specific, take a look at your Perfectionism Self-Inquiry again (page 31).

2. **Uncover the hidden need, value, or desire associated with your algorithm.** How? There are several questions you can ask yourself to hone in:

What is the opposite of this algorithm?
What if things weren't so hard?
What if no one's looking?
What unmet need is my fear or belief obscuring?
What do I need to feel calm in my body?
What needs my undivided attention?
What would I really want to do if there were no constraints?
What would I do if I knew I couldn't fail?
What would I do even if I tried and failed?
What do I say "Yes, but . . ." to?
What do I secretly desire to be or do?
What means the most to me above all else?
What would I do if I had one month/year to live?
What are my strengths, gifts, or superpowers?

3. **Create a new algorithm.** It can be helpful to use a non–first person self-distancing approach (refer back to Step 2, Validation, for a refresher), as if you are a coach to your Plus One or other inner minions who need your attention. For example, *You are worthy.* Or if you feel you want to own a new trait, use a declarative I statement, *I am worthy.*

Here is a list of declarative I statements I've collected over the years from clients and students. See if any resonate and then tailor the statement to suit yourself.

- I can see my mistakes without shaming or blaming.
- I am willing to see my imperfections for what they are: human.
- I am my own best friend.
- I can turn toward my inner critic with care and understanding.
- I give myself grace.
- I can recognize my inner critical voice as an outdated habit of mind that has been trying to help me in ways that no longer serve me.
- I commit to living with more ease and joy while still striving for excellence.
- I am aware of my expectations for myself and others.
- I can be kind to myself just as I would be toward a loved one or friend in need.
- I can call on positive affirmations that are authentic and true for me.
- I am ready to allow for the full range of emotions to coexist and to ride the waves.
- I can appreciate how my nervous system signals to me and not get trapped by exaggerated fears.
- I can appreciate the small steps.
- I am worthy (brilliant, successful, open, whole, forgiving, innovative . . . you name it).
- I allow myself to see the gray areas in life and see more than one perspective.
- I'm ready to ask for help, feedback, and accountability without dread.
- I recognize that I am part of a community and not alone.
- I'm ready to relax and play more.
- I'm ready to trust my inner strengths and not rely on outer approval for self-worth.
- I recognize that self-compassion is a strength and not a weakness.

The key element is that your statement needs to feel true from the intuitive body level. You know it when you feel it.

Questions to consider include:

> *What attitudes and actions will I take to install a new algorithm that is easy to remember?*
> *What unhelpful behaviors or habits will I let go of?*
> *What attitude or heart quality do I want to cultivate instead?*
> *What inner strength(s) do I want to grow over the next month? Over the next year?*
> *What rings true to my core?*

4. **Write it out.** Grab your journal or have paper and pen handy. Give yourself ten to twenty minutes to reflect on what limiting belief or behavior you are ready to let go of and play with some ideas. It's OK to be messy, cross things out, and land on a few new algorithms or mantras. That's because varied experiences call for nuanced self-talk and it's good to have choices. Then, when you are ready, write your commitment statement with clarity and confidence. Let's pull one example from the Perfecting subcategory of the Perfectionism Self-Inquiry.

Current Habit/Trait	Irritability or impatience with others
Old Algorithm/Self-Talk	I find others irritating when they don't understand me.
Hidden Need, Value, Desire	To feel seen or understood; respect
Inner Strength	Leadership

New Algorithm/Self-Talk	*I am calm and connected.*
	Don't take it personally.
	It's OK to speak from your heart.
	Effective leaders connect rather than perfect.

Commitment Statement

I commit to expressing myself with calm and patience. I will do this by checking in with my nervous system, connecting with my heart, and pausing before I speak.

Over the next month, I will name and appreciate the small wins and the efforts of others.

Over the next year, I will practice listening to my inner wisdom and will be present when listening to others, too.

I envision myself being someone people look up to because I am a good role model.

I will walk the talk.

As a bonus step, say the statement aloud and gently tap the middle of your brows with two fingers (the third eye area) five to seven times to energetically seal in the positive statement. Even better, do this at least once a week.

Finding the Heart of the Matter

In a speech he gave to a stadium full of fans, Kobe Bryant eloquently explained the power of making a commitment to yourself. He said:

> Those times when you get up early and you work hard . . . Those times when you stay up late and you work hard . . . Those times when you don't feel like working . . . You're too tired. You don't want to push yourself, but you do it anyway. That is actually the dream. That's the dream. *It's not the destination, it's the journey* [emphasis mine]. If you can understand that, then what you will see happen is you won't accomplish your dreams. Your dreams won't come true. *Something greater will.*[9]

That something greater is the commitment you make to yourself and the journey you embark on as a result of that commitment. With his words, Bryant invites you to make space for the stumbles, missteps, and grit that drive meaning and purpose. It's something much bigger than the self, and it may well take some time to unfold. What's that "something greater" for you? What actions can you commit to in the long game of your life? Can you cultivate poise and patience when things get challenging?

Some clever marketing researchers at Stanford University's Graduate School of Business studied what helps people accomplish their goals once they set them. They looked at what helps people maintain goals and what benefits are gained from the experience.[10] After all, for many people, once a personal goal is accomplished, it's easy to move on to something else or revert to old habits and forget about what worked. For example, running a marathon is a big goal. You may or may not do that ever again. Or say you got a new job after many interviews and feel both relieved and pleased, but may not necessarily consider what you learned about yourself in the process as you go headfirst into working.

The Stanford researchers were interested in what supports postgoal motivation by observing what happens when people are asked to view their pursuit of a goal as either a journey or a destination. Across six studies that surveyed a wide array of participants, from US college students to business executives in Africa, the researchers asked people to reflect on a goal they accomplished or were close to attaining (for example, adopting a healthy diet, or achieving a physical accomplishment, an academic goal, or a business goal).[11] They followed up at a later point to assess if the goals or lessons learned were sustained. Participants were randomized into one of three groups—one that was asked to reflect on their successful goal as completing a journey; one that was asked to view their goal as reaching a destination; and a control group. Across the studies, viewing the pursuit of a goal as journey (vs. a destination) led to a greater sense of personal growth and increased chances that behaviors were sustained.

The takeaway? Reflecting on the steps you take and the lessons you learn along the way matters, not just the achievement—or the dream, as Kobe Bryant tried to convey to his fans. Of course, goal pursuit may require some grit, defined by psychologist Angela Duckworth as passion and perseverance toward a goal. But embodying a sense of purpose and meaning is just as important. This was the case for Mariah, the college freshman faced with the reality that she couldn't breeze through college like she had in high school. Once she realized that she had to learn to study in different ways and ask for help, things began to turn around. Her goal was to maintain her high GPA, but the process required new tactics. Mariah made her new mantra "You can do hard things." She also made a commitment to learn new study habits and ask for help when needed. At the same time, she was sure to build in time for the things she loved. Not only did Mariah put in the effort to turn things around, but she also did something very important—she put joy back in the center of her life.

Making a Vow Reflection #2: Small Wins

Think back to a time when you met a goal you had to put true effort into reaching, and you felt pleased, proud, or happy as a result. This doesn't need to be some epic accomplishment. Maybe it was something that would be easy or ordinary for someone else but was a challenge for you. Maybe it was a particular moment that shifted something for you—speaking up, trying out for something, sticking with a plan, finishing a project, asking for help, or stretching yourself in some way.

Next, immerse yourself in this experience like you are watching a replay.

- What went well? What didn't go well?
- What did you learn?
- What is memorable about the situation?
- What do you feel in your body as you remember it?
- What aspects can you apply to other areas of your life?
- What inner strengths did this moment help you grow now that you look back?

To derive even more benefit from this exercise, share what you learned with others. I've seen the power of sharing your story firsthand in the Overcoming Perfectionism groups I lead—as one participant reflects on their experiences in meeting challenges, the energy reverberates from person to person throughout the room. Your example can inspire others, and as others share their own experiences, it can inspire you to keep going.

Making Meaning in Daily Life

Positive psychology is a vibrant subfield of study that looks at the factors that contribute to human flourishing. It asks expansive questions on what well-being is and how people cultivate emotions that lift them up rather than bring them down.

Rather than trying to diminish the hard stuff, the focus of positive psychology is how to be resilient amid life's inevitable trials and tribulations and add meaning to your journey. Psychologist Barbara Frederickson refers to this as the *broaden and build* theory of positive emotions, where the intentional experiencing of positive emotions helps to restore and revitalize, triggering the Green Zone of calm and connection and the Blue Zone of inspired productivity.[12] Many studies confirm the benefits of igniting positive emotions, through activities such as engaging in a loving-kindness meditation, doing kind acts for others, or expressing gratitude. In other words, positive psychology is all about bringing forward the qualities of heart. What positive psychology does not espouse is toxic positivity. Rather, it illuminates the truth that well-being is not replacing the negative with the positive, an either-or proposition; it is learning to make space for all the good, bad, and ugly, with compassion, patience, and perspective.

This is exactly what Mariah decided to do. So she began to make time to sing with her pink rhinestone-adorned karaoke mic. During these at-home singing jams, she was doing more than having fun and releasing stress. She was instilling meaning in her life. It kept her energetic vibration at a higher level and modulated her heart coherence. It helped her prioritize positivity in her life. And that meant she turbocharged her efforts to find her way to happy achieving. Studies show that when people find habitual ways to create positive experiences, they exhibit greater well-being.[13] This may sound obvious on the surface, but due to our tricky brains, people habitually focus on the stressors in life rather than the delights, like Chloe was prone to do.

When Kobe Bryant said that when you commit to moving toward your goals, your dreams won't come true *but something greater will*, he was imploring us to go deeper and see the larger meaning of our desires and actions. Finding meaning and purpose are human needs that go beyond self-interest. Positive psychology researcher Pninit Russo-Netzer, who studies meaning-making, has observed through several studies that prioritizing meaning is a distinct and complementary contributor to well-being.[14] It is not just making sure that you do the fun stuff in life, however essential that is, but to construct meaningful experiences in everyday life. Prioritizing positivity helps with short-term gains, like happiness and other beneficial emotions, whereas intentionally engaging in meaningful experiences contributes to an overall sense of coherence in life. Russo-Netzer goes even further: "Holding a set of personal values that gives one a sense of meaning or being familiar with sources of meaning in life may not be the whole story. . . . If this value is not translated into action through structuring daily life accordingly, it may not benefit well-being. Prioritizing meaning is more oriented toward experiencing meaning and embodying it in daily lives."[15]

Moreover, researchers Shigehiro Oishi and Erin Westgate conducted seven studies and identified a third dimension of what it means to live a good life that is not often captured in Western-centric measurements of happiness.[16] Their various studies included one that surveyed people across nine countries and codified the content of newspaper obituaries.[17] They found that a satisfying, meaningful life, and a "psychologically rich" life, relies on an openness to change and flexibility in the face of surprise. This includes such elements as novelty, interest, curiosity, time, spontaneity, energy, exploration, perspective change, and wisdom. All in all, this begs the question as you pause to identify your own needs, desires, values and strengths: *How are you living into them?*

Turning Inner States into Durable Traits

It's one thing to identify your needs, desires, values, and strengths as an essential step. It's quite another to convert these human longings and aspirations into beneficial and meaningful experiences that, in turn, become lasting traits. Traits are durable, stable, and reliable, whereas states are transitory experiences that largely arise from relatively brief interactions. For instance, when Mariah picks up her mic and blares her favorite song, she evokes a state of glee. It's temporary and she moves on to the next activity in her life. The more Mariah includes singing into her daily life, the more likely singing becomes a habit that enriches her soul and is a part of her character.

Psychologist Rick Hanson offers a compelling way to "take in the good" and make such experiences stick. Drawing on the underlying neural mechanisms for how we learn new things, Hanson spells out how to develop inner strengths. In a process called *positive neuroplasticity training*, he suggests that noticing or having a positive experience is an important first step, called "activation." But there is a necessary second step that involves deliberately capitalizing on how the nervous system learns, called "installation." Hanson created the HEAL framework as a recipe for turning passing states into durable traits.[18]

Step 1: Activation

H = *Have a beneficial, useful, or positive experience*. In other words, notice when something beneficial is spontaneously occurring. Or deliberately create a positive state. For example, go for a workout or try some of the energy practices in this book because you know it's good for your body, or intentionally focus on qualities of the heart like self-compassion or gratitude, calling a friend, or simply stopping to smell the roses.

Step 2: Installation

E = *Enrich the experience*. Intentionally prolong or intensify the experience by savoring it, calling on all the senses, which can heighten the salience of the experience and prime certain regions of the brain that enhance memory to create an internal representation. This step releases juicy neurochemicals like norepinephrine and promotes synaptic connections (plasticity).

Basically, you make the beneficial experience into an immersive Omnimax theater scene in your mind, body, and heart.

A = *Absorb the experience.* Intentionally, "take in" the experience into your body and focus on what is rewarding about it. This can initiate a dopamine squirt that fosters memory consolidation, like a mental Instagram. Neurochemical rewards are very sticky, and the brain remembers the good feelings and images. By amplifying the experience, you are imprinting it in the nervous system and energy pathways. This may help with installing a new beneficial algorithm.

L = *Link positive and negative content.* Considered optional, this step acknowledges that all may not be well in your internal and external worlds. Yet you can purposely draw attention to a beneficial or useful experience in the present moment, what Hanson refers to as the "foreground of awareness." At the same time, you can allow what is difficult and painful to recede to the "background of awareness." It's zooming in on what's beneficial, leaving the uncomfortable material out of focus for a moment. An "even though" statement can also help. For example, "Even though I feel crushed by my lab research results, I completely and deeply accept myself and know I have friends supporting me who remind me to make time to chill and have fun." This linking requires *kindsight*—viewing life experiences with tenderness and understanding.

Making a Vow Reflection #3:
Prescribe Positive Action

You may be familiar with the popular euphemism "Be the change you wish to see in the world." This rings true when you consider that learning anything new means putting in the effort—what I refer to as *joyful effort* when it comes to positive action. It may not be easy, but the effort is worth it because the brain will change based on your actions.

Here we are trying to connect head and heart, allowing for greater integration. Drawing on heart intelligence and your highest self, take a moment to reflect on an inner strength you want to grow. Place a hand or both hands over your heart and tune inward. Take a few breaths. Because you have the power to bring positive change into your experience, and to the world, what inner strength do you want to cultivate? What brings meaning into your life? Name it. Imagine one way you can begin to grow this inner strength in the next twenty-four hours or over the next week . . . and plug it into your calendar.

Kayla's Story, Part 2

Toward the end of Kayla's academic studies, she was asked to present her sustainability design project as part of a university-wide scholars' program across the disciplines. It was a TED Talk format, and she had six minutes to present and one month to prepare. It was a perfect storm for the part of her that she called Cold Feet. Initially, Kayla asked for "the big guns," a referral for antianxiety medication to deal with the sheer panic of the Red Zone she was in. This was a viable option, yet it was one that may not help her *learn* how to manage her nerves and *trust* in her own inner resources. She knew her stuff inside and out. The content wasn't the issue. It was the vulnerable part of her that feared social humiliation that is so common with performance anxiety. With her vow written out and framed on her wall, it was time to take action. She decided to go to a local Toastmasters meetup where members of the audience practice giving a small talk. That was courageous and what psychologists would refer to as an emotional exposure technique.

But even before that bold move, which her Cold Feet could easily opt out of, she needed to tend to the emotional dysregulation triggered by the fear of reputation annihilation. Just the thought of the upcoming talk caused panic. She needed to do the body work *before* the emotional work. So Kayla committed to practicing a lovely energy technique of crossing the hands over the heart, called Heart Assisted Therapy® (HAT), developed by psychologist John Diepold.[19] (See the Get Connected exercise on page 199.) It involves three rounds of three breaths with overlapping hands over the heart. The crossing of hands over the heart helps with vagal tone and heart coherence.

Kayla decided to do this heart energy exercise whenever she sat with her cat Smokey for a few minutes, which naturally already had a calming effect. This pairing of two activities—the habit of sitting with her cat in her lap along with the new hands over heart sequence—is called habit stacking. Since doing something new often is a matter of fits and starts, inserting the new habit in an already established routine makes it more likely to stick over time.

Kayla's fear about her future speaking engagement entailed addressing a stop-start paradox (or psychoenergetic reversal). Her self-defeating behavior of avoidance understandably offered temporary relief but caused further procrastination and anxiety. Another part of her also felt excited about sharing her work. So she used the heart crossing exercise to focus on the upcoming talk while repeating the following acceptance phrases to calm her nervous system:

Deep in my heart I love and accept myself even though I feel overwhelmed.

Deep in my heart I love and accept myself even though I can get nervous with public speaking.

Deep in my heart I love and accept myself even though I have this desire to opt out but knowing that I'll be proud of myself after I present.

Kayla practiced this and eventually shifted her acceptance phrases to imagining her future self speaking in front of an audience and feeling at ease: *Deep in my heart I love and accept myself knowing I have something valuable to share with others.* When she could recognize that what she had to share was much greater than herself, and that she was a channel for her unique message about sustainability, her Inner Monica and Cold Feet calmed down.

A few months later, Kayla shared the public link of her talk, and I was floored with how smoothly it went. If she was nervous, it did not show. She stood in her own power. Kayla did the work. She made a vow to herself, challenged herself to take some scary steps, and tended to the mind-body-heart connection. Importantly, she cultivated several inner strengths that will serve her for a very long time. She stepped into the flow.

Happy Achiever Tools: Making a Vow

You've been getting clarity about what matters to you and how you want to live your life in ways that bring more ease and joy. It's a wonderful unfolding and the following tools can help you step into alignment in mind, body, heart, and soul.

GET GROUNDED: HUG YOUR BRAIN

One of my all-time favorite techniques from Eden Energy Medicine is the Neurovascular Hold, what I call a "brain hug." (*Neuro* refers to the brain and *vascular* refers to blood flow.) The brain hug enables you to get calm, think more clearly, and encourage your energy pathways to flow in harmony. It's excellent in calming a worried mind and to try before falling asleep too. Many stressed clients and I have sat facing each other while holding our heads in this posture. Sometimes the simplest strategy is the most elegant. Here's how to do it:

1. Place one hand over the front of your forehead.
2. Place the other hand at the back of your head toward the occipital ridge at the lower skull. Breathe for a few minutes. Ahhh . . .

After a few moments you will likely feel calmer, still, and supported. You may also find that you naturally linger longer in this posture due to the sense of relief, like when a cool compress soothes a fever.

GET ENERGIZED:
SUPERCHARGING YOUR SUPERPOWERS

Striving for excellence is what many perfectionists desire. Most of us muscle through with brain power, persistence, and determination. Perfectionists are constantly navigating the Blue Zone of motivation and are often in an overenergized state. It's also natural to dip into the Red Zone of panic or anger when things don't go as planned, or an algorithm of not being good enough that then lights up the brain circuitry of self-criticism. Like Kayla, we can change that.

Several physical spiritual traditions offer body positions that keep you grounded and connected. Think of sun and moon salutations, and the mountain pose, in many yoga flow practices. You may be familiar with the "power pose" made popular by Amy Cuddy in her TED talk, which is akin to standing in a Wonder Woman or Superman posture with hands on hips, or a cheerleader's victory pose with both arms extended up in a V shape. Think of the statue of Lady Liberty representing freedom. These poses fire up elegance, empowerment, and excellence. One of my favorite postures is Donna Eden's Heaven Rushing In.[20] It's a wonderful energy exercise to connect up your radiant circuitry. Here's how to do it:

1. Standing tall, rub your hands together, and shake your fingers toward the ground. Rest your hands on the top of your legs for a few breaths. Visualize sending your energies into the ground, as if you are plugging into the earth.
2. Take an inhale as you circle your arms up over your head and then lower your hands to a prayer position at your chest. Exhale.
3. Take another deep inhale and stretch both arms to the sky into a letter V position. Look up toward the heavens, making a sacred connection between earth and sky. Hold for one minute or so.

4. As you hold, visualize that you are part of the universe, whole and expansive, inviting in the radiant, healing energies.

5. After a minute, exhale slowly, gather your arms to your heart area, as if you are scooping in the good vibes, which supports greater heart coherence.

6. You may feel a shift or even receive guidance or a positive affirmation. And if not, just imagine that you are aligned with the universe and receptive to inspiration that may appear at a later time when you least expect it.

7. Take some final deep breaths to send the energies throughout your body and to any areas that may need some extra TLC.

This is also a wonderful exercise to do when standing in the woods or on a beach to make a connection to the vastness of the life force energy.

GET CONNECTED: A HEART OF GOLD

Heart Assisted Therapy® (HAT) is a gentle touch technique in energy psychology that is thought to augment heart coherence and vagal tone. As with other energy psychology techniques, such as tapping, HAT combines touch with verbalization of what's known as an acceptance statement. You can tailor your acceptance phrase to match whatever is happening in your current experience that is causing stress.

This technique takes about three minutes, and the steps are as follows (adapted from the basic recipe for HAT to promote self-regulation):

1. Notice the current intensity level of whatever you're experiencing on a 0 to 10 scale (0 = no intensity, 10 = highest intensity).

2. Round 1: Cross your hands directly over the center of your heart area. It doesn't matter which hand is over the other.

3. Quiet the mind and focus your attention on something in front of you, like a spot on the floor or wall. Your eyes can be open. Take three normal breaths while keeping your hands over your heart.

4. Round 2: Reverse your hands over your heart and take another three natural breaths.

5. Round 3: Reverse your hands for the final time and take three natural breaths.

Repeat the 3x3 breath sequence again, but this time, *repeat your acceptance statement* with each breath. Be creative and discover what feels right for you. Here are some prompts:

Deep in my heart I love and accept myself, even though . . . [I am/feel_____].

I completely and deeply accept myself, even though . . . [I am/feel_____].

Even though . . . [I am/feel_____], I completely and deeply accept myself.

Repeat a final set of three rounds for a final energetic cleanse. Notice if there is any change in intensity. Keep practicing for several weeks or as a daily infusion of self-care. Keep in mind this is not medical intervention. It's simply a self-regulation skill using gentle touch that can help with de-stressing whenever you feel a spike in emotions, fears, and concerns. Plus, as little as twenty seconds of a hand on the heart repeated daily for one month improves well-being, so it's worth a try.[21]

You are accumulating a treasure trove of methods and strategies to transform the negative effects of perfectionism and assuage the inner critical voices so they can find more ease and play. The last step, Sparking the Energy of Excellence, will help integrate the learnings as you go along on your journey to being a happy achiever.

9

Step 6

E, Spark the Energy of Excellence

*When you are in harmony with yourself, you are in
harmony with everyone else.*

— Debbie Ford

No one was more confused than me about my panic attack the day
that I had it. "Tara, just breathe," I told myself on the gurney as
I was driven off to the local ER, while my little girls stood watching in
confusion. I lay in the hospital bed hooked up to various monitors, just
relieved I wasn't having a stroke. Later, a visit to a neurologist assured
me that I did not have a brain tumor. My reflexes were working, and all
lab tests were normal. The neurologist chalked it up to stress. "Try to
relax," the nurses repeatedly told me.

As time went on, my panic attack eventually made more sense to
me. For months afterward, prickly sensations from the right side of my
skull scattered across my cheekbones, quivering at the top of my lip as
if I had walked into a spider's web. These physical sensations were ever
present, yet there was no obvious reason why I felt them. I feared I
might be losing my mind. I was constantly irritated and frustrated by
this mystery symptom.

One day, when walking around the town pond at dusk with my
girls, I remembered a story my mother would tell my sister and me on
humid summer evenings when the sky turned pink and purple. "Oh,
look, the angels are baking cookies!" Sharing this with my own two
children helped for some reason. A tinge of warmth swelled from deep

within. I surrendered to the heavens and called on the ministry of angels. "Angels, help me," I silently prayed.

I heard a quiet response, "It's going to be OK." I didn't know where the message was coming from, but I didn't care. I felt comforted, and I knew something had to change. I just wasn't quite sure what. No doubt life was stressful with a career, student loans, a mortgage, small kids, and the tiresome family burdens that trailed me from childhood and set the path toward becoming a psychologist. From an early age I absorbed many messages. *Don't be so sensitive! Stop complaining. What a temper! Be grateful to have clothes on your back. Life is a struggle. There's never enough. It could be worse! Hard work pays off. Education is your ticket out.* And on and on. But I was adding way too many second arrows of suffering along the way.

As a child, my family members told me I was defiant or feisty, depending on the source. I was also born pigeon-toed, a common condition called severe metatarsus adductus. I had casts on my legs, followed by a brace between my shoes, and wore costly corrective shoes to remedy the problem. (No wonder I was a frustrated toddler!) Later, I often stormed out of the house with a sleeping bag and stuffed leopard in tow to stew in a pine grove at the edge of the yard. Like Luis, I had a young Tiny Terror part that I now call Scarlett, who was easily triggered into a Red Zone. I also had a ten-year-old part I named Tax Collector, who was charged with reminding Daddy about the child support checks that inevitably bounced. There was the Bookworm part, who championed the strategy I now call "Education as the defense against the dark parts." That part showed up when I was in middle school, gawky and awkward, knowing she'd never make the popular girls' list. This Bookworm effectively squashed the angry parts and made the choice to work her tail off to get to college—spawning the compulsive striver and self-oriented perfectionist in me.

I didn't get to know these parts and how they tried to protect me until much later. But the walk around the pond that evening was my first call to self-compassion. There would be many more moments inviting me to quell the inner critics, face the stressors with grace, and do something radically different.

In my quest to understand why my face felt the way it did, I saw a dentist who attributed my physical pain to trigeminal neuralgia, a nerve condition that affects the side of the face. The sensation of spider webs tingling from ear to lips was real. I wasn't making it up. From there, I launched into a healing journey that included acupuncture, chiropractic care, and yoga. I knew little of the skills in this book, but I was on my way to discovering them.

At the time, I was working as a research scientist in behavioral health technology, at what some of us in the field call a grant writing mill. Perfectionists, I've discovered, find the ideal professions to reinforce perfectionist traits, requiring exacting attention to detail with often uncertain outcomes. I often joked I was the Queen of the Resubmit, because we were groomed to keep submitting innovation grants even in the face of rejections by a review panel of anonymous scientists. I developed a thick skin to such rejections, which were often quite subjective, and just went back at it. I could relate when Luis, the neuroscientist, remarked to me, "My career is the perfect storm of an unrelenting focus on precision." But it was a comment by my younger daughter, Josie, one evening before bedtime when she was eight years old that did me in. "Mommy, is your job writing emails all day?"

Josie's innocent question stopped me. How many times over the years did I say, "I'll be right up after I send an email!" As if corresponding with a collaborator was more important than tucking my daughter in. As if reviewing "track changes" on yet another document couldn't wait. As if my children's need to cuddle with Mommy was at the bottom of the priority list.

I had to get my head on straight. Or rather, connect my head with my heart. My facial nerve pain signaled that I was totally out of balance, and the answers would not spring from my brain but from my body, not from my conscious mind but from unconscious energy patterns. Judith Swack, a pioneer in the field of energy psychology and one of my healers, calls it "healing from the body level up."[1] And that's exactly what I needed to do.

As I began tending to my energy by recommitting to my yoga practice and learning to meditate, slow but seismic shifts helped me overcome the negative effects of perfectionism and create the EVOLVE method. Over time, I created sacred space and community to regulate and coregulate my emotions (E, Step 1), validated my experiences (V, Step 2), practiced kindfulness and self-compassion (O, Step 3), explored inner parts work (L, Step 4), committed to change, found clarity, and practiced kindsight (V, Step 5), and eventually stepped outside of my traditional training as a psychologist to learn, adopt, and begin to teach basic energy psychology skills to self-regulate and unlock self-sabotaging blocks (E, Step 6). Although each of the EVOLVE steps is helpful and necessary, I've found that it's this final step that creates a lasting awakening and healing from perfectionism.

The Goal of Step 6: Spark the Energy of Excellence

The energy of excellence is not about constant striving for the perfect life. The energy of excellence is balanced, flexible, and heart-centered. It is nourished by your deep well of personal resources. The goal of this last step, E for Energy of Excellence, is to illuminate your inner resources and so many other hidden gems. After all, the world needs you to shine your bright light.

And what is your bright light? It's your energy.

I introduced the concept of energy in chapter 2 and ever since then, you've been supercharging your energy as you've gone on this journey of befriending yourself—whether you've realized that's what you've been doing or not. When your unique energy patterns are in balance, your mind, body, heart, and spirit are aligned—and primed— for success. You transform your perfectionism into the energy of excellence, and then you can meet your need for belonging and bring your best to whatever you seek to do without a high cost to your overall being. This is why my definition of perfectionism intentionally includes the word *energy*: *Perfectionism is the paradox created by the need for belonging—and fear of rejection—paired with unrealistic expectations for achievement and approval that sap your energy or life force.*

Psychologist Anodea Judith, in *Charge and the Energy Body*, states that "we, as energetic beings, can tap into an infinite field of energy far greater than our amazing little bodies can hold."[2] It's a wonderful prospect to consider. In Step 6, you will begin to dip your toes into your energetic potential. You will begin to clear energetic blocks with "emotional acupuncture," and ultimately create upward spirals of energy. I hope you trust me to guide you, and more importantly, trust your own inner guidance system.

By now you might feel a little more confident in your ability to befriend yourself as you heal the negative effects of perfectionism. But if there is one thing that seems to befuddle people even more than self-kindness, it is how to trust themselves more. In the face of uncertainty, this can feel very hard. "How can I trust my vibes?" Kayla lamented more than once when finding herself in moments of indecision. Asher also struggled with chronic self-doubt. Daria had a hard time letting go of control. Mariah had to reinvent herself by learning new skills, and Justin resisted having a soft heart. Chloe, Luis, and Reed all shared some form of compulsive striving to meet their own unrealistic expectations. I, too, still contend with limiting beliefs. It's part of the human condition. As writer and embodiment coach Prentiss Hemphill so aptly states, "Perfectionism is a commitment to habitual self-doubt." And what is self-doubt? It is an energetic block from the past.

Self-trust is being true to yourself and standing in your integrity no matter your missteps in life or what your inner doubter has to say. It's all too easy to second-guess your own intuition or succumb to others' opinions. And now that you have committed to a new vow in the previous step, it's time to take a leap of faith, tune into your vibes, and ultimately live into your true potential. Trusting yourself may be the final hitch in releasing energetic blocks of perfectionism.

However, self-trust is one of those things that you can't just magically do. It's not like flipping a switch. It's more about experiencing many micro-moments of believing in yourself, regulating your nervous system, quieting your mind to access your intuition, and then trying out new ways of stepping into alignment with who you are becoming. No matter where you begin, it is important to create time and space in your life to practice the Happy Achiever Tools you've been learning throughout this book—what I call creating your sacred container.

"Container" describes safe boundaries and space to allow new things to grow. In my profession, the material and immaterial space in which a therapist and client sit together is a container. So is an agreement for expectations in a support group. My Overcome Perfectionism workshops include the edict, "What is shared in the room stays in the room, but what is learned can be shared out of the room." This ensures confidentiality of personal struggles yet also inspires practical acts of compassion for oneself and others in daily life. The container is also a metaphor for structuring creative endeavors, such as writing workshops, art programs, camps, sports, and any other inspired effort that requires commitment and the support of allies. If you ever participated in a trust fall you know that certain agreements had to first be in place. Establishing a container for yourself is a way to foster consistency, which creates new inner algorithms for trust and self-care—so essential for perfectionists. And before you know it, a healthy habit for self-compassion is born.

After the innocent email comment by Josie, here's what I did to create a container for my healing: I took over a small space in the house as my sanctuary. I painted the room a soft lavender, collected my favorite books, knickknacks, photos, essential oils, a candle or two, and claimed it as my space. Daylight glittered through the old poured-glass windowpanes. I hung a hotel doorknob sign that read "Do not disturb." It was where I planned to journal, listen to music, and just chill.

Of course, that didn't happen. Not exactly.

But over time I grew into that space. I gradually added a soft throw, fresh cut flowers in a handmade ceramic vase from a client, and a photograph of me at age five. In the photo, I am missing my two front teeth. The photo immediately evokes a sense of warmth and tenderness, and reminds me to honor the young parts of myself who overcame many obstacles in life. Sometimes, I just take a breath and wink at that little girl, communicating "I got your back." I cultivated a trust in myself to take care of my motley crew of parts.

In fact, the room exuded a calming energy that spread throughout the whole house, even though, despite my efforts, my girls still ran through it unabashedly. My husband would sit down on the couch at the end of a day, and the dog would sleep by my feet. It had a gravitational pull like a vortex. Eventually, it became a place for my private practice. Then our girls grew up and we moved away. Now I have a very small corner with a meditation cushion, but my established "container" has proven to be very portable.

Spark the Energy of Excellence Reflection #1: Create Sacred Space

When you create cues in your environment that support a useful or beneficial habit, it simply makes it easier to do. You begin to fill your sacred container with the essential ingredients and leave out the rest. Just like having your sneakers ready at the door or fresh fruit on the table makes it easier to exercise and eat healthy. Consider creating a ritual or routine for yourself every day in the same place: a room, a nook, a park bench, or a favorite path for walking. You can call it whatever you want: centering practice, chill corner, getting grounded, intentional space, me time, mindful moment, meditation, sanctuary, or sacred pause. If you travel often, you can bring an item that represents your intention. After all, your practice is as portable as your breathing. Your practice could be as little as five to ten minutes. It simply requires you to quiet the mind's chatter, to acknowledge the inner parts that may be activated or need some TLC, and to allow your true self a few moments of peace and quiet. Having this container allows for new things to grow, which is what happened as I learned to balance my energy and unblock my psychoenergetic reversals.

Learning Emotional Acupuncture

After learning how to assuage the fireworks in my face, I began to consider pain in a new way—as pools of energy that get stuck, or become overactive or underactive. Metaphysically, my trigeminal neuralgia was an invitation to reconnect my head and heart. I've found the various energetic practices remove the element of self-judgment, in part because the skills are gentle and add an element of personal control.

As my nerve pain eased over time with the help of traditional acupuncture, I was later introduced to tapping from master teacher Ingrid Dinter when we found each other in a business coaching class. Ingrid was part of the intervention team in the first randomized controlled study using tapping, or Emotional Freedom Technique (EFT), with veterans with PTSD.[3]

The effectiveness of EFT is backed by significant and growing scientific evidence.[4] EFT is not a stand-alone therapy but is often blended into traditional counseling, mind-body medicine, and palliative care to help clients reduce distress, regulate their nervous system, and find quick relief in the moment. Clinical EFT is also used to help people integrate past traumatic experiences and core negative beliefs that still affect present day life, work, and relationships. EFT is essentially a body-based stress reduction system and a safe and efficient way to get out of a Red Zone.[5] Tapping is often used as therapeutic homework between therapy sessions, and there are apps and videos to guide a self-help approach. It's an ideal tool for perfectionists because tapping combines building distress tolerance, addressing limiting beliefs, and cultivating self-acceptance.

Tapping involves using a fingertip or two to stimulate particular acupoints located on your head, other hand, and torso. When Ingrid first led me through an EFT sequence on our bus ride back from New York to Boston, I thought it was too silly and simple to be effective. In truth, I was more self-conscious than anything because tapping does look odd to an outsider—it's like watching a baseball pitcher and catcher emit pitch signs. I might have alleviated years of aches and pains, as well as internal and external dramas, if I had latched on to EFT back then. The instructions for the tapping skills literally had me physically tapping on the very areas of my face that were inflamed, as if tapping were invented for my condition!

The truth of the matter is perfectionists, myself included, often don't have patience to practice the little things, but when done consistently they can generate big results. If you have an impatient inner doubter or skeptic, that's OK. Now that I'm trained in the modality, I consider it a staple in the Happy Achiever Tool kit, especially for perfectionistic self-saboteurs. Plus, it's very easy to learn and practice on your own.

In chapter 2, I described Daria, the lawyer, who practiced tapping to help her with her inner critic. It's a compassionate approach that enables you to hold a painful thought, emotion, or experience with self-acceptance by repeating phrases such as "Even though I feel unworthy of happiness, I completely and deeply accept myself," while you gently tap specific spots on your body. You also experienced hints of this technique with "even though" compassion statements and tapping in the Step 1 Happy Achiever Tools, including the Code Switch and the Quick Reset. In this chapter, I offer a fuller tapping routine that you can do on your own—but consider it "EFT lite." If we were sitting together, I would be leading you in what might seem like a "Simon Says" game. I speak and tap and you repeat and tap. Here, you can practice this tapping routine using the illustration of the acupoints as a guide. If anything, tapping does no harm, so you have nothing to lose. If tapping causes more distress for some reason, then stop. Eventually, you may be interested in finding a practitioner who offers the standardized clinical EFT to do deeper healing work.

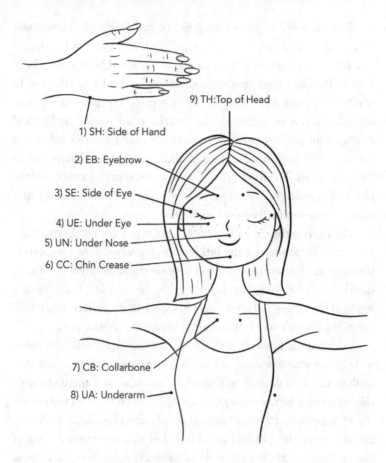

1) SH: Side of Hand
9) TH:Top of Head
2) EB: Eyebrow
3) SE: Side of Eye
4) UE: Under Eye
5) UN: Under Nose
6) CC: Chin Crease
7) CB: Collarbone
8) UA: Underarm

What Is Tapping and How Does It Work?

Tapping involves acupressure points along a number of the meridian pathways in Traditional Chinese Medicine. The points are associated with electromagnetic fields in the body and organs. Tapping is thought to regulate the nervous system through stimulation of an electrical signal via connective tissue that travels to neural circuits in the brain that maintain limiting beliefs, traumatic memories, and emotional arousal. In this way, tapping may help with emotion regulation, memory reconsolidation, and overall well-being.[6] At minimum, tapping involves a combination of stimulating acupressure points while simultaneously using words or imagery.[7] You don't even need to know what the points are associated with in the body for the tapping to work. Moreover, any of the Happy Achiever Tools can help harmonize your energies *before* you even begin a tapping session, including breathing skills, placing hands over the heart, and Eden's Daily Energy Routine.[8]

The basic recipe begins with a gentle tapping, about seven to ten quick taps on each point, beginning on the pinky side of one hand (1), at the brow between the eyes (2), at the far side of eye and just below the brow's edge (3), under the eye (4), above and below the lips (5 and 6), an inch below the collarbones (7), a few inches under an armpit at lower rib (8), and at the top of the head (9). EFT practitioners may use slightly different points, have variations in sequence, and begin or follow up with other light touch gestures to integrate the tapping. For our purposes with EFT lite, you can follow the recipe below (see the scripts in Appendix B or visit a demonstration on my website www.perfectionistsdilemma.com).

It may feel awkward at first, but once you know the pattern, it becomes second nature. As you identify a target concern for tapping, you verbally pair an "even though" statement of the fear, concern, or aspiration with an acceptance statement, as you will identify in Reflection #2.

Energy of Excellence Reflection #2: Finding Your Acceptance Statement

At first it may help to have some writing materials available to remember your setup statement. The classic acceptance statement is "I deeply and completely love and accept myself," or simply "I love and accept myself." In my experience with perfectionists, they'll resist using an acceptance statement at first. This is often because self-acceptance and self-love are core issues. Using a "choice" statement is a good alternative. If nothing lands from the list below, consider something you might grow into over time. You decide what works for you, but it is important to grow toward unconditional acceptance no matter how tentative. Even if it feels awkward, just try one acceptance statement on for size.

I accept myself deeply and completely.

I deeply and completely accept (love) myself.

I love and accept myself anyway/just as I am.

I'm working on accepting myself.

I accept how I feel at this moment.

I deeply and completely accept that these are my feelings.

I honor/acknowledge/respect how I feel.

I know I'm doing the best I can.

I know I've been trying to protect myself.

I feel compassion for myself.

I'm OK right now.

I'm a good person.

I choose to love and accept myself anyway.

I choose to appreciate making positive changes.

I choose to recognize how perfectionism gets in my way.

I choose to honor my worth.

Create your own acceptance statement.

Clearing Perfectionist Blocks

Now that you've come this far, you're ready to directly address an energetic block (or, as we covered in Step 4, a psychoenergetic reversal)—a mind/body pattern that keeps you stuck even though it's trying to solve a problem. Remember, these patterns have to do with experiences and beliefs related to worthiness, scarcity, a conviction that a goal is impossible, a fear that you don't have what it takes (compared to others), and competing motivations among your parts. You can think of this as a pesky predictive pattern in the brain with deep energetic roots.

Remember, you now have skills to be safely challenged and to navigate the Red, Blue, and Green Zones. Recall how in Step 1 you identified your brand of stress, noticed your triggers as well as the various sensations in your body, common emotions, and negative thoughts without judgment. In Step 2, you validated your feelings and experiences without trying to minimize them. In Steps 3 and 4 you opened your heart to your personal Plus One and other inner critics with self-compassion, learning to care for them instead of banishing them. In Step 5, you drilled down to your values, what is meaningful to you, and committed to inspired action. All these steps are important groundwork for taking this next step of clearing blocks and letting your energy flow. Yet you can't change your behavior until you change your feelings or beliefs—and the energetic charge associated with them. As Anodea Judith states, "Our beliefs fixate our charge, keeping it bound, just as we bind charge into the muscles and tissue of the body. The point is not to get rid of the charge, but to keep the charge and change the belief."[9] Your energy flows while your limiting belief dissolves.

To help you do just that, I invite you to focus on a paradoxical perfectionist habit that is holding you back from either reaching a dream or overcoming a challenge that you know can free you to live more authentically. A common example is the start-stop pattern or the perfectionism-procrastination dilemma. Once you have one identified, you're going to use tapping to release the energetic lock.

Let's get to it.

What's Your Current Dilemma?

Think of a thought pattern you've been getting stuck in lately. If you aren't sure what that might be, refer back to the Perfectionism Self-Inquiry and pick a theme of perfecting, pleasing, performing, or producing that is keeping you from a desired goal. Or you could start with a typical quandary for perfectionists: *Do I go for it or do I play it safe?*

Notice if your Plus One or another part is the main player. There may also be two parts of you in a tug-of-war—gridlocked somewhere in your internal family system where the fear is lodged. Tapping helps to neutralize the underlying emotions and beliefs, and quells the fight/flight/freeze reactivity. Why does this matter? If you are stuck in fear, you can't even imagine the possibilities for something different, exciting, or wonderful. Fear short-circuits inspiration. And you may have fears that directly contradict each other, such as a fear of failure and a fear of success. For many people, it's both. As perfectionism researcher Patrick Gaudreau stated, "Perfectionist strivers are motivated to attain success, but they are also daunted by fear of failure."[10] Now you can take a closer look and begin to untangle a perfectionist dilemma.

DESCRIBE THE SABOTAGING BEHAVIOR

Get curious about what's blocking you in your life now and drill down to the emotional charge, such as anger, confusion, fear, humiliation, rejection, shame, and so on. (You might get mad and hate yourself for naming it. That's OK. Draw on your budding emotional courage and self-compassion.) Then take a journal or notebook and answer the questions below:

1. Where do you notice any feeling or sensation in your body now as you consider your self-sabotage?
2. If you know the sabotage behavior may be linked to a past event, give it a title, for example, "The time my boss yelled at me" or "The time I froze in front of the class."

3. What is the *positive solution* you are seeking? How is the sabotage behavior protective (that is, a positive outcome when you avoid failure)? In other words, what is the potential benefit if you *don't* change? What feels *safe* about keeping the status quo?

4. Or consider the opposite: What is the *negative solution* you are avoiding? If you actually *succeeded* at your intended goal, what are you afraid of (that is, a negative outcome if you're great)? In other words, what is the potential *cost, consequence,* or *damage* if you actually do well? Dig deep. You clearly want success—and may even have it—but aren't *experiencing* success. You may be afraid at some level that you can't keep it up, that the bar keeps getting higher, or you may be afraid of exposure or rejection. You may worry that others will see you differently or may become upset or jealous. Ironically, being successful may cause an identity crisis.

5. Decide on your target for tapping. Give it a simple title or storyline. A familiar example is *I'm afraid of rejection.*

6. Create two sets of mini reminder phrases for the tapping sequence you are about to experiment with—one batch that describes your distress (so that you can reduce those sensations) and one set that captures the positive benefits you are seeking to create (so you can amplify them). Mini reminders are little phrases that capture the essence of the block you want to clear, release, or heal, and they help you stay emotionally engaged as you tap. A mini reminder describes your felt experience in the *present moment* as you acknowledge the situation, such as qualities of your emotions, sensations, a memorable cue, or a belief. Examples for tapping down the negative charge (decreasing distress) might include *heat in my body, tightness in my chest, feeling frozen/exposed, sense of embarrassment/shame/fear/anger/rejection, being called out for my mistake, in trouble again.* Examples for tapping up the positive charge (increasing vitality) might include words like *releasing* the heat in my body, *letting go* of my

embarrassment, *healing* my shame, or a brief affirmation like *ready to go for it* or *it's my time to shine*. State your mini reminders as simply as you can as they will serve as anchor points for tapping on the face and body.

7. Measure your current level of distress or discomfort due to your target concern, on a 0 to 10 intensity scale with 0 being "not at all" distressed and 10 being "extremely" distressed. This is called a subjective unit of distress (SUD) rating. You'll also check in on your SUD rating after you've done a round of tapping. This simply allows you to notice if there are any differences after tapping on a target fear or block, which eventually (and ideally) drops down to 1 or 0. Typically, the energy of distress feels contracted—both emotionally intense and physically tense.

8. Now you have the building blocks to create a setup statement to begin a tapping round, which starts with tapping on the side of the nondominant hand. This setup statement is the prelude to the rest of the tapping round where you will use the mini reminder phrases to keep momentum as you neutralize the fears. The setup statement helps you get out of the starting gate. It helps you to develop some distance from the self-sabotaging problem by befriending it in an encouraging manner.

CREATE A SETUP STATEMENT

Here is the format of a setup statement:

> Even though I am/have/believe/feel
> [_____],
> [*your target concern/issue/conflict*]
> +
> I choose to love and accept myself anyway.
> [*or your acceptance statement of choice*]

A setup statement has two parts:

1. The first part is the "even though" statement to draw attention to the negative aspect of your experience. For example, "Even though I'm afraid of being critiqued," "Even though a part of me feels I have to be perfect to be loved," or "Even though my striving for excellence is killing me."
2. The second part is your preferred self-acceptance statement you just identified in Reflection #2.

You can stick to one setup statement phrase or have two to three variations on the same target since perfectionism, as we know, is complex. But start simple at first. You will see how these statements flow in the examples below.

BE CLEAR ABOUT WHAT YOU WANT INSTEAD

EFT master teacher Carol Look calls perfectionism a "dream killer."[11] Therefore, a key component in tapping is also keeping your dream alive. Refer back to your revised algorithms, your *why*, and your commitment statement from Step 5. Identify what matters most to you, the impact or positive effect you want in the world and the feeling that arises when you contemplate that effect. You know it when you feel it, but oftentimes you need to list several aspects of your desired goal that excite you, not just one or two. Go for five to ten reasons why this goal is important, meaningful, or inspiring. No overthinking, just let the reasons flow.

Similarly, give yourself a rating about what excites you. One of my friends, Kitty Hooper, a nurse and Eden Energy practitioner, calls this a *Subjective Unit of Vitality*, which I have adopted. As you begin to access the expansive energy of excellence, it will tick up to a 10.

With tapping, not only do you reduce the negative charge of distress, you can also ignite the uplifting charge of inspiration. Practically, you are tapping down the fear until it's no longer activated and tapping up the excitement until the inspiration feels aligned with mind, body, heart, and spirit. If your fear-based distress is at an 8 but your joyful vitality is at 2, the tricky brain will prioritize the fear. So you must first practice with tapping down on the negative, which may take several rounds or even days and weeks of daily tapping. Tapping helps you shift the ratio—or as Ted Lasso offered, reverse the curse. Fear will lose its grip, freeing up your energetic container to refill with the energy of excellence, which is flexible, fluid, light, spacious, aspirational, and is associated with a host of pleasant states and emotions.

To bolster the positive effect in your daily life, it helps to gather allies around you, who can encourage your future self and supercharge your intentions. That's what students in my Overcome Perfectionism workshops did for each other.

Examples from Our Perfectionist Companions

Let's look at some examples from our fellow perfectionists and how they might create setup statements for their perfectionism blocks.

KAYLA'S DILEMMA

For Kayla, who struggles with socially prescribed perfectionism, playing small is safer than the possibility of becoming a successful architect. After all, being recognized for her innovative designs could result in being seen and exposed. It feels safer to stay in place than to level up. Her habit of deficit thinking fueled by negative social comparison is a major block. Her Cold Feet part is doing double duty by avoiding both failure and success. Kayla has her commitment statement from Step 5 and she's clear on what she wants to activate, which is "unapologetically sharing my work without caring about the opinions of others." Tapping can help her release the energetic hold that keeps her dilemma alive and well.

> **Protective Behavior:** My self-sabotage of procrastination avoids the pain of being called out as a mediocre architect (a fear of criticism).

Emotion/Sensation: Anxious. Butterflies in the belly.

Positive Solution: I push off being critiqued, which buys me time (her solution to fear of failure).

Negative Solution: By staying unnoticed I won't offend people or make them envious or angry (her solution to a fear of recognition/success).

Target for Tapping: I'm afraid of being critiqued by people in my field.

Aspirational Goal: My innovations can impact how we plan and build and change how we live and work. I know what I want to do in my life and it is bigger than me. I care about making a difference and I don't want to hold back anymore. I want to share my work with confidence. I feel excited imagining it.

Intensity Ratings: Distress = 8, Vitality = 4

Possible Setup Statements for Kayla (when tapping the side of hand):

- Even though I'm afraid to stop tweaking and tinkering with my work because I'm afraid of being critiqued, I deeply and completely accept myself.
- Even though I hate the part of me, my Cold Feet, who waits until the last possible moment to produce results, and I know I'm protecting myself from rejection, I deeply and completely accept myself.
- Even though the thought of standing out makes me so anxious and gives me butterflies, I deeply and completely accept myself.

Mini Reminder Statements (when tapping the points on head and body):

(–) afraid of being critiqued | my anxiety | these butterflies | I'm at an 8

(+) ready to step up | I'm proud of my work | I love what I do | excited

LUIS'S DILEMMA

For Luis, the neuroscientist, his self- and other-oriented perfectionism creates exactly what he doesn't want. By alienating his collaborators with unreasonable demands, he risks damaging his reputation and losing the very respect and validation he craves. No doubt he loves his line of research and can see the potential outcomes for patients. His Tiny Terror part, however, is a fierce protector that turns Luis into his own worst enemy. Yet he yearns for love and authentic connection. For Luis, "perfect is the enemy of the good."

> **Protective Behavior:** My relentless work ethic and demand for excellence ensures I am respected and at the top of my game (to combat his fear of annihilation).
> **Emotion/Sensation:** I am tense and lonely.
> **Positive Solution:** You can always count on me to produce flawless work (his solution to a need for recognition and validation).
> **Negative Solution:** I stand apart from colleagues and have few friends, so no one can hurt me (his solution to past attachment wounds).
> **Target for Tapping:** I must be perfect to be loved.
> **Aspirational Goal:** I know my work matters, but I don't feel that I matter. I want to matter to people and I want to learn how to connect in healthy ways. I'm ready to let go of the hostility I carry because I want to find a partner, have kids someday, and start my own company. I want to relax, be likable, and have more pleasure in my life even though I'm not totally sure how to change.
> **Intensity Ratings:** Distress = 10, Vitality = 1
> **Possible Setup Statements for Luis (when tapping the side of the hand):**
>
> • Even though I work harder than anyone I know, and I'm convinced nobody seems to care, and they may even reject me, I choose to accept who I am and how I feel.

- Even though I'm unsure of how to change, I'm willing to take some steps—even though it scares me—to accept who I am and how I feel.
- Even though a younger part protects me from feeling hurt and I know where it comes from, I feel connected to my work because it can make a difference in people's lives—which really inspires me. I accept who I am and how I feel.

Mini Reminder Statements (when tapping the points on head and body):
(–) must be perfect | tense | lonely | Tiny Terror shows up
(+) ready to change | appreciating my protector | healing my wounds | inspired

DARIA'S DILEMMA

Daria, high in self-oriented perfectionism, is convinced that she needs to work harder and do more. She suffers from the diminishing rate of return analogy offered by Canadian researcher Gaudreau.[12] As Daria depletes her body budget, lives in a Red Zone of fear, exhausting her internal resources, she's more anxious, sleep deprived, and risks making mistakes. She notices other new lawyers are better adjusted and have personal lives. She wants that for herself too.

Protective Behavior: Being busy is how I know I am needed and worthy (her need for belonging).
Emotion/Sensation: I am exhausted.
Positive Solution: Overcommitting to work projects proves what a dedicated lawyer I am and proves that I'm more than just good enough (her solution to fear of failure and rejection).
Negative Solution: Being miserably productive, even if it means losing sleep and time with friends, keeps me distracted from feeling anything at all (a setup for isolation and burnout).
Target for Tapping: Striving for excellence is killing me.

Aspirational Goal: My dream is to create a life and a law practice that allows me to create my own schedule, travel the world, and do international work. I care about making a positive difference in people's lives. I know I need to put in my time as a new lawyer but don't want it to kill me. I want more freedom, fun, and friends. I feel happy imagining my future self.

Intensity Ratings: Distress = 9, Vitality = 3

Possible Setup Statements for Daria (when tapping the side of the hand):

- Even though I learned growing up that I had to be perfect to be loved, I'm learning to love and accept myself anyway.
- Even though it's hard to accept not being perfect—and I know it's a trap—I'm learning to love and accept myself anyway.
- Even though I'm afraid to let up and to rest—no wonder I'm a workaholic!—I choose to love and accept myself anyway.

Mini Reminder Statements (when tapping the points on head and body):

(−) must prove myself | overcommitted | exhausted | distracted
(+) feeling free | ready to release the block | allowing rest | happy

See how personalized the tapping process is? There is both art and science to the technique. As you identify your brand of self-sabotage and create your setup statements, you can begin to tap on your target behavior. In her Clarity In Action program, EFT master Carol Look cautions that if your fear is stronger than your desire, the fear will win out every time. So tap down the fear until it feels boring, and tap up your aspirational goal until it feels like a no-brainer to make positive changes.

Next, you are invited to tailor a general tapping script to your experience. You may find rather quickly, or over consistent practice, that the tension eases and the intensity ratings recalibrate. One tapping round is usually under two minutes. You can string a few rounds together as you get the hang of it and allow the process to flow. You can include this practice as part of your 3x4 Mindful Minutes tool from Step 1.

Tapping Cliffs Notes

Get Ready

1. Choose the self-sabotage target (thoughts, feelings, actions) and express it in a simple "target for tapping" title.
2. Describe the aspirational state or goal you want instead. (Recall your commitment statement from Step 5.)
3. Be aware of the underlying positive and/or negative solution to your self-sabotage behaviors.

Get Set

4. Give yourself a self-rating of how intense the state of *distress* feels about the target (0 to 10 scale) as well as a self-rating on how intense the state of *vitality* feels about the desired aspiration you want to experience in the future.

Go

5. Perform the (–) sabotage tapping round by repeating your setup statements (up to three) as you tap on the side of your hand. (You may do several rounds to tap down the distress.)
6. Use the various mini reminders on the rest of the tapping points.
7. Perform the (+) aspirational tapping round with an affirmative setup statement as you tap on the side of your hand, or skip this setup and go right to (+) reminders.
8. Use various affirmative mini reminders on the rest of the tapping points.
9. Reassess your (0 to 10) self-rating and notice any shifts.
10. Do a daily practice for several weeks until tapping feels like second nature.

Tapping Away the Sabotage

You now have the components of the setup statement, which includes the "even though" stem plus the acceptance phrase, and the illustration of the acupoints. In the following scripts you're invited to try two rounds. Round 1 invites you to tap on the fear or block. You can use the personalized "even though" statements you just created for yourself, or follow the general script to get the hang of it. Round 2 invites you to tap on the aspirational goal, or you can follow along with the provided script. (See Appendix B for tapping scripts for each of the EVOLVE steps. You can also watch me do a tapping round at www.perfectionistsdilemma.com.)

While this may seem weird at first, I invite you to practice tapping over the next month and notice the experience. Keep in mind, tapping is not a "one and done" skill. Even as I wrote the pages here I had to tap on a few fears, including limiting beliefs around "not knowing enough yet," "what if they hate it," and "it's too late to be successful." The wonderful thing about these energy tools is that they are like daily vitamins. Find the practices that suit you and keep them up. You will find that your perfectionism eases and your energies will feel balanced.

SABOTAGE TAPPING ROUND

Target for Tapping: I must be perfect to be loved.

Side of hand: Repeat the following setup statements, focusing on the negative elements.

- Even though a part of me strives to be perfect all the time, I completely and deeply love and accept myself anyway.
- Even though I'm convinced I need to keep improving, I completely and deeply love and accept myself anyway.
- Even though this belief comes from an old algorithm of "not good enough" that I learned growing up, I completely and deeply love and accept myself anyway.

Mini Reminder Phrases:

- **Eyebrow:** This belief that I'm not good enough.
- **Side of eye:** It's from my childhood/culture.
- **Under eye:** It's exhausting.
- **Under nose:** It's simply not true.
- **Chin:** But a part of me still believes it.
- **Collarbone:** I'm tired of endless striving.
- **Under arm:** A part of me is just afraid I'll get criticized.
- **Top of head:** I'm ready to release this block.

Take a deep breath. What is the emotional charge? You can move on if your distress rating has decreased at all. If not, repeat the tapping round a few times, making adjustments in your wording as needed.

ASPIRATIONAL TAPPING ROUND

Side of hand: Repeat variations of a setup statement that feel authentic, focusing on the positive change elements.

- Even though I'm dealing with some perfectionism, I feel excited about following my vision—and when I make some mistakes along the way, I choose to love and accept myself anyway.
- Even though I'm scared I'll fail and that's what's been blocking me, I know I can make a real difference and I'm ready to release the fear.
- Even though I'm nervous about making a change, I know that's a normal feeling, and I accept where I am in my life right now.

Mini Reminder Phrases:

- **Eyebrow:** I appreciate all my efforts and hard work.
- **Side of eye:** I want a life that is more balanced.
- **Under eye:** I'm excited to be free of compulsive striving.
- **Under nose:** I choose to release the burden of not-good-enough.
- **Chin:** It's an old pattern I don't need.

- **Collarbone:** I've accomplished a lot already.
- **Under arm:** It feels good to be kinder to myself.
- **Top of head:** I'm ready for change.

Take a deep breath and tune in. Check if your vitality rating has shifted or increased. If not, that's OK. You may need to tap down the distress more until it feels neutralized. You can tweak the phrasing, fine-tune your reminder phrase, and continue for a few rounds.

Creating Upward Spirals

As I created more energetic spaciousness in my life, more serenity and serendipity appeared. I began to creep up toward the happy achiever quadrant in the Perfectionism Matrix. In particular, learning about energy modalities inspired me to expand my well-being tool kit. I believe that energy medicine and energy psychology methods—with their deep traditional and cultural roots from the world over—are at an inflection point. I liken this evolution to how mindfulness practices from Eastern wisdom traditions entered into the medical and mental health field forty years ago and are now standard fare. As the evidence-base for EFT and other practices grow, so too will the varied practices spread. Energy master Donna Eden writes, "The return of energy medicine is one of the most significant cultural developments of the day, for the return of energy medicine is a return to personal authority for health care, a return to the legacy of our ancestors in harmonizing with the forces of nature, and a return to practices that are natural, friendly, and familiar to the body, mind, and soul."[13] Doesn't that sound good?

The fact is that people who suffer the negative effects of perfectionism need more remedies at their disposal that go beyond traditional mental health interventions. We tend to overemphasize the mind and tend to thoughts and limiting beliefs, at the expense of the body, heart, and spirit. In fact, if anything, we perfectionists need to lighten up and have some fun.

This brings me to an energy medicine method that can lift the spirits.

When I learned about an energy system called *radiant circuits* as described by Donna Eden, I fell in love with the name.[14] They are like happiness molecules. Radiant circuits, briefly mentioned in the Ignite Joy exercises in Step 3, serve the body as energetic emissaries that jump around as needed to intervene whenever internal disturbances arise. Those disruptions often involve the triple warmer meridian (see chapter 5), the energy pathway that is engaged in survival tactics associated with the fight/flight/freeze response. As Eden describes it, the triple warmer meridian is like a military general who mobilizes the body's energy systems to ward off danger, often taking an all-hands-on-deck approach. Tending toward overprotection and false alarms, triple warmer energy taxes your inner resources and keeps you in the Red Zone. And now you've learned some skills to calm it.

"If triple warmer mobilizes your 'inner militia,'" Eden writes, "the radiant circuits mobilize your 'inner mom.' They support, inspire, strengthen, and cajole all your organs and energy systems to function as a tightly knit family."[15] Referred to as "strange flows" and "wondrous wires" by Chinese healers, radiant circuits intuitively sense where they are needed, and they also instantly respond to your thoughts. Had I known this when my trigeminal neuralgia developed, I could have enlisted radiant circuits energies by visualizing them as helpers to that area of my body. Does this sound too woo to be true? It's not. As you've been learning all along in this book, your mind, including your imagination, mental scripts, and images, can influence your energies. Eden notes, "Your chemistry follows your thoughts and your radiant circuits are the energetic link."[16]

So what does this all mean for the perfectionist? For starters, keep your radiant circuits flowing. How? By getting yourself into the

Green Zone of calm and connection. Support your inner mom and take care of these versatile energies. Since radiant circuits aren't associated with acupuncture points of their own like meridians, you can jump start them in ways other than tapping. And you've already got a running start with many of the Happy Achiever Tools that are inspired by Eden Energy Medicine and other methods. So far these include:

Step 1: The Hook-Up, Zip-Up
Step 2: Compassionate Imagery, Antistress Smoothie
Step 3: Hand on Heart, Self-Compassion Break
Step 4: Secret Self-Hug, Blow Out, Reboot with Crisscrossing
Step 5: Supercharging Your Superpowers, Heart Assisted Therapy

At the end of this chapter, you will have even more to add to your Happy Achiever Tool kit.

Energy of Excellence Reflection #3: Go Out and Play

If there is one single prescription I'd give a perfectionist, it is to *go out and play*. Think about it. Your Plus One and other inner protectors are smaller parts of you that are locked in a survival state. It's exhausting. They need recess time. They need nap time. They need to be silly without a care in the world. They need to sing and dance. They need a hug. And these parts need to know they matter to you. Like any child.

Sometimes referred to as *prescribing positivity* in psychology interventions, engaging in beneficial experiences raises your vibrational frequency, harmonizes your energies, and gets your radiant circuits flowing. Keep in mind, these activities are not about achieving happiness. For example, you may not feel overjoyed or happy while doing a strenuous workout, but you know it is good for you and you feel better for doing it. And unlike procrastination, such as mindlessly scrolling social media, binging on streaming TV, or whatever dawdling activity you might use to avoid your life and the challenges that come with it, being *intentional* about beneficial activities and positive distractions promotes overall well-being. This also requires action.

What are beneficial activities you can consistently engage in to ignite your radiant circuits? See if you can name at least ten activities. Sometimes the activities aren't much fun but you know they are good for you, like eating green veggies, doing squats, balancing your bank account, and clearing out clutter—and yet you feel rejuvenated afterward. Other activities are joyful, like seeing friends, hugging, taking a bubble bath, dancing, singing, or hiking in nature, to name but a few.

Your Inner Evolution from Perfectionism to Excellence

When you shift your energy away from constant striving to being present and openhearted, you begin to release the energetic lock of limiting beliefs, stuck emotions, and burdened inner parts. It requires both *intention* and *attention*. This may be what spirituality psychologist Lisa Miller describes as a shift in perspective from *achievement awareness* to *awakened awareness*—from a self-focused lens to a big picture lens on what life is showing you.[17] Both kinds of awareness are important and call on different inner resources. When you can travel the lanes of Blue and Green Zones with ease, life feels more like being in cruise control and you can enjoy the ride. Miller, who studies what spiritual experiences look like in the brain, delineates a trifecta of awakened brain regions. She refers to them as the "neural docking station of love, unity, and guidance." What a wonderful image when considering that we've been transforming the inner algorithms associated with perfectionism toward the radiant energies of excellence. As you learn to harmonize your energies and connect with your head with your heart, you will discover you are a spark of the universe.

We need your bright light.

Happy Achiever Tools: Spark the Energy of Excellence

You are trying so many new skills! Something may be connecting for you. This final set of tools is intended to keep your energies harmonized. All of these will give you a good jump start on sparking the energy of excellence. (Appendix A summarizes all the tools.)

GET GROUNDED: MAKE SPACE IN YOUR BODY

In the spirit of creating sacred space in your home, you can also create a conduit of energy in your body, from your toes to your crown, from earth to sky. Stretching is a basic physical activity that underlies basic good health, is essential for athletes, and is the foundation of yoga movement. Intuitively, stretching encourages flexibility in mind, body, and spirit. And yet modern work life is largely sedentary with a hyperfocus in workstations or hunched over computers or phones—a sure recipe for poor posture, muscle tension, and achy joints. The side stretch is common to many warm-ups and workouts. A favorite of mine, in part because of the name and in part because I have found it to work, is Donna Eden's exercise Connecting Heaven and Earth.[18] This exercise helps to clear out old energies to make way for new and eases transitions between daily tasks. Done regularly, it can foster alignment in your life. It activates the spleen meridian and ignites the radiant circuit energies, like an upward spiral of good vibes.

Simply stand with your feet about shoulder width apart or wider for more balance. You can also use the support of a wall or do this while sitting in a chair.

1. Rub your hands and shake them out toward the ground, readying yourself for releasing any stuck energies.
2. Begin with hands at rest on top of your thighs as if you are grounding into the earth.
3. As you inhale slow and deep, spread both your arms wide up to the sides and then up over your head until your palms touch.
4. Slowly bring hands down in prayer position to rest at your heart area. Exhale.
5. On the next full inhale, raise your right hand up, stretching the torso, while the left hand pushes down. It's as if you are holding up the sky with your right hand and pushing down the earth with your left. Hold the inhale as long as it feels comfortable and notice the nice stretch along the right side of your body.
6. Exhale. And return your hands to prayer position.
7. Begin to stretch the other side of your torso, inhaling as you reach your left hand overhead and pushing down with your right hand, holding your breath for a moment at the top, and notice the nice stretch along the left side of your body. Gently release back to center prayer position as you slowly exhale.
8. Repeat twice on each side.
9. After the stretches, slowly fold forward at the waist, reaching for your toes or shins with knees slightly bent. Take two deep breathes while hanging in a rag doll position, grabbing opposite elbows, before returning to standing.
10. While rolling up to standing position, you can make figure-eight motions with your arms or roll your hands up over each other, up over your head and to the side, as if you are fluffing up your energies.

Naturally, discontinue if you feel dizzy. Most likely you may feel a stretch along the sides of your body, lower back, and hips. It's wonderful to practice in the mornings to help you feel more energized, motivated, and ready to go about your day, or anytime you feel a need for a reset.

GET ENERGIZED: IN THE FLOW

Healthy energy runs in patterns of infinity circles in your body, criss-crossing in a fluid and graceful manner. Yet it can get trapped in moving in more linear patterns. Often you might not be aware that your energies are scrambled. You might notice you are stressed, tired, or overworked but not make the connection to energy patterns. If energies aren't flowing with ease, it is very hard to find peace of mind and ease in the body, and you may be prone to burnout or illness. Your energies likely aren't flowing in the right direction. This can happen if you get stuck in overthinking or brain fog, experience anxiety or low mood, or notice that your fight/flight/freeze response is overly activated. Or you may be taking on the negative energies from other people (who might be cranky or give off a bad vibe) or find your environment to be stressful, not to mention the pressure cooker living in a culture that glorifies beauty, success, status, and wealth. In other words, your subjective vitality rating is in the pits. If this is the case, your energies may be flowing in right and left parallel lines from head to toe, rather than crossing naturally between the right and left brain hemispheres and your body. This is what Donna Eden calls a "homolateral energy pattern."[19] You might even notice you are klutzy or uncoordinated.

One test to see if you may be in a homolateral energy pattern is to try and march in place and tap your knees with the opposite hands, which is usually a natural motion like when walking or swimming. If this marching motion feels hard or more awkward than might be typical, it is likely that you need to get your energy flowing properly. I find this rigid pattern is common when students are pulling all-nighters, over-studying at computers, missing quality sleep, and chronically worried. You can have an energy medicine practitioner assess you, but you can also do a simple exercise to get the energetic juices flowing properly again.

1. Jump-start your energies with the four thumps exercise from Step 1 and the crisscrossing exercises from Step 4, or the superpower stance from Step 5, or the standing stretch described on page 231. You can also ground first by gently spooning the bottom of your feet with a stainless-steel spoon to reset the north-south magnetic polarities in your body. Simply use the back of a spoon and rub your soles in circles or figure-eights for thirty seconds or so.

2. Begin with a counterintuitive homolateral march in place. Tap your right knee with the right hand, and your left knee with the left hand about twelve times for each leg as you breathe. If this homolateral march feels too hard or unstable, you can also sit or lie down as you do it. The last thing you want to do is strain yourself more. Make it easy.

3. After twelve leg lifts in this awkward pattern, begin a *crossover march* by tapping your opposite hand to each knee, like you might do in aerobics class or a sports warm-up. Do this twelve times for each side. This likely feels more natural to do. (If you are sitting or lying down, simply tap the leg with the opposite hand.)

4. Repeat the counterintuitive march twelve times.

5. Repeat the crossover march twelve times.

6. In a final round, anchor the crossover pattern with a final twelve repetitions.

Do this daily a few times over a few weeks. You can add your favorite upbeat music to make it more fun. Eventually your energies will begin to feel more balanced and coordinated.

Since I spend so much time talking with clients and students about difficult life issues, my energies can easily get homolateral. It doesn't help that I can be sedentary from sitting or feel rushed with writing up clinical notes. A few minutes of marching between client sessions, topped off with an energetic hook-up (one of the Happy Achiever Tools in Step 1), really helps.

GET CONNECTED: LOVING-KINDNESS MEDITATION

There's something magical that happens when you intentionally pair your energy with elevated emotions associated with caring, gratitude, kindness, and love. Your inner mom ignites radiant circuits. One beautiful practice is a loving-kindness or metta meditation (LKM), derived from Eastern wisdom traditions. Translated from the Pali word *metta*, which means friend or friendliness, loving-kindness meditation cultivates compassion from the inside out. It is like a blessing or prayer.

Doing a LKM practice daily for as little as seven weeks also has been shown in research studies to promote well-being, reduce self-criticism, and enhance structural changes in the brain networks associated with greater integration of perspective, emotional regulation, and social affiliation.[20] Below is a simplified variation of a loving-kindness meditation in three rounds. Give yourself five to ten minutes. (You can also listen to my guided loving-kindness meditation at www.perfectionistsdilemma.com.)

1. Wherever you are, find a posture of dignity and strength, with a sense of a strong back and open heart.

2. Draw your attention to where your breathing is the easiest to access. Perhaps through your nostrils, or in the rise and fall of your chest or belly. Notice the natural cadence of your breathing and embodied sensations. Or rather than focusing on the breath, notice your body sitting or your feet supported by the earth. Allow stillness to settle in for a minute or two.

3. Bring to mind an image of someone you care about, someone who brings you joy just thinking about them—a child, pet, or kind spiritual being.

4. Allow feelings of comfort and ease to arise. Notice an inner smile of appreciation. Imagine a safety net of love surrounding both you and this caring being.

5. Repeat the following phrases twice, directing friendly wishes toward this being:

Postscript

Good, you are awake. Your eyes blink like stars.

— Kyle Potvin

When I imagine sitting around a campfire with Asher, Chloe, Justin, Kayla, Luis, Mariah, and Reed, I feel a deep sense of kinship. I hope you feel that sense of connection too. They are you and you are them. The deep and innocent need for love and belonging is part of the human condition. For some of us, it manifests as perfectionism, and as we well know, this is not one singular experience.

Perhaps you too can now visualize your parts gathered around an inner campfire. Or maybe you see something more like Ted Lasso and his AFC Richmond players huddled around a barrel of flames on the sports field. Or some other image of inclusion that holds space for your Plus One and the other inner critics and protectors you are getting to know—just as your friends in this book have identified their companions: Cold Feet, FOMO, Grumpire, Leech, Inner Monica, Tiny Terror, and Twisted Sister, among others.

I hope you are discovering that when your unique energy patterns are in balance, your mind, body, heart, and spirit are aligned for success. The sparks of energy crackle in your life as you choose to live consciously, install new algorithms, and create soul habits for life with the EVOLVE method. You are becoming a happy achiever by embracing excellence as a process, not an end result—with greater ease, kindness, and joy. Of course, the EVOLVE steps serve as guideposts to help you on your journey in overcoming the negative effects of perfectionism. The more you engage with the practices, the greater the likelihood of living in alignment with your values and purpose. I am here with you and offer you the following blessing.

> ### PERFECTIONIST'S BLESSING
> May you *embody the present moment* as you meet life's challenges.
>
> May you remember to *validate your experiences* with patience and understanding.
>
> May you *open your heart* to all the imperfect parts of you that need tending and healing.
>
> May you *love your inner critic* so you can transform anxiety and fear into self-acceptance and self-compassion.
>
> May you *make a vow* to yourself and commit to radical self-care as you strive to create a meaningful life.
>
> May you *spark the energy of excellence* by aligning your mind, body, heart, and spirit.
>
> May you evolve into *a happy achiever* as you recognize that you already contain all the inner resources you'll ever need to thrive.

Perhaps you discovered some hidden resources along the way too, as you read though this book. While you have many inner gems and are wired to cultivate many rich resources throughout your life, three assets that weave through the EVOLVE method are your inner worth, your inner humanity, and your inner leadership. I mentioned these in the introduction, but now that you've come this far, you're ready to revisit them.

Inner worth, or a basic sense of being OK, helps you treat yourself with respect, care, and safety. While your inner critics are busy managing the show of your life, under all that activity in the pursuit of perfection lies the essence of your basic goodness. Even if it feels buried or nascent, your worthiness for love and belonging is a birthright. And you've been tending to this strength all along in this book by opening up to your vulnerability and fears.

When I began my own energy work some very surprising things showed up. With the guidance of my energy practitioner, Judith, who uses a kinesiology muscle testing technique, I discovered I was seduced by a common limiting belief. She called it the Wizard of Oz overtangle, based on the classic story by L. Frank Baum, *The Wonderful Wizard of Oz*. Essentially, my life was akin to traveling down the yellow brick road searching for something I thought I was missing. Just like the character Dorothy and her friends, I had always been looking for some secret sauce—more knowledge, expertise, uniqueness—*outside* of myself and never felt I was getting anywhere. My pursuit of a perfect life was an unending treasure hunt for gold—or put differently, success and fame. And it was all an illusion.

One of the most challenging questions Judith posed was "What do you actually want?" I was mute. I could not articulate what I wanted for myself and immediately a part of me felt ashamed. She kept peppering me with the same question, and I was stone-faced. My voice was blocked. Why?

As we gradually uncovered in that session, I was holding on to secrets from the past, which included irrevocable loss, heartbreak, and grief in my family of origin. But I was also blocking out the truth of the present moment: I have the essential ingredients to be successful and happy. And there is no magic out there. The lessons were twofold. First, it's OK to be sad and grieve the losses that I could not help. Second, I was exactly where I needed to be to discover my true self.

I was stirred up, to say the least. Judith then guided me through a simple visualization in which I released the old beliefs and emotional burdens I'd been carrying. That energy session illuminated something I didn't have access to before, not even in all the phases of my own therapies or mental health training. In the days that followed, I focused on self-care with tapping and tended to the parts of me that now had permission to speak. The shifts that came afterward were big—including publishing this book. Through this process, I came to understand inner worth as a hidden gem waiting to be uncovered, and I hope that you have too. And that you've started to feel some of the shifts that come from recovering this particular gem.

Inner humanity, or a wellspring of self-compassion, is a powerful antidote to shame. It helps you forge meaningful relationships—with yourself and others.

If I hadn't cultivated the practice of mindfulness and self-compassion over the years, I would have left the session with Judith with an attitude of skepticism and sarcasm. I felt intense shame when I couldn't answer the simple question of what I wanted to do with my life at my age. My perfectionism, and the shame I was hiding, felt like the armor that Brené Brown describes, "Perfectionism is a twenty-ton shield that we lug around thinking it will protect us when, in fact, it's the thing that's really preventing us from taking flight."[1] It is one of the first quotes I use in my Overcome Perfectionism workshops. Perfectionism, to me, is gold-plated armor.

The last thing a perfectionist will allow is vulnerability. Somewhere on my particular yellow brick road, I paused to do the inner work, especially learning mindful self-compassion and tending to my motley crew of parts. As mentioned earlier, parts work is what many Internal Family System therapists refer to as spiritual re-parenting, which is tending to the needs, feelings, and experiences that went unmet or unacknowledged in childhood, were diminished by trauma, or infected by cultural pressures to conform. This work is truly about befriending yourself.

In particular, I acknowledged common humanity—knowing I was not alone with my struggles. I also practiced being kinder in general, which was the inspiration for my first book, The Kindness Cure. Because kindness toward oneself is so challenging for perfectionists, I hope the Happy Achiever practices will melt your armor and let your humanity shine forth.

Inner leadership, or a resilient and courageous orientation to life, empowers you to advocate for yourself, find strength in failure, connect with a sense of purpose, and experience joyful effort in your life pursuits. By trusting in your worth and humanity, you also begin to trust in yourself, see your endeavors as truly valuable no matter the external outcome, and lead your life from the inside out.

When you cultivate inner leadership you also grow outer leadership. There is some compelling research to support that the most impactful qualities of a leader are the "soft" skills: self-awareness, mindfulness and compassion.[2] Not exactly what most people might think. When we are exclusively achievement-focused, the gaze of our attention is toward the future. We risk missing out on the life lessons, delights, and small wins that often happen without even trying. A kind of spiritual awakening unfolds.

I've come to believe that all energy seeks harmony within oneself, between living things, and with some source or intelligence greater than ourselves. Just looking up at a clear night sky gives me a comforting sense of belonging. When we recognize that energy, or life force, is ever present, it becomes possible that our obstacles, and barriers, and struggles can be healed or transformed. This doesn't mean problems are magically solved and there is no pain. But suffering evolves into compassion.

In his slim volume *A Lamp in the Darkness*, psychologist Jack Kornfield writes, "When we realize that things are fundamentally uncertain, we come to trust in the unfolding of our individual lives with the vastness of all time and space."[3] If you start with the premise that everything changes, and you have at your disposal your own inner resources to handle the changes, you begin to trust your inner leadership. Your light will shine.

When I reflect on a turning point in my journey to overcome the negative effects of perfectionism, it was the energy work, perhaps more than anything, that helped me release the unconscious algorithms and illusions. Sometimes I see Judith like Glinda the Good Witch. She didn't give me some magical elixir, she just illuminated what was already there. My old beliefs that I was not expert enough or that I was missing some essential ingredient—and led me down the never-ending path of being a student and a seeker—evaporated. The spell was broken.

Whenever Judith ends a healing session, she exclaims "Poof!" This makes me laugh and reinforces the absurdity of my old beliefs. My little parts appreciate the playfulness too. Now if I find myself on some yellow brick road, it's much easier to stop and click my heels knowing I'm exactly where I need to be.

And you are too.

APPENDIX A

The EVOLVE Steps: Tracking Your Inner Evolution

Use the following pages to support your efforts in being safely challenged in overcoming the negative effects of perfectionism and tending to your inner critics with compassion. You can create your own recipe from the tool tracker for cultivating the energies of excellence. You can also download the EVOLVE tracker PDF at www.perfectionistsdilemma.com.

Reflections

1. Take the Perfectionist Self-Inquiry (page 31): List the algorithms and/or self-talk you resonate with or create your own.
2. Locate yourself on the Perfectionism Matrix (page 47).
3. Name your Plus One and other inner protectors.
4. What do the Red, Blue and Green Zones look like for you? How do you feel, think, and act in each one?
   a. My Red Zone is when I . . .
   b. My Blue Zone is when I . . .
   c. My Green Zone is when I . . .
5. Who are your supports as you practice these tools?

Happy Achiever Tool Tracker

Use the following table to track any reflections and Happy Achiever Tools you try. When you try a skill, keep at it for a few days to a week, and write down what you notice. See if your vitality rating changes from before and after you try.

Step 1: E, Embody the Present Moment	Not for Me	Ready to Try
Types of Mindful Meditation Practices (pick one)	_____	_____
Reflection #1: What's Your Brand of Stress?	_____	_____
Reflection #2: Making New Guesses	_____	_____
Get Grounded: 3x4 Mindful Minutes	_____	_____
Get Energized: A Quick Reset	_____	_____
Get Connected: Code Switch	_____	_____

Step 2: V, Validate Your Experience	Not for Me	Ready to Try
Reflection #1: Attention Grabbers	_____	_____
Cultivating Kindsight	_____	_____
Reflection #2: No Wonder!	_____	_____
Reflection #3: Being in the Driver's Seat	_____	_____
Get Grounded: RAIN Technique	_____	_____
Get Energized: Antistress Smoothie	_____	_____
Get Connected: Imagine a Kind Being	_____	_____

Step 3: O, Open Your Heart	Not for Me	Ready to Try
Reflection #1: Self-Compassion Break	_____	_____
Reflection #2: Have a Puppy Mind	_____	_____
Reflection #3: Giving Voice to Self-Compassion	_____	_____
Get Grounded: A Compassionate Voice	_____	_____
Get Energized: Ignite Joy	_____	_____
Get Connected: Heart Energy	_____	_____

Before, Vitality Rating (0–10)	What I Noticed	After, Vitality Rating (0–10)
_____	_____	_____
_____	_____	_____
_____	_____	_____
_____	_____	_____
_____	_____	_____

Before, Vitality Rating (0–10)	What I Noticed	After, Vitality Rating (0–10)
_____	_____	_____
_____	_____	_____
_____	_____	_____
_____	_____	_____
_____	_____	_____

Before, Vitality Rating (0–10)	What I Noticed	After, Vitality Rating (0–10)
_____	_____	_____
_____	_____	_____
_____	_____	_____
_____	_____	_____
_____	_____	_____

L, Love Your Inner Critic	*Not for Me*	*Ready to Try*
Reflection #1: Dabble with Mind Mapping	____	____
Reflection #2: Deflecting the Arrows of Self-Sabotage	____	____
Reflection #3: Don Your Spiritual Space Suit	____	____
Get Grounded: A Secret Self-Hug	____	____
Get Energized: Blow Off Steam	____	____
Get Connected: Reboot with Crisscrossing Energies	____	____

V, Make a Vow	*Not for Me*	*Ready to Try*
Reflection #1: Reverse Engineering a Limiting Belief	____	____
Reflection #2: Small Wins	____	____
Reflection #3: Prescribe Positive Action	____	____
Get Grounded: Hug Your Brain	____	____
Get Energized: Supercharging Your Superpowers	____	____
Get Connected: A Heart of Gold	____	____

E, Spark the Energy of Excellence	*Not for Me*	*Ready to Try*
Reflection #1: Create Sacred Space	____	____
Emotional Acupuncture (Tapping Away the Sabotage)	____	____
Reflection #2: Finding Your Acceptance Statement	____	____
Creating Upward Spirals	____	____
Reflection #3: Go Out and Play	____	____
Get Grounded: Make Space in Your Body	____	____
Get Energized: In the Flow	____	____
Get Connected: Loving-Kindness Meditation	____	____

Before, Vitality Rating (0–10)	What I Noticed	After, Vitality Rating (0–10)
_____	_____	_____
_____	_____	_____
_____	_____	_____
_____	_____	_____
_____	_____	_____

Before, Vitality Rating (0–10)	What I Noticed	After, Vitality Rating (0–10)
_____	_____	_____
_____	_____	_____
_____	_____	_____
_____	_____	_____

Before, Vitality Rating (0–10)	What I Noticed	After, Vitality Rating (0–10)
_____	_____	_____
_____	_____	_____
_____	_____	_____
_____	_____	_____
_____	_____	_____
_____	_____	_____

APPENDIX B

EVOLVE Tapping Scripts

When you begin a self-guided practice of tapping, there are a few things to keep in mind:

- **Stick with it.** Don't give up too early if you don't see immediate results.
- **Track your intensity ratings before and after your rounds in a notebook or journal.** Practice makes progress.
- **Focus on tapping on the distress target before tapping on the positive target or outcome you desire.** In other words, don't ignore the stickiness of negation emotions, thoughts, or experiences that keep your fight/flight/freeze responses engaged (Red Zone). These can take time to tend and mend. Tapping sends a calming signal to your brain that it's safe to address your distress (notice, name, nurture). You may even experience an emotional release (like crying or another physiological experience). Once a troublesome target is neutralized (in one session or over many), then direct your attention to building up the positives you want to focus on.
- **Be aware of psychoenergetic reversals and be mindful of your Plus One or inner protectors.** Psychoenergetic reversals are why keeping a symptom might serve a hidden purpose or secondary gain (avoidance or attention), and your Plus One or any inner

protectors might put up a fight or resistance. Be curious and encouraging toward yourself and those parts.

- **Avoid switching your target too often.** Focus on one area of concern first, and don't move too quickly to another concern. Tapping is about being specific to your concern, so tailor a tapping round to your experience!

- **Take advantage of videos, scripts, and apps online.** Some practitioners have different variations for the tapping order (such as starting or ending on the top of the head, or skipping it altogether) or may add in other preparation steps such as using an energy balancing technique. Don't worry. As long as you hit all the main meridian points of the basic tapping protocol, you are doing just fine. You can also adjust the tapping reminders phrases as needed to be as authentic and true to your lived experience. No need to do this perfectly! The Tapping Solution App and TheTappingSolutionChannel on YouTube are both great places to start.

- **Notice any memories or "aha" moments.** These might reveal important nuances about the symptom or habit you are addressing, which may become another tappable target.

- **Always feel empowered to ask for help.** If you struggle with mental health concerns, trauma, or chronic conditions, you may like to find a qualified tapping coach or practitioner to help you.

The following are generic scripts related to the main themes covered in the EVOLVE steps. You can modify as needed and customize your mini reminder phrases. Remember to settle on a setup statement for a script that contains the problem statement as well an acceptance statement that feels true to you, which you will repeat three times while tapping on the side of your hand.

Even though I am/have/believe/feel _____
[*your target concern*]

+

_____ [*your acceptance statement of choice*].

See Step 6 to review options and the illustrations of points (page 210).

E: Embody the Present Moment Tapping Script

This step helps you increase your body awareness, get out of your head, and listen to the wisdom your body is trying to share with you. Understanding how the nervous system works and your brand of stress reactions is key. Tapping is a great way to soothe the stress response.

Target for Tapping: Giving a presentation/being exposed
Give yourself an intensity rating 0–10.

- **Side of hand (x3):** Even though I am so nervous about my presentation—what if I bomb?—I choose to completely love and accept myself anyway.

Mini Reminder Phrases:
- **Eyebrow:** So nervous.
- **Side of eye:** Feeling nauseous thinking about it.
- **Under eye:** What if I bomb?
- **Under nose:** So nervous.
- **Chin:** Of course, I'm nervous.
- **Collarbone:** I really want to do well.
- **Under arm:** Just a case of the nerves.
- **Top of head:** What if I don't get so nervous this time? That's possible too.

Repeat the above. Or if intensity rating becomes very low or zero, move on to a positive round.

Mini Reminder Phrases:
- **Eyebrow:** I know my stuff.
- **Side of eye:** The slides are the easy part.
- **Under eye:** I can breathe through it.

- **Under nose:** I can remind myself that I'm a messenger.
- **Chin:** It's less about me.
- **Collarbone:** It's more about what I have to offer.
- **Under arm:** People are rooting for me.
- **Top of head:** It's totally possible everything will be alright!

Take a deep breath. Place hands on heart. Notice if your intensity rating has changed. Repeat the rounds, altering phrases and words as needed.

V: Validate Your Experiences Tapping Script

This step helps you name your experiences and bring them into your awareness. As you recognize thoughts, emotions, and sensations as normal responses to stress and where they come from (e.g., internalization of judgment, past failures or setbacks, family, societal or systemic factors), you begin to free yourself from harsh algorithms and accept your past and present self with understanding.

Target for Tapping: Imposter feelings about doing something new or challenging
Give yourself an intensity rating 0–10.

- **Side of hand (x3):** Even though I'm afraid others will judge me for not being good enough, I know I'm doing the best that I can.

Mini Reminder Phrases:
- **Eyebrow:** Feeling freaked out.
- **Side of eye:** Not sure I fit in.
- **Under eye:** It's so uncomfortable.
- **Under nose:** I've been criticized in the past.
- **Chin:** And I know where my fear stems from.
- **Collarbone:** But I deserve to be here.

- **Under arm:** I've done many hard things before.
- **Top of head:** It's OK to be new at something.

Repeat the above. Or if intensity rating becomes very low or zero, move on to a positive round.

Mini Reminder Phrases:
- **Eyebrow:** I forget that it's OK to be a beginner sometimes.
- **Side of eye:** I can have a beginner's mind.
- **Under eye:** I can be curious.
- **Under nose:** I can trust myself.
- **Chin:** I can be awkward.
- **Collarbone:** It's OK not to know everything at the get-go.
- **Under the arm:** I'm actually a quick learner.
- **Top of head:** I'm just at the beginning of a new adventure.

Take a deep breath. Place hands on heart. Notice if your intensity rating has changed. Repeat the rounds, altering phrases and words as needed.

O: Open Your Heart Tapping Script

This step helps you be kinder toward yourself. When you begin to befriend the negative voices in your head, you begin a deep process of self-compassion and cultivate heart coherence, the ultimate antidote to shame and unhelpful survival strategies.

Target for Tapping: Beating myself up all the time and feeling ashamed of my imperfections
Give yourself an intensity rating 0–10.

- **Side of hand x3:** Even though I have this habit of beating myself up—and I know it's a part of me that feels scared—I am learning to love and accept myself.

Mini Reminder Phrases:

- **Eyebrow:** A part of me is scared.
- **Side of eye:** It tells me I should be better, do better, feel better.
- **Under eye:** "Who do you think you are?"
- **Under nose:** "What makes you so special?"
- **Chin:** "Don't count on anyone to help you."
- **Collarbone:** Feeling unworthy.
- **Under the arm:** That part of me hides my shame.
- **Top of head:** It's been around for a long time.

Repeat the above. Or if intensity rating becomes very low or zero, move on to a positive round.

Mini Reminder Phrases:

- **Eyebrow:** I'm learning to love that part.
- **Side of eye:** To care for it.
- **Under eye:** It's been hurt.
- **Under nose:** I can care for it now.
- **Chin:** I can honor its resilience.
- **Collarbone:** I take care of this part of me.
- **Under the arm:** I'm ready to heal this part.
- **Top of head:** It feels good to care for myself in new ways.

Take a deep breath. Place hands on heart. Notice if your intensity rating has changed. Repeat the rounds, altering phrases and words as needed.

L: Love Your Inner Critic Tapping Script

This step helps you to heal. Because self-love often—and sadly—feels so foreign to so many of us, resistance to self-compassion will undoubtedly arise. As you continually practice courage, compassion, and connection, you will find that tapping can help with the backlash you may encounter along the way (from your parts or from others in your life as you begin to change).

Target for Tapping: My critical Plus One (or other part) that gets in my way by keeping me small
Give yourself an intensity rating 0–10.

- **Side of hand x 3:** Even though I have this critical voice in my head about achieving my dreams, and I know it's trying to protect me from failure, I completely and deeply accept myself.

Mini Reminder Phrases:
- **Eyebrow:** My Plus One is always on guard.
- **Side of eye:** "Keep pushing!"
- **Under eye:** "Don't let up."
- **Under nose:** "If you slow down you can't catch up."
- **Chin:** I'm exhausted.
- **Collarbone:** I can't do another thing.
- **Under the arm:** But if I rest, I may fall behind.
- **Top of head:** It's so hard to be kind to myself.

Repeat the above. Or if intensity rating becomes very low or zero, move on to a positive round.

Mini Reminder Phrases:
- **Eyebrow:** This critical voice.
- **Side of eye:** I know where it comes from.
- **Under eye:** I'm ready to release the need to be perfect.
- **Under nose:** My Plus One is just afraid to rest.
- **Chin:** I don't have to give up my value for excellence.
- **Collarbone:** Yet, I can release the strain and stress.
- **Under the arm:** I am ready for my Plus One to trust me.
- **Top of head**: I'm doing my best and it's OK to rest.

Take a deep breath. Place hands on heart. Notice if your intensity rating has changed. Repeat the rounds, altering phrases and words as needed.

V: Make a Vow Tapping Script

This step helps you cultivate a new habit of self-care. By committing to change and putting in joyful effort, you will learn to identify values, clarify your purpose, and discover new possibilities for yourself. Creating a ritual helps create new cues for self-care. Writing a vow helps to take consistent action for sustainable change.

Target for Tapping: Committing to self-care
Give yourself an intensity rating 0–10.

- **Side of hand x3:** Even though I judge myself whenever I want to be kind to my mind and body, I choose to appreciate making positive changes.

Mini Reminder Phrases:
- **Eyebrow:** I can be so hard on myself.
- **Side of eye:** If I can't do something perfectly, why bother trying?
- **Under eye:** That is an old algorithm.
- **Under nose:** I can get trapped by my harsh inner voice.
- **Chin:** "You don't have what it takes."
- **Collarbone:** "You never stick with self-care."
- **Under the arm:** "You give up too easily."
- **Top of head:** I can be *so* hard on myself.

Repeat the above. Or if intensity rating becomes very low or zero, move on to a positive round.

Mini Reminder Phrases:
- **Eyebrow:** Being hard on myself is what helped me achieve.
- **Side of eye:** It's hard to let up on that habit.
- **Under eye:** I want to lighten up.
- **Under nose:** I can be kinder to myself.
- **Chin:** I honor my mind and body.
- **Collarbone:** I don't have to be perfect to befriend myself.
- **Under the arm:** I can start small.
- **Top of head:** I'm proud of myself for prioritizing self-care.

Take a deep breath. Place hands on heart. Notice if your intensity rating has changed. Repeat the rounds, altering phrases and words as needed.

E: Energy of Excellence Tapping Script

Through daily practice of self-care and kindsight you will become fluent in directing your attention to the sweet spot of belonging and energy flow. The negative effects of perfectionism will readily dissolve when you begin to recognize the pattern, and the happy achiever in you will thrive.

Target for Tapping: Doubts about being happy or ever being fulfilled
Give yourself an intensity rating 0–10.

- **Side of hand x3:** Even though being successful is important to me, it's also very stressful; I accept who I am and how I feel.

Mini Reminder Phrases:
- **Eyebrow:** I'll tell myself I don't have what it takes.
- **Side of eye:** That there's something missing.
- **Under eye:** But I'm learning to trust myself more.
- **Under nose:** I allow all my parts to be heard and witnessed.

- **Chin:** I welcome all the feelings I have about success and failure.
- **Collarbone:** I hold all these thoughts and feelings with compassion and courage.
- **Under the arm:** I'm learning to feel confident in who I am, not just in what I accomplish.
- **Top of head:** I have all the resources inside me to create a meaningful life.

Repeat the above. Or if intensity rating becomes very low or zero, move on to a positive round.

Mini Reminder Phrases:
- **Eyebrow:** I know that self-criticism doesn't work.
- **Side of eye:** That's just a younger part who needed understanding and encouragement.
- **Under eye:** I can do that for myself now.
- **Under nose:** I choose to give myself permission to make mistakes.
- **Chin:** Not skip over the little wins and everyday delights.
- **Collarbone:** I trust that I will figure things out and be kind to myself along the way.
- **Under the arm:** I'm excited to step into a future of happy achieving.
- **Top of head:** I already feel the sweet spot between effort and ease.

Take a deep breath. Place hands on heart. Notice if your intensity rating has changed. Repeat the rounds, altering phrases and words as needed.

APPENDIX C

Resources

You can find free resources on my website for various Happy Achiever practices at www.perfectionistsdilemma.com. Below are relevant resources that informed this book and may offer further insights on research, training, and education on various topics.

Energy Medicine and Psychology

Association for Comprehensive Energy Psychology (US)
https://www.EnergyPsych.org
Eden Method (Donna Eden)
https://edenmethod.com/
Daily Energy Routine (Donna Eden)
https://edenmethod.com/daily-energy-routine/
EFT Universe (Dawson Church, PhD)
https://efttraining.org/
EFT HQ (AUS) (Peta Stapleton, PhD)
https://www.evidencebasedeft.com/
EFT International
https://eftinternational.org/
Healing From the Body Level Up (Judith Swack, PhD)
https://www.hblu.org/
The Tapping Solution
https://www.thetappingsolution.com/

Internal Family Systems

IFS Institute
https://ifs-institute.com/

Mindfulness

American Mindfulness Research Association
https://goamra.org/
Cambridge Health Alliance Center for Mindfulness and Compassion
https://www.chacmc.org/
Mindful Institute for Emerging Adults
https://mindfulnessinstituteforemergingadults.com/

Perfectionism

The Perfectionism & Psychotherapy Lab (Paul Hewitt, PhD)
https://hewittlab.psych.ubc.ca/

Self-Compassion

Center for Mindful Self-Compassion
http://www.CenterforMSC.org
Compassionate Mind Foundation (UK; Paul Gilbert, PhD)
https://www.compassionatemind.co.uk/
Self-Compassion with Dr. Kristin Neff
https://self-compassion.org/

Science and Mind/Body Medicine

Emotion and Self-Control Lab, University of Michigan,
(Ethan Kross, PhD)
https://selfcontrol.psych.lsa.umich.edu/research/
Harvard Intergroup Neuroscience Lab (Mina Cikara, PhD)
https://www.intergroupneurosciencelaboratory.com/
Interdisciplinary Affective Science Laboratory

(Lisa Feldman Barrett, PhD)
https://www.affective-science.org/
National Center of Complementary and Integrative Health
https://www.nccih.nih.gov/
Polyvagal Institute (Stephen Porges, PhD)
https://www.polyvagalinstitute.org/
Spirituality Mind Body Institute
https://spiritualitymindbody.tc.columbia.edu/

GRATITUDE

Love is patient, love is kind.

— *1 Corinthians 13:4*

The seeds for this book were planted many years ago in the messy garden of my life. My life is still blessedly unruly, and tending to it requires patience and compassion. I'd like to think I've got the hang of it by now, but many things prove to be unpredictable. Perfectionism, to me, is like a rose in the garden. Sophisticated. Intoxicating. Charming. Beautiful to ponder yet prickly to touch. Roses can climb or ramble. They require maintenance, a trellis or structure, good soil and sunlight, and judicious pruning. Roses symbolize beauty, love, passion, promise, purity, friendship, hope, joy, achievement, and every conceivable human emotion. The variety is impressive and the caretaking challenging.

We teach best what we most need to learn. I see my work with perfectionists as a continual practice of being both teacher and student. And as the universe seems to have designed my life, I attract other perfectionists quite easily. The people who seek me out, attend my workshops, and identify with perfectionism begin what will become a lifelong habit of tending and befriending. It's like community gardening for high achievers. This book is dedicated to the vulnerability and courage of my client and students.

Naturally, I could never do this tending without the many gardeners in my own life who hand me the gloves, trowel, rake, hose, barrel, and bug spray. I am blessed with a devoted family: my husband, Steve, and daughters, Sophie and Josie, who make me laugh and cry, nourish me, and honor my imperfections. (Josie and Steve created the illustrations.) My mother, *Omi* to her five grandchildren, is my first teacher of compassion. *Meine Mutter ist die Stimme des Mitgefühls. Danke von ganzem Herzen.* My steadfast and dear friends Bornali Basu, Kristen Darcy, Christine Gardiner, Jennifer Granquist, Elaine McNamara, and Kate Sweetman although far away remain close in in spirit.

Writing never came easy to me, with a tough and a tenacious Plus One at my side. But once I discovered that it was OK to be a beginner, teachers began to appear. Many thanks to the Gateless Writing Method, developed by Suzanne Kingsbury, and Gateless teachers Terri Trespicio and Becky Karush. During the pandemic, their writing salons offered a refuge, soothing my inner critics and allowing many of the anecdotes in this book to burst forth. It was through a writing salon that I met Kate Hanley, a writer and editor extraordinaire who helped me "evolve" my method and develop this book. And as the roses ramble, many thanks to psychologists Chris Willard and Beth Kurland who led me to literary agent Dani Segelbaum of Arc Literary Management. She championed *The Perfectionist's Dilemma* manuscript that led me to Laura Apperson, my editor at Alcove Press. It's been a joy to work with Laura and her team, especially Thasheemariei Fantauzzi Perez, who diligently and kindly copyedited various drafts.

The first iteration of "Overcome Perfectionism Through Self-Compassion" was an audio course on the Insight Timer meditation app, now with over 12,000 students, that launched my quest to help others heal from perfectionism. The Insight Timer platform is a gift to the world, truly. After I arrived at Harvard University's Counseling and Mental Health Service in 2019, I began to offer in-person workshops on perfectionism, with the blessing of the senior director, Barbara Lewis, MD. We weathered the COVID pandemic with live online workshops and the seeds were planted for an offshoot, *Befriending the Inner Critic.* This series was specifically designed for graduate students, whose challenges and needs are unique to this period in academic life and emergent career choices. Feedback from online listeners and university students helped shape the curricula, and I am forever indebted to them. The robust body of perfectionism research spearheaded by Paul Hewitt and Gordon Flett decades ago, and contemporary perspectives by researchers Thomas Curran and Patrick Gaudreau among others, gives gravitas to the pervasive and multifaceted experience of perfectionism—and that there is no one-size-fits-all approach to healing from its negative effects.

My blend of practices in overcoming perfectionism stem from an alchemy of rich sources. This includes the trainings offered by Center for Mindful Self-Compassion, cofounded by psychologists Christopher Germer and Kristin Neff, in particular Mindful Self-Compassion for Teens created by Karen Bluth and Lorraine Hobbs, and the Self-Compassion in Psychotherapy (SCIP) program. The SCIP "Turquoise" international peer group continues to meet monthly, in part because we "vow" to reassess and renew commitment to the practice and teaching of self-compassion. Blessings to Ceara Clark, Christian Gerber, Katherine Moss, Lori Pine, Naomi Tucker, and Sharon Smart. I have immense gratitude for the work of Holly Rogers, founder of the Mindfulness Institute for Emerging Adults (formerly known as Koru Mindfulness) and author of *The Mindful Twenty-Something*. I occasionally teach MIEA's Mindfulness for Beginners course via the Center for Wellness and Health Promotion at Harvard University Health Services, a wonderful primer for mindfulness practices.

The foundation for my own practice and teaching of mindfulness and compassion is firmly rooted in the two-year program developed by Jack Kornfield and Tara Brach, the Mindfulness Meditation Teacher Certification program (Sounds True). Closer to home, the Center for Mindfulness and Compassion at Cambridge Health Alliance, Cambridge, Massachusetts, serves as a beacon of excellence for research and application of contemplative practices into health care and underserved communities. Thank you to Zev Shuman-Olivier, Susan Pollak, and Paula Gardiner, among others, for their dedication. Over ten years ago I embarked on the professional training The Daring Way™, based on the research and writing of Brené Brown, whose teachings on imperfection, shame, vulnerability, and courage continue to resonate for me and my students. The teachings of Rick Hanson, Deb Dana, and Paul Gilbert—particularly on the tricky brain, the ANS, and the mind-body connection—are foundational in my work as a therapist.

I finally came around, during the strange pandemic reprieve, to get formal training in Internal Family Systems (IFS), the beautiful method developed by psychologist Richard Schwartz. After working to heal inner critics, my own and others, for decades, learning the IFS model was like coming home. Everything I learned until then fell into place. Perhaps I waited too long—or the timing was just right. I'm particularly grateful to therapist Carolyn Sass, an IFS program assistant in my Level 1 training, who reviewed my chapter on "Love Your Inner Critic."

What can I say of my covey of healers and good witches? I bow to Judith Swack (Healing from the Body Level Up™), Julie Fowler, (Simple Energy), and the late EFT master Ingrid Dinter, who first introduced me to tapping; to the Association for Comprehensive Energy Psychology for leading me to Carol Look, Lynn Mary Karjola, and EFT trainings, and for providing access to the evidence-based studies, standards, and ethics in practicing a relatively new field of mind-body methods; and to Donna Eden and David Feinstein, founders of Eden Energy Medicine, for opening a whole new world of effective practices for accessing the wisdom of the body and energy; and to Jennie Mulqueen, MDiv, and the Women Song community, who raise my vibes and radiant circuit energies at every gathering at the Ames Chapel in Hingham, Massachusetts.

BIBLIOGRAPHY

Barrett, Lisa Feldman. *How Emotions are Made: The Secret Life of the Brain.* New York: Harper, 2017.

Barrett, Lisa Feldman. *Seven and a Half Lessons About the Brain.* New York: Mariner Books, 2021.

Brach, Tara. *Radical Acceptance: Embracing Your Life with the Heart of a Buddha.* New York: Bantam Books, 2004.

Brach, Tara. *Radical Compassion: Learning to Love Yourself and Your World with the Practice of RAIN.* New York: Viking Life, 2019.

Brown, Brené. *The Gifts of Imperfection: Let Go of Who You Think You're Supposed to Be and Embrace Who You Are.* Center City, MN: Hazelden, 2010.

Bryant, Kobe, and Pau Gasol. *The Mamba Mentality: How I Play.* New York: Farrar, Straus and Giroux, 2018.

Burns, David D. *Feeling Good: The New Mood Therapy.* New York: William Morrow, 1999.

Childre, Doc, Howard Martin, and Deborah Rozman. *Heart Intelligence: Connecting with the Intuitive Guidance of the Heart.* 2nd ed. Cardiff, CA: Waterfront Digital, 2022.

Cousineau, Tara. *The Kindness Cure: How The Science of Compassion Can Heal Your Heart and Your World.* Kind Minds, 2024.

Curran, Thomas. *The Perfectionism Trap: Embracing the Power of Good Enough.* London: Scribner, 2023.

Dana, Deborah. *Polyvagal Exercises for Safety and Connection: 50 Client-Centered Practices.* New York: Norton, 2020.

Dispenza, Joe. *Becoming Supernatural: How Common People Are Doing the Uncommon.* Carlsbad, CA: Hay House, 2017.

Eden, Donna, and David Feinstein. *Energy Medicine: Balancing Your Body's Energies for Optimal Health, Joy and Vitality.* New York: Tarcher Perigee, 2008.

Feinstein, David, and Donna Eden. *Tapping: Self-Healing with the Transformative Power of Energy Psychology.* Boulder, CO: Sounds True, 2024.

Ford, Debbie. *The Dark Side of the Light Chasers: Reclaiming Your Power, Creativity, Brilliance and Dreams.* New York: Riverhead Books, 1998, 2010.

Germer, Christopher. *The Mindful Path to Self-Compassion: Freeing Yourself from Destructive Thoughts and Emotions.* New York: Guilford, 2009.

Germer, Christopher, and Kristin Neff. *Teaching the Mindful Self-Compassion Program: A Guide for Professionals.* New York: Guildford, 2019.

Gilbert, Elizabeth. *Big Magic: Creative Living Beyond Fear.* New York: Riverhead Books, 2015.

Gilbert, Paul. *The Compassionate Mind: A New Approach to Life's Challenges.* Oakland, CA: New Harbinger, 2009.

Hanson, Rick. *Hardwiring Happiness: The New Brain Science of Contentment, Calm, and Confidence.* New York: Harmony, 2013.

Hewitt, Paul, Gordon Flett, and Samuel Mikail. *Perfectionism: A Relational Approach to Assessment, Treatment, and Conceptualization.* New York: Guilford, 2017.

Jha, Amishi P. *Peak Mind: Find Your Focus, Own Your Attention, Invest 12 Minutes a Day.* New York: HarperOne, 2022.

Karjala, Lynn M. *Healing Everyday Traumas: Free Yourself from the Scars of Bullying, Criticism and Other Old Wounds.* Roswell, GA: Psychology Innovations, 2022.

Kolts, Russell L. *CFT Made Simple: A Clinician's Guide to Practicing Compassion-Focused Therapy.* Oakland, CA: New Harbinger, 2016.

Kornfield, Jack. *A Lamp in the Darkness: Illuminating the Path Through Difficult Times.* Boulder, CO: Sounds True, 2014.

Kross, Ethan. *Chatter: The Voice in Our Head, Why It Matters, and How to Harness It.* New York: Crown, 2021.

Levine, Amir, and Rachel Heller. *Attached: The New Science of Adult Attachment and How It Can Help You Find—and Keep—Love.* New York: Tarcher, 2010.

McKeown, Greg. *Effortless: Make It Easier to Do What Matters Most.* New York: Crown Currency, 2021.

Miller, Lisa. *The Awakened Brain: The Psychology of Spirituality.* London: Penguin Random House UK, 2021.

Neff, Kristin. *Fierce Self-Compassion: How Women Can Harness Kindness to Speak Up, Claim Their Power and Thrive.* New York: Harper, 2021.

Neff, Kristin. *Self-Compassion: The Proven Power of Being Kind to Yourself.* New York: William Morrow Harper Collins, 2011.

Porges, Stephen W. *The Polyvagal Theory: Neurophysiological Foundations of Emotions, Attachment, Communication, and Self-Regulation.* Norton Series on Interpersonal Neurobiology. New York: Norton, 2011.

Rosenberg, Marshall. *Nonviolent Communication: A Language of Life. Life-Changing Tools for Healthy Relationships.* 3rd ed. Encinitas, CA: Puddle-Dancer, 2015.

Schwartz, Richard C. *Introduction to Internal Family Systems.* 2nd ed. Boulder, CO: Sounds True, 2023.

Schwartz, Richard C. *No Bad Parts: Healing Trauma and Restoring Wholeness with the Internal Family Systems Model.* Boulder, CO: Sounds True, 2021.

Siegel, Daniel J. *The Developing Mind: How Relationships and the Brain Interact to Shape Who We Are.* 3rd ed. New York: Guilford, 2020.

NOTES

INTRODUCTION

1. Devasmita Chakraverty, "A Cultural Impostor? Native American Experiences of Impostor Phenomenon in STEM," *CBE—Life Sciences Education* 21, no. 1 (2021): article 15, https://doi.org/10.1187/cbe.21-08-0204; B. Methikalam et al., "Asian Values, Personal and Family Perfectionism, and Mental Health Among Asian Indians in the United States," *Asian American Journal of Psychology* 6, no. 3 (2015): 223–232, https://doi.org/10.1037/aap0000023.
2. Thomas Curran, *The Perfectionism Trap: Embracing the Power of Good Enough* (London: Scribner, 2023), 13.
3. Lisa Feldman Barrett, *How Emotions Are Made: The Secret Life of the Brain* (New York: Harper, 2017), 287.

CHAPTER 1

1. Thomas Curran and Andrew P. Hill, "Perfectionism Is Increasing Over Time: A Meta-analysis of Birth Cohort Differences from 1989 to 2016," *Psychological Bulletin* 145, no. 4 (2019): 410–429, https://www.apa.org/pubs/journals/releases/bul-bul0000138.pdf.
2. The majority of published studies on perfectionism were primarily conducted in the United States, the UK, and Canada. Interestingly, the stark increase in socially prescribed perfectionism is correlated with the introduction of smart-phone technology in 2007. See Thomas Curran, *The Perfectionism Trap: Embracing the Power of Good Enough* (London: Scribner, 2023), 136.
3. Carmen Iranzo-Tatay et al., "Genetic and Environmental Contributions to Perfectionism and Its Common Factors," *Psychiatry Research* 230, no. 3 (2015): 932–939.

4. AS TV Online, "Where Did Kobe Bryant's 'Black Mamba' Nickname Originate?" January 26, 2022, https://en.as.com/en/2022/01/26/nba/1643203491_137407.html. According to the online article, "That's when he introduced the idea of an alter ego and 'Black Mamba' was born. Inspired by the code name of an assassin in the cult favorite film, Kill Bill by Quentin Tarantino, Bryant sought to not only reinvent himself but create a means of deflecting the intense backlash that he had begun to face."

5. Stacy Quick, "Perfectionism vs. OCD: How to Tell the Difference," Treat My OCD, November 7, 2023, https://www.treatmyocd.com/blog/perfectionism-vs-ocd-how-to-tell-the-difference.

6. Kobe Bryant, *The Mamba Mentality: How I Play* (New York: Farrar, Straus and Giroux, 2018), 125.

7. Chris Ballard, "Kobe Bryant May Never Be Happy, and Perhaps That's What Makes Him Great," *Vault, Sports Illustrated* (online), May 14, 2014, https://vault.si.com/vault/2012/05/14/where-does-greatness-come-from.

8. Paul Hewitt et al., "The Interpersonal Expression of Perfection: Perfectionistic Self-presentation and Psychological Distress," *Journal of Personality and Social Psychology* 84, no. 6 (2003): 1303–1325, https://doi.org/10.1037/0022-3514.84.6.1303.

9. Dana Harari et al., "Is Perfect Good? A Meta-analysis of Perfectionism in the Workplace," *Journal of Applied Psychology* 103, no. 10 (2018): 1121–1144, https://doi.org/10.1037/apl0000324; Brian Swider et al., "The Pros and Cons of Perfectionism, According to Research," *Harvard Business Review* December 27, 2018, https://hbr.org/2018/12/the-pros-and-cons-of-perfectionism-according-to-research.

10. Brené Brown, *The Gifts of Imperfection: Let Go of Who You Think You're Supposed to Be and Embrace Who You Are* (Center City, MN: Hazelden, 2010), 56.

11. Curran, *The Perfectionism Trap*, 70.

12. Patrick Gaudreau et al., "Because Excellencism Is More Than Good Enough: On the Need to Distinguish the Pursuit of Excellence from the Pursuit of Perfection," *Journal of Personality and Social Psychology* 122, no. 6 (2022): 1117–1145, https://doi.org/10.1037/pspp0000411.

13. Gaudreau et al., "Because Excellencism Is More Than Good Enough," 1118.

14. Gaudreau et al., "Because Excellencism Is More Than Good Enough," 1118.

15. Gaudreau et al., "Because Excellencism Is More Than Good Enough," 1145.

16. Gaudreau et al., "Because Excellencism Is More Than Good Enough," 1118.

17. Patrick Gaudreau, "On the Distinction Between Personal Standards Perfectionism and Excellencism: A Theory Elaboration and Research

Agenda," *Perspectives on Psychological Science* 14, no. 2 (2019): 197–215, at 200, https://doi.org/10.1177/1745691618797940.

18. Gaudreau, "On the Distinction Between Personal Standards Perfectionism and Excellencism," 203.

19. Lisa Feldman Barrett, *Seven and a Half Lessons About the Brain* (New York: Mariner Books, 2021), 31.

20. Paul Rozin and Eugene B. Royzman, "Negativity Bias, Negativity Dominance, and Contagion," *Personality and Social Psychology Review* 5, no. 4 (2001): 296–320, https://doi.org/10.1207/S15327957PSPR0504_2.

21. Lisa Feldman Barrett, *How Emotions Are Made: The Secret Life of the Brain* (New York: Harper, 2017), 72–73.

22. Barrett, *Seven and a Half Lessons About the Brain*, 104–105.

23. Barrett, *How Emotions Are Made*, 71.

24. Social scientists and emotion experts use various terms to describe similar concepts about the importance of understanding the nuances of emotional experiences and the skill of emotional regulation for optimal wellbeing. Daniel Goleman writes about "emotional intelligence" or EQ, Susan David refers to "emotional agility", and Lisa Barrett Feldman uses the phrase "emotional granularity."

25. Amir Levine and Rachel Heller, *Attached: The New Science of Adult Attachment and How It Can Help You Find—and Keep—Love.* (New York: Tarcher, 2010); Ross A. Thompson, Jeffry A. Simpson, and Lisa J. Berlin, eds., *Attachment: The Fundamental Questions* (New York: Guilford, 2021).

26. Oxana Mian et al., "Associations Between Exposure to Adverse Childhood Experiences and Biological Aging: Evidence from the Canadian Longitudinal Study on Aging," *Psychoneuroendocrinology* 142 (August 2022), https://www.sciencedirect.com/science/article/pii/S0306453022001627.

27. Psychologists Paul L. Hewitt and Gordon L. Flett have led the charge in understanding the complexity of perfectionism for over three decades. For further reading, see: Paul Hewitt and Gordon Flett, "Perfectionism in the Self and Social Contexts: Conceptualization, Assessment, and Association with Psychopathology," *Journal of Personality and Social Psychology* 60 (1991): 456–470, https://pubmed.ncbi.nlm.nih.gov/2027080/; Paul Hewitt, Gordon Flett, and Samuel Mikail, *Perfectionism: A Relational Approach to Assessment, Treatment, and Conceptualization* (New York: Guilford, 2017).

28. Martin Smith et al., "The Perniciousness of Perfectionism: A Meta-analytic Review of the Perfectionism-Suicide Relationship," *Journal of Personality* 86, no. 3 (June 2018): 522–542, https://doi.org/10.1111/jopy.12333; Martin Smith et al., "Why Does Socially Prescribed Perfectionism Place People at Risk for Depression? A Five-Month, Two-Wave Longitudinal Study of the Perfectionism Social Disconnection Model," *Personality and Individual Differences* 134 (November 2018): 49–54, https://doi.org/10.1016/j.paid.2018.05.040.

29. Swider et al., "The Pros and Cons of Perfectionism."

30. Gordon Flett and Paul Hewitt, "Reflections on Three Decades of Research on Multidimensional Perfectionism: An Introduction to the Special Issue on Further Advances in the Assessment of Perfectionism," *Journal of Psychoeducational Assessment* 38, no. 1 (2020): 8, https://doi.org/10.1177/0734282919881928.

31. National Academies of Sciences, Engineering, and Medicine, *Social Isolation and Loneliness in Older Adults: Opportunities for the Health Care System* (Washington, DC: National Academies Press, 2020), https://doi.org/10.17226/25663.

32. Curran, *The Perfectionism Trap*, 216.

33. There are a number of research-based perfectionism assessments which you can find online and in research articles. The Perfectionism Self-Inquiry list is gathered from the author's workshop participants and serves as a reflection tool only. See, for example, G. L. Flett and P. L. Hewitt, "Still Measuring Perfectionism After All These Years: Reflections and an Introduction to the Special Issue on Advances in the Assessment of Perfectionism," *Journal of Psychoeducational Assessment* 34 (2016): 615–619.

34. Bryant, *The Mamba Mentality*, 33.

CHAPTER 2

1. David Feinstein and Donna Eden, *Tapping: Self-Healing with the Transformative Power of Energy Psychology* (Boulder, CO: Sounds True, 2024), 13.

2. Feinstein and Eden, *Tapping*.

3. Lisa Feldman Barrett, *How Emotions Are Made: The Secret Life of the Brain* (New York: Harper, 2017), 73.

4. Lisa Feldman Barrett, "How to Understand Emotions," interview with Andrew Huberman, *Huberman Lab*, podcast, October 15, 2023, https://www.hubermanlab.com/episode/dr-lisa-feldman-barrett-how-to-understand-emotions.

5. Paul Gilbert, *The Compassionate Mind: A New Approach to Life's Challenges* (Oakland, CA: New Harbinger, 2009).

6. The Association for Comprehensive Energy Psychology (ACEP) defines energy psychology as a family of methods "that combine cognitive interventions with somatic techniques that influence the human bio-energy systems such as meridians, chakras and the biofield to elevate physical, mental, emotional and spiritual well-being." ACEP, https://www.energypsych.org.

7. Donna Eden and David Feinstein, *Energy Medicine: Balancing Your Body's Energies for Optimal Health, Joy and Vitality* (New York: Tarcher Perigee, Penguin Random House, 2008); David Feinstein and Donna Eden, "Six Pillars of Energy Medicine: Clinical Strengths of a Complementary

Paradigm," *Alternative Therapies in Health and Medicine* 14, no. 1 (2008): 44–54.

8. Association for Comprehensive Energy Psychology (ACEP), "Quick Facts: The Science of Energy Psychology," updated August 2023, https://www .energypsych.org/researchdb8c71b7#ResearchQuickFacts.

9. Emerging research attempts to map the Chinese meridians to a Western explanatory model. Acupressure points appear to correspond with bundles of vascular nerves of soft connective tissue that pass through fascia in the primary vascular system and send afferent signals to parts of body and brain. See Norbert Maurer et al., "Anatomical Evidence of Acupuncture Meridians in the Human Extracellular Matrix: Results from a Macroscopic and Microscopic Interdisciplinary Multicentre Study on Human Corpses," *Evidence-Based Complementary and Alternative Medicine*, March 21, 2019, https://www.ncbi.nlm.nih.gov/pmc/articles/PMC6448339; Zhang-Jin Zhang, Xiao-Min Wang, and Grainne M. McAlonan, "Neural Acupuncture Unit: A New Concept for Interpreting Effects and Mechanisms of Acupuncture," *Evidence-Based Complementary and Alternative Medicine*, vol. 2012, doi.org/10.1155/2012/429412.

10. Two approaches I gravitated to are Eden Energy Medicine and EFT. Both are complementary and alternative medicine modalities with a growing evidence base in research studies. The techniques allow you to recruit the body's subtle energy pathways to harmonize and heal your body and mind. See David Feinstein, "Six Empirically-Supported Premises About Energy Psychology: Mounting Evidence for a Controversial Therapy," *Advances in Mind-Body Medicine* 35, no. 2 (2021): 17–32, https://irp.cdn-website.com /d7d8897f/files/uploaded/Feinstein.pdf.

CHAPTER 3

1. Lisa Feldman Barrett, *How Emotions Are Made: The Secret Life of the Brain* (New York: Harper, 2017).

2. Richard C. Schwartz, *No Bad Parts: Healing Trauma and Restoring Wholeness with the Internal Family Systems Model* (Boulder, CO: Sounds True, 2021).

3. Debbie Ford, *The Dark Side of the Light Chasers: Reclaiming Your Power, Creativity, Brilliance and Dreams* (New York: Riverhead Books, 1998, 2010), 99.

CHAPTER 4

1. Stefan Hofmann and Angelina Gómez, "Mindfulness-Based Interventions for Anxiety and Depression," *Psychiatric Clinics of North America* 40, no. 4 (2017): 739–749, https://doi.org/10.1016/j.psc.2017.08.008; Bassam

Khoury et al., "Mindfulness-Based Therapy: A Comprehensive Meta-analysis," *Clinical Psychology Review* 33, no. 6 (2013): 763–771 https://pubmed.ncbi.nlm.nih.gov/23796855/.

2. Amishi P. Jha, *Peak Mind: Find Your Focus, Own Your Attention, Invest 12 Minutes a Day* (New York: HarperOne, 2022).

3. Tara Brach, *Radical Acceptance: Embracing Your Life With the Heart of a Buddha* (New York: Bantam Books, 2004).

4. Administration for Strategic Preparedness and Response (ASPR), "Individual Resilience," accessed May 1, 2024, https://aspr.hhs.gov/at-risk/Pages/individual_resilience.aspx.

5. Aljoscha Dreisoerner et al., "Self-Soothing Touch and Being Hugged Reduce Cortisol Responses to Stress: A Randomized Controlled Trial on Stress, Physical Touch, and Social Identity" *Comprehensive Psychoneuroendocrinology* 8 (2021), https://doi.org/10.1016/j.cpnec.2021.100091; Tobias Esch and George B. Stefano, "The Neurobiological Link Between Compassion and Love," *Medical Science Monitor* 17, no. 3 (2011): 65–75, https://doi.org/10.12659/msm.881441; Eli S. Susman et al., "Daily Micropractice Can Augment Single-Session Interventions: A Randomized Controlled Trial of Self-Compassionate Touch and Examining Their Associations with Habit Formation in US College Students," *Behaviour Research and Therapy* 175, (2024), https://doi.org/10.1016/j.brat.2024.104498.

6. Viktoriya Maydych, "The Interplay Between Stress, Inflammation, and Emotional Attention: Relevance for Depression," *Frontiers in Neuroscience* 13 (April 2019): 384, https://doi.org/10.3389/fnins.2019.00384.

7. Daniel J. Siegel, *The Developing Mind: How Relationships and the Brain Interact to Shape Who We Are*, 3rd ed. (New York: Guilford, 2020).

8. Lisa Feldman Barrett, *How Emotions Are Made: The Secret Life of the Brain* (New York: Harper, 2017).

9. Cleveland Clinic. "The Gut-Brain Connection," accessed May 1, 2024, https://my.clevelandclinic.org/health/body/the-gut-brain-connection; Jana Vasković, "Nervous System," Kenhub, last reviewed November 3, 2023, https://www.kenhub.com/en/library/anatomy/the-nervous-system.

10. Joseph Dispenza, *Becoming Supernatural: How Common People Are Doing the Uncommon* (London: Hay House, 2017), 67.

11. Brian J. Kenny and Bruno Bordoni, "Neuroanatomy, Cranial Nerve 10 (Vagus Nerve)," StatPearls, updated November 7, 2022, https://www.ncbi.nlm.nih.gov/books/NBK537171.

12. Sylvain Laborde, Emma Mosley, and Julian F. Thayer, "Heart Rate Variability and Cardiac Vagal Tone in Psychophysiological Research—Recommendations for Experiment Planning, Data Analysis, and Data Reporting," *Frontiers in Psychology* 8 (2017): 213, https://doi.org/10.3389/fpsyg.2017.00213.

13. Stephen W. Porges, *The Polyvagal Theory: Neurophysiological Foundations of Emotions, Attachment, Communication, and Self-Regulation*, Norton Series on Interpersonal Neurobiology (New York: Norton, 2011).
14. Deborah Dana, *Befriending Your Nervous System: Looking Through the Lens of Polyvagal Theory*, audio CD, unabridged, Sounds True, June 23, 2020.
15. Deborah Dana, *Polyvagal Exercises for Safety and Connection: 50 Client-Centered Practices* (New York: Norton, 2020).
16. Barrett, *How Emotions Are Made*, 82.

CHAPTER 5

1. Raisa Bruner, "Here's Why Taylor Swift Is Re-Releasing Her Old Albums," *TIME*, October 27, 2023, https://time.com/5949979/why-taylor-swift-is-rerecording-old-albums.
2. Russell L. Kolts, *CFT Made Simple: A Clinician's Guide to Practicing Compassion-Focused Therapy* (Oakland, CA: New Harbinger, 2016).
3. Lisa Feldman Barrett, *Seven and a Half Lessons About the Brain* (New York: Mariner Books, 2021), 71.
4. Nadja Doerig et al., "Neural Representation and Clinically Relevant Moderators of Individualized Self-Criticism in Healthy Subjects," *Social Cognitive and Affective Neuroscience* 9, no. 9 (2014): 1333–1340, https://doi.org/10.1093/scan/nst123; Olivia Longe et al., "Having a Word With Yourself: Neural Correlates of Self-Criticism and Self-Reassurance," *NeuroImage* 49, no. 2 (2010): 1849–1856, https://doi.org/10.1016/j.neuroimage.2009.09.019.
5. Theodore Powers et al., "The Effects of Self-Criticism and Self-Oriented Perfectionism on Goal Pursuit," *Personality and Social Psychology Bulletin* 37, no. 7 (2011): 964–975, https://doi.org/10.1177/0146167211410246.
6. Dana Harari et al., "Is Perfect Good? A Meta-analysis of Perfectionism in the Workplace," *Journal of Applied Psychology* 103, no. 10 (2018): 1121–1144, https://doi.org/10.1037/apl0000324.
7. Longe et al, "Having a Word with Yourself," 1855.
8. Rick Hanson, "Learning to Learn from Positive Experiences," *Journal of Positive Psychology* 18, no. 1 (2023): 142–153, https://www.tandfonline.com/doi/epdf/10.1080/17439760.2021.2006759.
9. David D. Burns described cognitive distortions, including in his classic and still widely circulated book *Feeling Good: The New Mood Therapy* (New York: William Morrow, 1999).
10. Sandra Silva Casabianca, "15 Cognitive Distortions to Blame for Negative Thinking," *Psych Central*, last updated January 11, 2022, https://psychcentral.com/lib/cognitive-distortions-negative-thinking.

11. The late Fred Rogers described the importance of emotional life aptly: "Anything that's human is mentionable, and anything that is mentionable can be more manageable. When we can talk about our feelings, they become less overwhelming, less upsetting, and less scary. The people we trust with that important talk can help us know that we are not alone." Fred Rogers, *The World According to Mister Rogers: Important Things to Remember* (New York: Hachette Books, 2003).

12. "'More than 50 percent of the cortex, the surface of the brain, is devoted to processing visual information,' points out [David] Williams, the William G. Allyn Professor of Medical Optics. 'Understanding how vision works may be a key to understanding how the brain as a whole works.'" Susan Hagen, "The Mind's Eye," University of Rochester, *Rochester Review* 74, no. 4. (March-April 2012); Nadine Dijkstra, Sander Bosch SE, and Marcel van Gerven, "Shared Neural Mechanisms of Visual Perception and Imagery," *Trends in Cognitive Sciences* 23, no. 5 (2019): 423–434, https://doi.org/10.1016/j.tics.2019.02.004

13. Carol Clark, "Earliest Look at Newborns' Visual Cortex Reveals the Minds Babies Are Born With," Emory University, Dilks Lab, Emory Department of Psychology, https://news.emory.edu/features/2020/03/esc-newborn-visual-cortex/, accessed May 2, 2024.

14. Katarzyna Zemla et al., "Investigating the Impact of Guided Imagery on Stress, Brain Functions, and Attention: A Randomized Trial," *Sensors* 23, no. 13 (2023): 6210, https://doi.org/10.3390/s23136210.

15. Samuel Moulton and Stephen Kosslyn, "Imagining Predictions: Mental Imagery as Mental Emulation," *Philosophical Transactions of the Royal Society B: Biological Sciences* 364, no. 1521 (2009): 1273–1280, https://doi.org/10.1098/rstb.2008.0314; Daniel J. Siegel, *The Developing Mind: How Relationships and the Brain Interact to Shape Who We Are*, 3rd ed. (New York: Guilford, 2020).

16. Joel Pearson, "The Human Imagination: The Cognitive Neuroscience of Visual Mental Imagery," *Nature Reviews Neuroscience* 20 (2019), https://doi.org/10.1038/s41583-019-0202-9; Joel Pearson and Stephen M. Kosslyn, "The Heterogeneity of Mental Representation: Ending the Imagery Debate," *Proceedings of the National Academy of Sciences of the United States of America* 112, no. 33 (2015): 10089-92, https://doi.org/10.1073/pnas.1504933112.

17. Kobe Bryant and Pau Gasol, *The Mamba Mentality: How I Play* (New York: Farrar, Straus and Giroux, 2018), 87.

18. Marius Vollberg, Brendan O'Connor, and Mina Cikara, "Activating Episodic Simulation Increases Affective Empathy," PsyArXiv. September 26, 2019, https://doi.org/10.31234/osf.io/r6wmx; Christine Wilson-Mendenhall, John Dunne, and Richard Davidson, "Visualizing Compassion: Episodic

Simulation as Contemplative Practice," *Mindfulness* 14, no. 10 (2023): 2532–2548.

19. Professor Mina Cikara runs the Harvard Intergroup Neuroscience Lab, which "uses social psychological and cognitive neuroscience approaches to study how group membership and prejudice change the course of social cognition." Learn more at http://www.intergroupneurosciencelaboratory .com. The studies on episodic simulation include: Brendan Gaesser, Yuki Simura, and Mina Cikara, "Episodic Simulation Reduces Intergroup Bias in Prosocial Intentions and Behavior," *Journal of Personality and Social Psychology* 118, no. 4 (2020): 683–705, https://doi.org/10.1037/pspi0000194; Marius Vollberg, Brendan Gaesser, and Mina Cikara, "Activating Episodic Simulation Increases Affective Empathy," *Cognition* 209 (2021): 104558, https://doi.org/10.1016/j.cognition.2020.104558.

20. Wilson-Mendenhall, et al., "Visualizing Compassion," 2532–2548.

21. Elizabeth Gilbert, *Big Magic: Creative Living Beyond Fear* (New York: Riverhead Books, 2015), 25.

22. Andrew Orvell, Ethan Kross, and Susan Gelman, "How 'You' Makes Meaning," *Science* 355, no. 6331 (2017): 1299–1302, https://doi.org/10 .1126/science.aaj2014; Igor Grossmann et al., "Training for Wisdom: The Distanced-Self-Reflection Diary Method," *Psychological Science* 32, no. 3 (2021): 381–394, https://doi.org/10.1177/0956797620969170; Ethan Kross and Ozlem Ayduk, "Self-Distancing: Theory, Research, and Current Directions," in *Advances in Experimental Social Psychology*, ed. John M. Olson (Cambridge, MA: Elsevier Academic Press, 2017), 81–136.

23. Ethan Kross, *Chatter: The Voice in Our Head, Why It Matters, and How to Harness It* (New York: Crown, 2021).

24. Rachel White et al., "The 'Batman Effect': Improving Perseverance in Young Children," *Child Development* 88, no. 5 (2017): 1563–1571, https://doi.org/10.1111/cdev.12695.

25. Soohyun Kim, "The Mind in the Making: Developmental and Neurobiological Origins of Mentalizing," *Personality Disorders: Theory, Research, and Treatment* 6, no. 4 (2015): 356–365, https://doi.org/10.1037/per0000102.

26. Longe et al., "Having a Word with Yourself," 1849–1856.

27. Elizabeth Gilbert, "Welcome to Letters from Love," Letters from Love Substack, accessed May 19, 2024, https://elizabethgilbert.substack.com/p /welcome-to-letters-from-love.

28. Sarah Ferguson, "Donald Olding Hebb," Canadian Association for Neuroscience, https://can-acn.org/donald-olding-hebb, accessed May 2, 2024.

29. Joseph Dispenza, *Becoming Supernatural: How Common People Are Doing the Uncommon* (London: Hay House, 2019), 67.

30. Cortland Dahl, Christine Wilson-Mendenhall, and Richard Davidson, "The Plasticity of Well-being: A Training-Based Framework for the

Cultivation of Human Flourishing," *PNAS* 117, no. 51 (2020): 32197–32206, https://doi.org/10.1073/pnas.2014859117.

31. Rick Hanson, *Hardwiring Happiness: The New Brain Science of Contentment, Calm, and Confidence* (New York: Harmony, 2013).

32. The RAIN skill was first developed by meditation teacher Michele McDonald, is widely taught in mindfulness meditation programs, and is the focus of Tara Brach's book, *Radical Compassion: Learning to Love Yourself and Your World with the Practice of RAIN* (New York: Viking Life, 2019).

33. Tara Brach, *Radical Acceptance: Embracing Your Life with the Heart of a Buddha* (New York: Bantam Books, 2004).

34. Donna Eden and David Feinstein, *Energy Medicine: Balancing Your Body's Energies for Optimal Health, Joy and Vitality* (New York: Tarcher Perigee, 2008), 253.

35. Joanne Kirby, Christina Tellegen, and Steven Steindl, "A Meta-Analysis of Compassion-Based Interventions: Current State of Knowledge and Future Directions," *Behavior Therapy* 48, no. 6 (2017): 778–792, https://doi.org/10.1016/j.beth.2017.06.003; Jing Lv et al., "The Effect of Four Immeasurables Meditations on Depressive Symptoms: A Systematic Review and Meta-Analysis," *Clinical Psychology Review* 76 (2020): 101814, https://doi.org/10.1016/j.cpr.2020.101814; Nicola Petrocchi et al., "The Impact of Compassion-Focused Therapy on Positive and Negative Mental Health Outcomes: Results of a Series of Meta-Analyses," *Clinical Psychology: Science and Practice*, 31 no. 2 (2024): 230-247, https://doi.org/10.1037/cps0000193.

CHAPTER 6

1. Laura Sanders, "A New 3-D Map Illuminates the 'Little Brain' Within the Heart," *Science News*, June 2, 2020, https://www.sciencenews.org/article/new-3-d-map-illuminates-little-brain-nerve-cells-within-heart; Neil Herring and David J. Paterson, "The Heart's Little Brain," *Circulation Research* 128, no. 9 (2021), https://www.ahajournals.org/doi/10.1161/CIRCRESAHA.121.319148; Thomas R. Verny, "The Significance of the Heart-Brain Connection," *Psychology Today*, February 4, 2022, https://www.psychologytoday.com/us/blog/explorations-the-mind/202202/the-significance-the-heart-brain-connection.

2. Howard Martin, *Engaging the Intelligence of the Heart*, TEDxSantaCruz, 2012, https://www.youtube.com/watch?v=A9kQBAH1nK4; Doc Childre et al., *Heart Intelligence: Connecting with the Intuitive Guidance of the Heart*, 2nd ed. (Dundee, UK: Waterfront Digital Press, 2022).

3. Cleveland Clinic, "Heart Rate Variability (HRV)," https://my.clevelandclinic.org/health/symptoms/21773-heart-rate-variability-hrv, accessed March 31, 2024.

4. Reena Tiwari et al., "Analysis of Heart Rate Variability and Implication of Different Factors on Heart Rate Variability," *Current Cardiology Reviews* 17, no. 5 (2021): e160721189770, https://doi.org/10.2174/1573403 X16999201231203854.

5. Kristin Neff, *Self-Compassion: The Proven Power of Being Kind to Yourself* (New York: William Morrow Harper Collins, 2011).

6. Greg McKeown, *Effortless: Make It Easier to Do What Matters Most* (New York: Crown Currency, 2021); Greg McKeown, "To Build a Top Performing Team, Ask for 85% Effort," *Harvard Business Review*, June 08, 2023, https://hbr.org/2023/06/to-build-a-top-performing-team-ask-for-85-effort.

7. Christopher Germer and Kristin Neff, *Teaching the Mindful Self-Compassion Program: A Guide for Professionals* (New York: Guilford, 2019), 100; Steven Hickman, "Safely Challenged: Self-Compassion and Mindfulness Enhancing Each Other," Dr. Steven Hickman Blog, August 12, accessed June 5, 2024, https://www.drstevenhickman.com/stuck-in -meditation/4zf71x72lio8fvrzbdtwi45dbj691i.

8. Shelley E. Taylor, "Tend and Befriend Theory," in *Handbook of Theories of Social Psychology*, ed. Paul A. M. Van Lange, Arie W. Kruglanski, and E. Tory Higgins, (London: Sage, 2012), 32–49, https://doi.org/10.4135 /9781446249215.n3.

9. J. David Creswell et al., "Self-Affirmation Improves Problem-Solving Under Stress," *PLOS ONE* 8, no. 5 (2013): e62593, https://doi.org/10.1371 /journal.pone.0062593; Janine Dutcher et al., "Self-Affirmation Activates the Ventral Striatum: A Possible Reward-Related Mechanism for Self-Affirmation," *Psychological Science*, February 25 (2016), 455–466, https:// doi.org/10.1177/0956797615625; Philine Harris, Peter R. Harris, and Eleanor Miles et al., "Self-Affirmation Improves Performance on Tasks Related to Executive Functioning," *Journal of Experimental Social Psychology* 70 (May 2017): 281–285, https://doi.org/10.1016/j.jesp.2016.11.011; David Sherman and Kimberly Hartson, "Reconciling Self-Protection with Self-Improvement: Self-Affirmation Theory," in *Handbook of Self-Enhancement and Self-Protection*, ed. Mark D. Alicke and Constantine Sedikides (New York: Guilford, 2011), 128–151; Jennifer Taber et al., "Optimism and Spontaneous Self-Affirmation Are Associated with Lower Likelihood of Cognitive Impairment and Greater Positive Affect Among Cancer Survivors," *Annals of Behavioral Medicine* 50 (2016): 198–209.

10. Doc Childre et al., *Heart Intelligence*, chapter 5, "Raising Our Vibration to Access Our Higher Potentials," 92.

CHAPTER 7

1. Richard C. Schwartz, *Introduction to Internal Family Systems*, 2nd ed., (Boulder, CO: Sounds True, 2023), 101.

2. Imposter phenomenon or syndrome was coined by Pauline Clance in 1978, to describe the fraudulent feelings experienced by high achieving women. It is not a mental disorder. Her measurement scale is the Pauline Rose Clance Impostor Phenomenon Scale (CIPS), https://paulinerose clance.com/pdf/IPTestandscoring.pdf, accessed June 5, 2024. Some research indicates that women and ethnic minorities experience imposter feelings due to marginalization and cultural biases about achievement and success. Pauline R. Clance and Suzanne A. Imes, "The Impostor Phenomenon in High Achieving Women: Dynamics and Therapeutic Intervention," *Psychotherapy: Theory, Research & Practice* 15, no. 3 (Fall 1978): 241–247, https://doi.org/10.1037/h0086006; Kevin Cokley et al., "An Examination of the Impact of Minority Status Stress and Impostor Feelings on the Mental Health of Diverse Ethnic Minority College Students," *Journal of Multicultural Counseling and Development* 41, no. 2 (2013): 82–95, https://doi.org/10.1002/j.2161-1912.2013.00029.x.

3. Juliana G. Breines and Serena Chen, "Self-Compassion Increases Self-Improvement Motivation," *Personality and Social Psychology Bulletin* 38, no. 9 (2012): 1133–1143.

4. Madeleine Ferrari et al., "Self-Compassion Interventions and Psychosocial Outcomes: A Meta-Analysis of RCTs," *Mindfulness* 10 (2019): 1455–1473, https://doi.org/10.1007/s12671-019-01134-6; Sara Dunne et al., "Brief Report: Self-Compassion, Physical Health and the Mediating Role of Health-Promoting Behaviours," *Journal of Health Psychology* 23, no. 7 (2016), https://doi.org/10.1177/1359105316643377; Meredith L. Terry and Mark R. Leary, "Self-Compassion, Self-Regulation, and Health," *Self and Identity* 10, no. 3 (2011): 352–362.

5. Christopher Germer, *The Mindful Path to Self-Compassion: Freeing Yourself from Destructive Thoughts and Emotions* (New York: Guilford, 2009).

6. Kristin Neff, *Fierce Self-Compassion: How Women Can Harness Kindness to Speak Up, Claim Their Power and Thrive* (New York: Harper, 2021).

7. Kristin D. Neff, "Self-Compassion, Self-Esteem, and Well-Being," *Social and Personality Psychology Compass* 5, no. 1 (2011): 1–12.

8. Schwartz, *Introduction to Internal Family Systems*, 101.

9. Internal Family Systems is a method developed by Richard C. Schwartz that I find most effective in understanding the inner critical voices. Excellent resources for the beginner include his books *Introduction to Internal Family Systems* (2nd ed.) and *No Bad Parts*, and the IFS Institute website, which is rich in resources, videos, and an IFS therapist directory: https://ifs-institute.com.

10. Richard C. Schwartz, *No Bad Parts: Healing Trauma and Restoring Wholeness with the Internal Family Systems Model* (Boulder, CO: Sounds True, 2021), 36.

11. Schwartz, *No Bad Parts*, 36.
12. Karen Grayson, "Actualizers: A 4th Type of Part in IFS," *IFS with Rennie*, April 3, 2023, https://www.ifswithrennie.com/post/actualizers-a-4th-type-of-part-in-ifs.
13. Schwartz, *Introduction to Internal Family Systems*, 36–51.
14. Susan Cain, *Bittersweet: How Sorrow and Longing Make Us Whole* (New York: Crown, 2022), 92.
15. Schwartz, *No Bad Parts*, 26.
16. Andrea Gibson, "A New Kind of Bucket List," *Things That Don't Suck*, November 14, 2023, https://andreagibson.substack.com/p/a-new-kind-of-bucket-list.
17. Lynn M. Karjala, *Healing Everyday Traumas: Free Yourself from the Scars of Bullying, Criticism and Other Old Wounds*, 2nd ed. (Roswell, GA: Psychology Innovations, 2022).
18. Robert Kegan and Lisa Lahey, "The Real Reason People Won't Change," *Harvard Business Review* (online), November 2001, https://hbr.org/2001/11/the-real-reason-people-wont-change.
19. Germer, *The Mindful Path*, 2009.
20. Jack Kornfield, *A Lamp in the Darkness: Illuminating the Path Though Difficult Times* (Boulder, CO: Sounds True, 2014), 66.
21. Donna Eden and David Feinstein, *Energy Medicine: Balancing Your Body's Energies for Optimal Health, Joy and Vitality* (New York: Tarcher Perigee, Penguin Random House, 2008), 80–90, 236, 241.
22. Eden and Feinstein, *Energy Medicine*, 270

CHAPTER 8

1. Marius Golubickis et al., "Knock Yourself Out: Brief Mindfulness-Based Meditation Eliminates Self-Prioritization," *Psychonomic Bulletin & Review* 30, no. 1 (2023): 341–349, https://doi.org/10.3758/s13423-022-02111-2; Erica Boothby et al., "The Liking Gap in Conversations: Do People Like Us More Than We Think?" *Psychological Science* 29 (2018): 1742–1756, https://pubmed.ncbi.nlm.nih.gov/30183512; *Hidden Brain*, "Mind Reading: How Others See You," with researcher Erica Boothby (The Liking Gap), https://hiddenbrain.org/podcast/mind-reading-how-others-see-you.
2. As of June 2024, Martha Postlethwaite's poem *Clearing* can be read at https://www.mindfulnessassociation.net/words-of-wonder/clearing-martha-postlethwaite.
3. Monica Guillen-Royo, "Human Needs," in *Encyclopedia of Quality of Life and Well-Being Research*, ed. Alex C. Michalos (Dordrecht: Springer, 2014), https://doi.org/10.1007/978-94-007-0753-5_1345.

4. Marshall Rosenberg, *Nonviolent Communication: A Language of Life*, 3rd ed. (Encinitas, CA: PuddleDancer, 2015); Marshall Rosenberg, "NVC Quotes," *Nonviolent Communication*, https://www.nonviolentcommunication.com /resources/mbr-quotes.

5. To learn more about the twenty-four character strengths as formulated by VIA Institute on Character, see https://www.viacharacter.org/character -strengths. The VIA Character Strengths survey is free to the public: https://www.viacharacter.org/character-strengths-via.

6. Richard Schwartz describes the eight Cs of self-leadership in *Introduction to Internal Family Systems*, 36–51.

7. Deborah Rozman, "Chapter 3: Attributes of Heart Intelligence," in *Heart Intelligence: Connecting with the Intuitive Guidance of the Heart*, ed. Doc Childre, Howard Martin, and Deborah Rozman, 2nd ed. (Dundee, UK: Waterfront Digital, 2022), 43–44.

8. The Ted Lasso "curse reverse" scene about the haunted training room can be watched on *Ted Lasso*, season 1, episode 6, "Two Aces" (Apple TV+, 2021), where Lasso states: "Gentlemen, I am, by nature, a believer. Ghosts, spirit guides, aliens. Still, I can't actually tell you what lives beyond our physical world and what doesn't. What I can tell you is that with the exception of the wit and wisdom of Calvin and Hobbes, not much lasts forever."

9. "It's not the destination, it's the journey" is a quote often attributed to Ralph Waldo Emerson, the American philosopher. See "Kobe Bryant On 'It's Not the Destination, It's the Journey,'" YouTube, https://www.youtube .com/watch?v=ThlxzwOck9Q.

10. Szu-Chi Huang and Jennifer Aaker, "It's the Journey, Not the Destination: How Metaphor Drives Growth After Goal Attainment," *Journal of Personality and Social Psychology* 117, no. 4 (October 2019): 697–720.

11. Huang and Aaker, "It's the Journey."

12. Barbara L. Fredrickson, "The Role of Positive Emotions in Positive Psychology: The Broaden-and-Build Theory of Positive Emotions," *American Psychologist* 56, no. 3 (2001): 218–226, https://doi.org/10.1037//0003-066x.56 .3.218

13. Rick Hanson, "Learning to Learn from Positive Experiences," *Journal of Positive Psychology* 18, no. 1 (2023): 142–153, https://www.tandfonline.com /doi/epdf/10.1080/17439760.2021.2006759.

14. Pninit Russo-Netzer, "Prioritizing Meaning as a Pathway to Meaning in Life and Well-Being," *Journal of Happiness Studies* 20 (2019): 1863–1891, https://doi.org/10.1007/s10902-018-0031-y.

15. Pninit Russo-Netzer, "Prioritizing Meaning," 1884–1885.

16. Shigehiro Oishi and Erin Westgate, "A Psychologically Rich Life: Beyond Happiness and Meaning," *Psychological Review* 129, no. 4 (2022): 790–811, https://doi.org/10.1037/rev0000317.

17. Shigehiro Oishi et al., "Happiness, Meaning, and Psychological Richness," *Affective Science* 1 (2020): 107–115, https://doi.org/10.1007/s42761-020-00011-z.

18. Rick Hanson, *Hardwiring Happiness: The New Brain Science of Contentment, Calm, and Confidence* (New York: Harmony, 2013), 59–62.

19. John Diepold, *Heart Assisted Therapy: Integrating Heart Energy to Facilitate Emotional Health, Healing, and Performance Enhancement* (Parker, CO: Outskirts Press, 2018); John Diepold and Gary Schwartz, "Clinical Effectiveness of an Integrative Psychotherapy Technique for the Treatment of Trauma: A Phase I Investigation of Heart Assisted Therapy," *EXPLORE* 18, no. 6 (2022): 698–705, https://doi.org/10.1016/j.explore.2022.07.002.

20. Donna Eden and David Feinstein, *Energy Medicine: Balancing Your Body's Energies for Optimal Health, Joy and Vitality* (New York: Tarcher Perigee, Penguin Random House, 2008), 26–27.

21. Aljoscha Dreisoerner et al., "Self-Soothing Touch and Being Hugged Reduce Cortisol Responses to Stress: A Randomized Controlled Trial on Stress, Physical Touch, and Social Identity" *Comprehensive Psychoneuroendocrinology* 8 (2021), https://doi.org/10.1016/j.cpnec.2021.100091.

CHAPTER 9

1. Judith A. Swack, PhD, biochemist/immunologist, master NLP practitioner, and mind/body healer, is a pioneer in the field of energy psychology and is the originator of Healing from the Body Level Up™ (HBLU), an innovative and powerful mind/body healing methodology with transformative results. https://hblu.org.

2. Anodea Judith, *Charge and the Energetic Body: The Vital Key to Healing Your Life, Your Chakras, and Your Relationships* (Carlsbad, CA: Hay House, 2018), 195.

3. Dawson Church et al., "Psychological Trauma Symptom Improvement in Veterans Using Emotional Freedom Techniques: A Randomized Controlled Trial," *Journal of Nervous and Mental Disease* 201, no. 2 (2013): 153–160, https://doi.org/10.1097/NMD.0b013e31827f6351.

4. Peta Stapleton, *The Science Behind Tapping: A Proven Stress Management Technique for the Mind and Body* (Carlsbad, CA: Hay House, 2021).

5. Dawson Church, *The EFT Manual* (Fulton, CA: Energy Psychology Press, 2019), 170.

6. David Feinstein and Donna Eden, *Tapping: Self-Healing with the Transformative Power of Energy Psychology* (Boulder, CO: Sounds True, 2024), 16. At the 16th Annual World Tapping Summit (2024), Drs. Feinstein and Stapleton individually reported on the advancements in EFT research at that time. There are over 300 studies and several metanalyses pointing to

the effectiveness of EFT for a variety of significant ailments. One explanation for the effectiveness of acupressure tapping for rapidly reducing mental and physical distress may be that the light pressure on an acupressure point on the skin generates an electrical signal that is nearly instantaneous and carried to remote areas of the body and brain though connective tissue, which is mediated by the semiconductor collagen. Other research, including dismantling studies, suggest that the acupressure component in a tapping protocol is the active ingredient (i.e., not due to placebo or nonspecific effects of most therapies, or due to the words in tapping scripts). "The Tapping World Summit 2024," presented by the Tapping Solution, produced by Nick Ortner, hosted by Jessica Ortner. Virtual online event, February 26 to March 7, 2024, https://www.thetappingsolution.com/blog/tapping-world -summit-2024. See also Donna Bach et al., "Clinical EFT (Emotional Freedom Techniques) Improves Multiple Physiological Markers of Health," *Journal of Evidence Based Integrative Medicine* 24 (2019 January–December): 2515690X18823691, https://doi.org/10.1177/2515690X18823691.

7. Feinstein, *Tapping*, 13.
8. A video of Eden's Daily Energy Routine can be found online: "Donna Eden's Daily Energy Routine, Official version," YouTube, Donna Eden Energy Medicine, https://www.youtube.com/watch?v=Di5Ua44iuXc.
9. Church, *The EFT Manual*, 203.
10. Patrick Gaudreau et al., "Because Excellencism Is More Than Good Enough: On the Need to Distinguish the Pursuit of Excellence from the Pursuit of Perfection," *Journal of Personality and Social Psychology* 122, no. 6 (2022): 1137.
11. Carol Look, "Clarity in Action Course," January 2024, https://www .carollook.com/.
12. Patrick Gaudreau, "On the Distinction Between Personal Standards Perfectionism and Excellencism: A Theory Elaboration and Research Agenda," *Perspectives on Psychological Science* 14, no. 2 (2019): 197–215, at 197, https://doi.org/10.1177/1745691618797940.
13. Donna Eden and David Feinstein, *Energy Medicine: Balancing Your Body's Energies for Optimal Health, Joy and Vitality* (New York: Tarcher Perigee, Penguin Random House, 2008), 4.
14. Eden and Feinstein, *Energy Medicine*, 241–272.
15. Eden and Feinstein, *Energy Medicine*, 260
16. Eden and Feinstein, *Energy Medicine*, 265.
17. Lisa Miller, *The Awakened Brain: The Psychology of Spirituality* (London: Penguin Random House UK, 2021), 182.
18. Eden and Feinstein, *Energy Medicine*, 266–268.
19. Eden and Feinstein, *Energy Medicine*, 250–251.
20. Xianglong Zeng et al., "The Effect of Loving-Kindness Meditation on Positive Emotions: A Meta-Analytic Review," *Frontiers in Psychology* 6,

no. 1693 (2015), https://doi.org/10.3389/fpsyg.2015.01693; Ben Shahar et al., "A Wait-List Randomized Controlled Trial of Loving-Kindness Meditation Programme for Self-Criticism," *Clinical Psychology & Psychotherapy* 22, no. 4 (2015): 346–356, https://doi.org/10.1002/cpp.1893.

POSTSCRIPT

1. Brené Brown, *The Gifts of Imperfection: Let Go of Who You Think You're Supposed to Be and Embrace Who You Are* (Center City, MN: Hazelden, 2010), 57.
2. Rasmus Hougaard and Jacqueline Carter, *The Mind of the Leader: How to Lead Yourself, Your People and Your Organization for Extraordinary Results* (Brighton, MA: Harvard Business Review Press, 2018); Rasmus Hougaard and Jacqueline Carter, "The 3 Qualities of a Successful Leader," *Potential Project*, https://www.potentialproject.com/insights/the-3-qualities-of-a-successful-leader, accessed June 5, 2024.
3. Jack Kornfield, *The Lamp in the Darkness* (Boulder, CO: Sounds True, 2014), 57.

INDEX